The Gawain-Poet
A Critical Study

The Gawain-Poet

A CRITICAL STUDY BY

A. C. SPEARING

*Fellow of Queens' College, Cambridge and
University Lecturer in English*

CAMBRIDGE

AT THE UNIVERSITY PRESS

1970

Published by the Syndics of the Cambridge University Press
Bentley House, 200 Euston Road, London N.W.1
American Branch: 32 East 57th Street, New York, N.Y.10022

© Cambridge University Press 1970

Library of Congress Catalogue Card Number: 72–112476

ISBN 0 521 07851 2

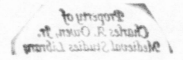

Printed in Great Britain by
W & J Mackay & Co Ltd, Chatham, Kent

Contents

Texts and abbreviations

Except where otherwise stated, I have quoted the following texts:

Purity, ed. R. J. Menner (New Haven, 1920).
Patience, ed. H. Bateson, 2nd edn. (Manchester, 1918).
Pearl, ed. E. V. Gordon (Oxford, 1953).
Sir Gawain and the Green Knight, ed. J. R. R. Tolkien and E. V. Gordon, 2nd edn., rev. Norman Davis (Oxford, 1967).
The Complete Works of Geoffrey Chaucer, ed. F. N. Robinson, 2nd edn. (Boston, Mass., 1957).

The Bible is quoted in Latin from the Vulgate and in English from the Douay version.

I have normalized the spelling of Middle English texts quoted, so as to eliminate ʒ and þ, and I have sometimes modified their punctuation where this seemed appropriate.

The following abbreviations are used in footnotes:

Benson L. D. Benson, *Art and Tradition in Sir Gawain and the Green Knight* (New Brunswick, 1965).
Borroff Marie Borroff, *Sir Gawain and the Green Knight: A Stylistic and Metrical Study* (New Haven, 1962).
Burrow J. A. Burrow, *A Reading of Sir Gawain and the Green Knight* (London, 1965).
EETS ES Early English Text Society, Extra Series.
EETS OS Early English Text Society, Original Series.
JEGP *Journal of English and Germanic Philology.*
Kean P. M. Kean, *The Pearl: An Interpretation* (London, 1967).
MLR *Modern Language Review.*
MP *Modern Philology.*
MS *Mediaeval Studies.*
PL *Patrologia Latina.*
PMLA *Publications of the Modern Language Association of America.*
RES n.s. *Review of English Studies,* new series.
Spec *Speculum.*

vi

Preface

This book is a study of four poems, two of which have been widely discussed by other scholars and critics. In writing about *Pearl* and *Sir Gawain and the Green Knight*, I have been deeply conscious of my indebtedness to these others, and in chapter 1 also I have often done little more than give a survey of facts and opinions about the *Gawain*-poet and his background. Throughout the book, indeed, I have frequently felt like a magpie making a ragged nest studded with other people's jewels. I hope that those from whom I have unwittingly stolen good ideas without acknowledgment will accept this general apology. I also owe a great deal to the Cambridge students with whom I have discussed the *Gawain*-poet in the last ten years, for their perspicacity in asking the right questions, their good sense in refusing to accept implausible answers, and their heartening enthusiasm for the poet's work. The first draft of this book was written while I was on sabbatical leave from my University and College posts, and I must express my gratitude to two of my colleagues at Queens' College, Dr John Holloway and Dr James Diggle, for standing in for me as Director of Studies in English and as Librarian while I was away. My greatest debt, as always, is to my wife, who over several years has discussed with me much of what is written here, has seen through many fallacies, and has encouraged me when I most needed encouragement.

The bulk of chapter 3 and a few paragraphs elsewhere were originally published in *Anglia*, LXXXIV (1966), 305–29, under the title '*Patience* and the *Gawain*-Poet', and I am indebted to the editors and publisher of *Anglia* for their permission to re-use the article here. At an earlier stage the same material formed a paper delivered to the Oxford University Medieval Society, to whose members I am grateful for their careful criticism, and also to the University of Essex Literary Society, some of whose members cheered me considerably with their flattering belief that I was myself the *Gawain*-poet. Parts of chapter 4 were originally published in *Modern Philology*, LX (1962–3), 1–12, under the title 'Symbolic and Dramatic Development in *Pearl*'. Intending contributors to *Modern Philology* may be interested to know that its publishers, the University of Chicago Press, subsequently, without consulting or even informing me, sold the right to reprint this article to the editor of an anthology to which I shall give no free publicity here. At an earlier stage this and other material in chapter 4 formed part of a thesis on medieval dream-poetry written under the supervision of Professor Elizabeth Salter, to whose help and encouragement I owe more than I can say.

Some important work on the *Gawain*-poet became available when this book was too near completion for me to be able to take adequate account of it. I would particularly mention Ian Bishop, *Pearl in its Setting* (Oxford, 1968), Charles Moorman, *The Pearl-Poet* (New York, 1968), and J. J. Anderson, ed. *Patience* (Manchester, 1969).

A.C.S.

Cambridge
July 1969

1

The Poet and His Background

The poems

For the purposes of this book, the phrase 'the *Gawain*-poet' means the author (or conceivably authors)[1] of the four poems which make up British Museum MS Cotton Nero A. x, art. 3. None of the four poems is known in any other manuscript; they are anonymous, and no author's name can convincingly be attached to them; there are no contemporary references to them;[2] and so, but for the chance survival of this single manuscript, we should not even know of the existence of what are generally agreed to be four poems among the finest in Middle English literature. In the manuscript the poems are without titles, but since they were first printed by the nineteenth-century scholars Sir Frederick Madden and Richard Morris they have generally been known as *Sir Gawain and the Green Knight*, *Pearl*, *Purity* (also called *Cleanness*), and *Patience*. All four are written in alliterative verse, but there are great differences among them in literary form. *Patience* and *Purity* are written continuously in long unrhymed alliterative lines, which sometimes seem to fall naturally into groups of four.[3] *Pearl* is in shorter alliterative lines divided into intricately rhymed twelve-line stanzas, the stanzas in turn being linked into groups of five by repetitions of words and phrases. *Sir Gawain and the Green Knight* is once more in long unrhymed lines, but these are divided into groups of irregular length, each concluding

---

[1] See below, pp. 32–40.

[2] There is no reason to suppose that the 'Anteris of Gawane' mentioned by Andrew of Wyntoun in about 1420 as being by 'Huchown of the Awle Ryale' is *Sir Gawain and the Green Knight*. For this suggestion, see G. Neilson, *Huchown of the Awle Ryale* (Glasgow, 1902).

[3] In the manuscript quatrains are marked off by ticks in the margin, and the division into quatrains is retained by some editors. But I do not believe that the poems themselves fall into quatrains regularly enough to justify this. For discussion, see M. Kaluza, 'Strophische gliederung in der mittelenglischen rein alliterirenden dichtung', *Englische Studien*, XVI (1891–2), 169–80; and Mabel Day, 'Strophic Division in Middle English Alliterative Verse', *ibid.*, LXVI (1931–2), 245–8.

1

with five short rhymed lines (the 'bob and wheel'). The poems also differ considerably in their subject-matter. Here, too, *Patience* and *Purity* stand together, each being a homily concerned with the virtue of its title, but illustrating it chiefly through examples taken from Scripture of the opposite vice. But whereas *Patience* is only 531 lines long, and deals solely with the story of Jonah and the whale, *Purity* has 1,811 lines and takes in three main stories exemplifying the punishment of impurity, namely Noah and the Flood, Sodom and Gomorrah, and Belshazzar's feast. *Pearl* belongs to a quite different medieval genre, that of the dream-poem, and gives what purports to be a first-person account of a vision of the other world, in which the narrator meets again a maiden from whom he has been separated by death. It is 1,212 lines long. And *Sir Gawain and the Green Knight* belongs to yet another medieval genre, that of chivalric romance. It is 2,530 lines long, and it tells of Gawain's acceptance of the Green Knight's challenge to a beheading game, of his temptation in a strange castle, and of the unexpected dénouement in which these two stories are linked.

The manuscript containing these four poems is generally dated at about 1400. All four are written in the same hand, but the number of scribal errors makes it impossible to suppose that this is the author's. The dating of their language is difficult, but it probably belongs to the second half of the fourteenth century. The late fourteenth century is also suggested by such internal evidence as the costumes, furnishings, armour and architecture described in the poems. All in all we may assume that the poems date from, say, the period 1360–95.[1] This is to say that they belong to the greatest period of medieval English literature, that great flowering in the second half of the fourteenth century which includes Chaucer, Langland, and Gower: the period when, for the first time since the Norman Conquest, there existed a cultivated English reading public which would support the production of imaginative literature written in its own language. One aspect of this fourteenth-century development was the movement known as the Alliterative Revival. From about 1340–50 onwards we find, alongside the rhyming, metrical poetry written in the South East by poets such as Chaucer and Gower, a considerable number of poems, mostly anonymous, written in largely unrhymed alliterative verse, and originating in areas more to the North and West. The best-known and probably, in its own time, the most

---

[1] These are the limits suggested by E. V. Gordon, ed. *Pearl,* p. xliv.

popular of these is *Piers Plowman* by William Langland, a West-countryman writing in London. Among other major works in alliterative verse, all dating from this period, are *Winner and Waster*, *The Parliament of the Three Ages*, *William of Palerne*, *The Wars of Alexander*, *The Destruction of Troy*, and the *Morte Arthure.* All of these, except possibly the last, seem to derive from the West-Midland area, and it is almost certain that the *Gawain*-poet also wrote in that area. For some time scholars have been agreed that the dialect of all four poems is the same, and that it belongs to the North-West Midlands (that is, roughly, the area including South Lancashire, Cheshire, West Derbyshire, Staffordshire and Shropshire). The Green Chapel in *Sir Gawain and the Green Knight* appears to be in this area, and the poet shows some knowledge of its topography. The earliest known owner of the manuscript is Henry Saville, a sixteenth-century gentleman from Yorkshire, which is near the right part of the country. More recently, Professor Angus McIntosh has argued that *Sir Gawain and the Green Knight* can be more narrowly localized as belonging to 'a very small area either in S.E. Cheshire or just over the border in N.E. Staffordshire'.[1]

The milieu

These poems, then, originate in an area remote from the metropolis and from the cultural influences which, especially under Richard II, radiated from the royal court, and they are written in a dialect and a type of verse which belonged to their own locality. A modern reader might well suppose that such poems could only be clumsily provincial pieces of work, possessing, no doubt, their own local strengths, but essentially naïve and unsophisticated. Some medieval readers might have shared this supposition. John of Trevisa, a Cornishman writing in 1387, shows to what a striking extent the cultural magnetism and cultural snobbery of London and the South already existed in the fourteenth century. He writes:

Al the longage of the Northhumbres [i.e. Northerners], and specialych at York, ys so scharp, slyttyng, and frotyng, and unschape, that we Southeron men may that longage unnethe undurstonde. Y trowe that that ys bycause that a buth nygh to strange men and aliens, that speketh strangelych, and

[1] 'A New Approach to Middle English Dialectology', *English Studies*, XLIV (1962), 1–11, p. 5.

also bycause that the kynges of Engelond woneth alwey fer fram that contray; for a buth more yturnd to the south contray, and yef a goth to the north contray, a goth with gret help and strengthe. The cause why a buth more in the south contray than in the north may be betre cornlond, more people, more noble cytés, and more profytable havenes.[1]

Chaucer too was likely enough to dismiss a town or village in this barbarian North as being 'Fer in the north, I kan nat telle where', and to look on an inability to compose alliterative verse as being a natural and indeed admirable characteristic in a southerner:

> But trusteth wel, I am a Southren man,
> I kan nat geeste 'rum, ram, ruf,' by lettre.[2]

In point of fact, however, this persistent anti-northern prejudice is a poor guide to the true nature of the *Gawain*-poet's work. To us, writing in northern dialect implies a deliberate provincialism, which, even if chosen out of affection rather than contempt, suggests a patronizing attitude towards what may patronizingly be called local 'culture'—an attitude like that expressed by the editor of the first separate edition of *Patience*:

It is necessary to harmonise our feelings with the atmosphere of the story or to approach it as a tale of wonder. Animated by such a sympathy, those who delight in the naïve charm of happy primitive faith will read with novel interest the story of Jonah related over five centuries ago by a Lancashire poet.[3]

In the fourteenth century it was still possible for dialects other than that of London to be literary languages, at least in their own areas, and to be written not, as another editor of *Patience* suggested, for 'simple folk',[4] but to create works of high art for aristocratic patrons. There is direct evidence to this effect in the case of one poem of the Alliterative Revival, *William of Palerne*. This is a romance translated from the French, and the translator both near the beginning and again at the end asks his audience to pray for the 'Erl of Herford, Sir Humfray de Bowne':

---

[1] From Trevisa's translation of Higden's *Polychronicon*, ed. Kenneth Sisam, *Fourteenth Century Verse and Prose* (Oxford, 1921), p. 150.

[2] In the first quotation the speaker is the Reeve (*Canterbury Tales*, I [A], line 4015); in the second, the Parson (*Canterbury Tales*, X [I], 42–3).

[3] *Patience*, p. vii. This passage is reprinted from the first edition of 1912.

[4] *Patience*, ed. I. Gollancz (London, 1913), gathering B, f. 4v.

For he of Frensche this fayre tale ferst dede translate,
In ese of Englysch men in Englysch speche.[1]

The Bohun family are known as patrons of fine manuscripts, some of which still survive; alliterative poems, too, were evidently among the luxury objects with which such fourteenth-century aristocrats brought beauty and entertainment to the lives of their families and courts. In general, there is every reason to suppose that the Alliterative Revival was fostered in the courts of great aristocrats of the West Midlands—men who may also, like the most powerful of them all, John of Gaunt, have held estates in other parts of the country, and have been closely in touch with the royal court in London.[2] About such provincial art there was nothing unsophisticated. We cannot place the work of the *Gawain*-poet in any specific court, as we can *William of Palerne*, but there is plenty of evidence in the poems themselves to indicate the courtliness of their milieu.

One kind of evidence lies in the nature of the manuscript itself. It is not a lavish example of scribal and pictorial art, like the surviving Bohun manuscripts, or like some English literary manuscripts of the early fifteenth century—the Ellesmere *Canterbury Tales*, for example, or the Corpus Christi *Troilus and Criseyde*. It is workmanlike without being elegant; but it does contain no fewer than twelve illuminations. These in turn are somewhat careless and clumsy, and are sometimes not very closely related to the passages they are supposed to illustrate—the one showing the Green Knight's arrival at Camelot, for example, does not depict either his greenness or his long hair. But Father Gervase Mathew has convincingly argued that the very presence of these illuminations suggests that the manuscript we have is a copy of something grander, something more like the Bohun manuscripts:[3]

Only the illuminations suggest the kind of manuscript of which it is a copy: slovenly executed, with figure-work curiously out of proportion, they are yet obviously related to the new experiments in the representation of natural scenery and of architectural background which marked sophisticated French court art at the turn of the century; they can be best explained as the clumsy copies of larger illuminations in a contemporary manuscript

---

[1] *William of Palerne,* ed. W. W. Skeat, EETS ES 1 (London, 1867), lines 165–8.
[2] For important recent work on the social milieu of the Alliterative Revival, see Elizabeth Salter, 'The Alliterative Revival', *MP*, LXIV (1966–7), 146–50 and 233–7.
[3] Gervase Mathew, *The Court of Richard II* (London, 1968), p. 117.

de luxe. On such an hypothesis the lost original behind the Gawain manuscript was... commissioned by a magnate of wealth.

We do not really need, however, even to look at the manuscript in order to see that it belongs to the courtly culture of fourteenth-century England (which was only part of an international culture radiating from the great courts of Western Europe). The poems themselves show everywhere a confident and detailed knowledge of courtly ways of life. We can see this at its most obvious in their treatment of the externals of life. Even when they are dealing with the remote world of the Old Testament, these poems, like all the art of the Middle Ages, 'medievalize' it—not deliberately, of course, but because medieval people imagined the past almost entirely in terms of the present. The past, then, is brought up to date, depicted in terms of the social world known to the artist and his public. The world depicted in the *Gawain*-poet's work is usually that of courts: of King Arthur and Sir Bertilak in *Sir Gawain and the Green Knight* (a pair of courts, one southern and one northern, tantalizingly suggestive of those of Richard II and of whichever lord was the poet's patron); of Belshazzar in *Purity*; and the 'court of the kyndom of God alyve' (445) in *Pearl*. This last may surprise us; but the poet, in a way characteristic of the Middle Ages, persistently sees heaven itself as an ideal court, the ideal of which earthly courts are imperfect copies. This is seen most explicitly in *Purity*:

> He is so clene in his corte, the Kyng that al weldez,
> And honeste in his housholde and hagherlych served,
> With angelez enorled in alle that is clene,
> Both wythinne and wythouten, in wedez ful bryght. (17–20)

In these courts described by the *Gawain*-poet, every detail rings true. What he offers is not the debased and exaggerated view of aristocratic life, seen from below stairs, that we find in medieval popular romances of the kind Chaucer parodies in *Sir Thopas*; it is the view of someone who knows courtly life through and through, and whose picture can be confirmed in detail not only from other works of art such as manuscript illuminations but also from bald contemporary records of aristocratic life such as the *Registers* of John of Gaunt.[1] We find this in the detailed descriptions of clothing and armour, especially in *Sir Gawain and the Green Knight*; or in

---

[1] See Elizabeth Salter, 'The Alliterative Revival', pp. 233–5.

such details as the description of Sir Bertilak's castle when Sir Gawain first sees it, glimpsed amid the forest, 'As hit schemered and schon thurgh the schyre okez' (772). It is a castle in the latest French fashion, elaborately pinnacled and chimneyed, exactly like the one in the illustration of September in the *Tres riches heures du duc de Berry*.

A similar knowledge is shown in the descriptions of great feasts in *Purity* and *Sir Gawain and the Green Knight*. The reader who knows anything of the *Gawain*-poet's work will remember the feasts at Camelot and at Sir Bertilak's castle, and so I quote instead the less familiar but no less brilliant description of Belshazzar's feast in *Purity*:

> When alle segges were ther set, then servyse bygynnes,
> Sternen trumpen strake steven in halle,
> Aywhere by the wowes wrasten krakkes,
> And brode baneres therbi blusnande of gold;
> Burnes berande the bredes upon brode skeles,
> That were of sylveren syght, and served therwyth,
> Lyfte logges therover and on lofte corven,
> Pared out of paper and poynted of golde,
> Brothe baboynes abof, besttes anunder,
> Foles in foler flakerande bitwene,
> And al in asure and ynde enaumayld ryche,
> And al on blonkken bak bere hit on honde.
> And ay the nakeryn noyse, notes of pipes,
> Tymbres and tabornes, tulket among;
> Symbales and sonetez sware the noyse,
> And bougounz busch batered so thikke. (1401-16)

Here the luxury and decorative ingenuity of the late-medieval feast are perfectly captured, along with a vigour which is often absent from medieval descriptions, with their tendency to mere enumeration—a vigour centring in a delight in noise, the mingled blarings and warblings drowned at last in the almost brutal rhythm of 'bougounz busch batered so thikke'. And, incidentally, these decorations of the food, 'pared out of paper', make it clear what the poet was thinking of in *Sir Gawain and the Green Knight* when he said of the castle that Gawain saw through the trees, 'pared out of papure purely hit semed' (802). Food-decorations like castles, castles like food-decorations: it is true indeed that in this courtly 'decorated' style, 'the aesthetic ideal of the visual *continuum* blurs any distinction

7

between major and minor arts. They all speak the same language'.[1]
And for this visual and plastic language the *Gawain*-poet has
invented a perfect verbal equivalent. But there is something more
than an effect of intricate decoration in such feast scenes. Feasts are
extremely common in medieval romance, chiefly no doubt through
their importance in aristocratic life. This importance derived not
only from the opportunity they gave for luxury and display—conspicuous consumption—but also from their function as a kind of
social sacrament, a symbol of the vital bonds by which society is held
together. A feast is not simply eaten, it is enacted as a kind of social
ritual, in which everything must be done with propriety, according
to a set pattern. This is an aspect of aristocratic life which the
Gawain-poet seems clearly to have known and felt from the inside.
The meal must begin at the right time; the social hierarchy must be
reflected in the seating; the very washing of hands before the meal
is a significant act, a rite of purification, to be performed 'worthyly':

> Alle this mirthe thay maden to the mete tyme;
> When thay had waschen worthyly thay wenten to sete,
> The best burne ay abof, as hit best semed. (*Gawain*, 71–3)[2]

The same decorum, though somewhat perverted, is observed even in
the pagan wickedness of Belshazzar's palace:

> When the terme of the tyde watz towched of the feste,
> Dere drowen therto, and upon des metten,
> And Baltazar upon bench watz busked to sete...
> Thenne watz alle the halle-flor hiled with knyghtes,
> And barounes at the sidebordes bounet aywhere,
> For non watz dressed upon dece bot the dere selven,
> And his clere concubynes in clothes ful bryght. (*Purity*, 1393–1400)

There follows the service of the first course, with the appropriate
music, 'with crakkyng of trumpes' (*Gawain*, 116). There is no lack
of mirth at these feasts, but it is not the disorderly mirth of peasants
(as depicted somewhat later in Breughel's paintings), but 'manerly
merthe' (*Gawain*, 1656); not the spontaneity of animals, but a truly
human order. And, of course, the power with which this courtly
decorum of feasting is felt and expressed by the *Gawain*-poet makes
all the more shocking the sudden breaking of decorum by some un-

---

[1] George Henderson, *Gothic* (Harmondsworth, 1967), p. 109.
[2] Cf. *Purity*, lines 89–92 and 114–16.

expected interruption, whether the appearance of the Green Knight at Camelot or the hand writing on the wall at Babylon.[1]

Another aristocratic entertainment of which the *Gawain*-poet shows a knowledge that bears witness to his inwardness with aristocratic life is the hunt. Like the feast, the hunt is a common theme of medieval poetry; and, like the feast, it is both an entertainment and something more than an entertainment: it too functions as a sacrament, a ritual by which violent energies are at once expressed and contained. Hunting was felt to be the most characteristic activity of the medieval aristocracy, the appropriate means by which in peacetime the aggressive instincts of what was still theoretically a warrior class might be given a dignified outlet. A useful outlet, too: wild animals really were enemies to a society based on agriculture, which is why Piers Plowman tells a representative of the knightly class that his role in the community must be to:

> go honte hardiliche to hares and to foxes,
> To bores and to bockes that breketh adoune menne hegges;
> And faite thy faucones to culle wylde foules;
> For thei comen to my croft my corn to defoule.[2]

Moreover, the hares, boars and bucks, if not the foxes, provided good food. The hunting scenes in *Sir Gawain and the Green Knight* show not just the common medieval love of hunting but an intense concern for technical perfection in every aspect of the hunt—a concern that the rite should follow exactly the order laid down in such missals of the chase as the *Master of Game* composed by the Duke of York in the early fifteenth century. There is a proper way of doing everything, even cutting up the dead beast, and knowledge of this way is a prerogative of the aristocracy and their skilled servants. Thus on the first day's hunting, after the slaughtered deer have been heaped up, it is the men of highest rank who organize the breaking up, and they have it done 'as the dede askez', in the right way:

[1] One might compare the intrusion of Banquo's ghost into the decorum of the feast at Forres, as a result of which Lady Macbeth can tell her husband: 'You have displaced the mirth, broke the good meeting/With most admired disorder' (*Macbeth*, III. iv. 108–9). The significance of feasts as a 'life-force' in Shakespeare has been discussed by G. Wilson Knight (*The Imperial Theme* [London, 1931]). In this, as in much else, Shakespeare is drawing on and enriching a medieval inheritance.

[2] *Piers the Plowman*, ed. W. W. Skeat (London, 1886), C. IX, lines 28–31. For 'bockes' (bucks), B, for which Skeat has probably used a better manuscript, reads 'brockes' (badgers).

> The best bowed therto with burnez innoghe,
> Gedered the grattest of gres that ther were,
> And didden hem derely undo as the dede askez. (1325-7)

The breaking up of the deer is completed 'by resoun' (1344), and on the next day the boar is disembowelled 'as hightly bisemez' (1612). For the appropriate performance of such ceremonial acts, skilled acolytes are needed, and the aristocracy are assisted by 'lerned' servants (1170), such as the 'wyye that watz wys upon wodcraftez' (1605) who disembowels the boar. An important part of their skill consists in knowing the right technical names for such things as horn and bugle calls, and the various parts of the inside of the dead animals. The technical vocabulary—words such as *mote*, *slot*, *gargulun*, *wesaunt*, *avanters*—forms, as it were, the liturgy of this aristocratic sacrament, and knowledge of it marks off the 'lerned' by birth or training. Malory in the fifteenth century was to attribute the invention of the techniques and terms of hunting to Sir Tristram:

as the booke seyth, he began good mesures of blowynge of beestes of venery and beestes of chaace and all maner of vermaynes, and all the tearmys we have yet of hawkynge and huntynge.

And so, he continues:

all jantyllmen that beryth olde armys ought of ryght to honoure sir Tristrams for the goodly tearmys that jantylmen have and use and shall do unto the Day of Dome, that thereby in a manner all men of worshyp may discever a jantylman frome a yoman and a yoman frome a vylayne.[1]

To judge the matter in these terms, we may conclude that the *Gawain*-poet was a 'jantylman' writing for 'jantylmen'; certainly, in being learned in the lore and language of hunting, he is fully identified with the aristocratic society for which he wrote. He delights in his learning, and the hunting scenes in *Sir Gawain and the Green Knight*, quite apart from their functions in the economy of the poem as a whole, joyfully celebrate the society he knew.[2]

His knowledge of aristocratic life is not confined to such vivid externals as feasting and hunting. It extends to the finer details of everyday behaviour, and to the values by which that behaviour was

---

[1] *The Works of Sir Thomas Malory*, ed. Eugène Vinaver (2nd edn., Oxford, 1967), I, 375.
[2] The poet's knowledge of hunting is studied by H. L. Savage, *The Gawain-Poet: Studies in his Personality and Background* (Chapel Hill, 1956).

governed. These are the same values that we find everywhere in medieval courtly literature: *trawthe, lewté, fraunchise, gentillesse, pitie*, and, above all, *cortaysye*.[1] *Cortaysye* is perhaps the central value of the courtly way of life, as indeed its name suggests: it is the virtue belonging to courts. It has a wide range of meaning, in which religious senses merge into secular, and the ethical may be delicately edged towards the erotic (as it is by the Lady in *Sir Gawain and the Green Knight*). In its religious sense, *cortaysye* is associated with the grace or mercy displayed by God and mediated by the Blessed Virgin. Heaven, we have seen, is itself a court, in which God is King and shows to mankind a 'cortesie more than covenant was'[2] in offering a remedy for the damnation demanded by mere justice. This heavenly *cortaysye* is explored most fully in *Pearl*, where Mary is 'Quen of cortaysye' (432) and has heaven, earth and hell in her dominion. The heroes of both *Pearl* and *Patience* find themselves unable to comprehend the full extent of this heavenly *cortaysye*. Justice is a more manageable concept, and they both complain that God is *too* merciful. Jonah rebukes God for extending his mercy to the repentant Ninevites, and remarks bitterly, 'Wel knew I thi cortaysye, thi quoynt soffraunce' (*Patience*, 417), and the Dreamer is shocked by the *cortaysye* that has made an earthly little child into a great lady in heaven, and exclaims, 'That cortaysé is to fre of dede!' (*Pearl*, 481). In its secular range of meaning, *cortaysye* includes thoughtfulness for others, refined manners, deference, the service of ladies, and elegant love-making. (In the *Romaunt of the Rose*, that seminal work on the courtly 'art of love', Curtesye is among the God of Love's followers, and is 'lemman' to a handsome and courageous knight.) This secular aspect of *cortaysye* is most fully explored in *Sir Gawain and the Green Knight*, whose hero was well known in medieval romance as the very paragon of this virtue:

> Gaweyn, the worthy,
> Was preised for his curtesy. (*Romaunt of the Rose*, 2209–10)

One way in which *cortaysye* readily shows itself is in forms of speech, turns of phrase nicely judged as being exactly appropriate to specific

---

[1] These and other courtly virtues are analysed by Gervase Mathew (*The Court of Richard II*). *Cortaysye* is studied by W. O. Evans, '"Cortaysye" in Middle English', *MS*, XXIX (1967), 143–57; and its place in the work of the *Gawain*-poet in an admirable essay by D. S. Brewer, 'Courtesy and the *Gawain*-Poet', in *Patterns of Love and Courtesy*, ed. John Lawlor (London, 1966), pp. 54–85.
[2] *Piers Plowman*, ed. W. W. Skeat (1886), C. xv. line 216.

social situations. Gawain's opening speech, in which he begs permission to take up the Green Knight's challenge, shows this at its
fullest,[1] but in Biblical scenes too—very remote, one might think,
from the idealized medieval courtliness of Camelot—the poet,
imagining a social encounter, also imagines the right forms of courtly
speech to accompany it. Thus in *Purity*, when God appears to
Abraham to tell him that he is going to destroy Sodom, Abraham is
given a suitably *cortays* form of address when he begins to persuade
him to spare the city. The words of apology given to Abraham in
the Bible might have seemed to a medieval poet and his audience
orientally extreme in their blunt self-abasement: 'Quia semel coepi,
loquar ad Dominum meum, cum sim pulvis et cinis' (Genesis xviii.
27) ('Seeing I have once begun, I will speak to my Lord, whereas I
am dust and ashes'). The poet expands this to give it a subtly
different medieval tone, suggesting not so much Jehovah and man
as a great prince and one of his council of lords:

> 'Aa! blessed be thow,' quod the burne, 'so boner and thewed,
> And al haldez in thy honde, the heven and the erthe;
> Bot for I haf this talke, tatz to non ille
> Yif I mele a lyttel more, that mul am and askez.' (*Purity*, 733–6)

Two of the phrases used in that gracious exordium, which flows so
elegantly on its repeated liquid sounds, reappear in *cortays* contexts
in other poems in the manuscript. Gawain says 'tas to non ille' (it
sounds a colloquial rather than a formal phrase) to the Lady when
he is apologizing for not having with him a suitable supply of gifts
from which to select a love-token for her (*Gawain*, 1811). And in
Pearl the Dreamer makes explicit the specifically courtly implications of the assertion 'I am only dust' when he says with great
deference to the Maiden:

> Thagh cortaysly ye carp con,
> I am bot mol and manerez mysse. 381–2)

The poet's reading

The *Gawain*-poet, then, possessed a sophisticated knowledge and
understanding of the courtly way of life and the values underlying
it. In considering the extent of his culture, we must also inquire

---

[1] See my analysis in *Criticism and Medieval Poetry* (London, 1964), pp. 39–42.

what he obtained from books. His place in the native literary tradition we shall discuss shortly; but his great contemporaries Chaucer and Gower were also men of wide literary and intellectual culture, based on reading in languages other than English. We know less about the *Gawain*-poet's reading than we do about, say, Chaucer's, because his surviving works are less voluminous, and he was in any case less ostentatious about his learning: he is not in the habit of telling us:

> The remenant of the tale if ye wol heere,
> Redeth Ovyde, and ther ye may it leere.
>
> *(Canterbury Tales*, III [D], 981–2)

But we can arrive at some conclusions about his reading. The authors of many of the major poems of the Alliterative Revival seem to have possessed knowledge of the two languages necessary to a medieval writer if he was to be truly a 'clerk': Latin and French, the most accessible language of the ancient world and the most developed, for literary purposes, of the modern. Langland quotes freely from both languages, while many of the other alliterative poems are translations from one or the other: *William of Palerne* from a French romance, *The Destruction of Troy* from the *Historia Destructionis Troiae* of Guido de Columnis, *The Wars of Alexander* from Leo's *Historia de Preliis*, and so on.

In Latin, *Purity*, *Patience* and *Pearl* all show the *Gawain*-poet's close familiarity with the Vulgate Bible. In the case of *Pearl* particularly, the poet displays a knowledge not only of the Apocalypse of St John, which is his main source, but of many other parts of the Bible, allusions to which he weaves together with great deftness. He may well have consulted Latin commentaries on the Apocalypse and on Genesis (for *Purity*) and Jonah (for *Patience*),[1] and he certainly makes use of such major traditional elements in Scriptural exegesis as the treatment of Jonah's descent into the whale as a type of Christ's descent into Hell, and of Abraham's three angels as a type of the Trinity. In general, though (and this is something we shall see when we examine *Patience* and *Purity* in detail), what most interested him was the literal sense of his Biblical sources rather than their typological or allegorical significance. So far we can accept Gordon's

---

[1] It has also been suggested by O. F. Emerson, 'A Parallel between *Patience* and an Early Latin Poem', *PMLA*, x (1896), 242–8, that *Patience* was influenced by a Latin poem, *De Jona et Ninive*, attributed to Tertullian; but the evidence for this is scanty.

view that, 'It would seem that the poet had read theological writings (as Chaucer did) without being himself a systematic theologian'.[1] *Pearl*, however, offers a slightly different picture. Here the discussion of the doctrine of grace may well owe something to the writings of fourteenth-century theologians such as the Englishman Thomas Bradwardine, and to the sources of these theologians' thought in such Fathers of the Church as St Augustine. The poem certainly shows a keen and informed interest in what now seem quite complex technical theological issues, though, as always, what chiefly concerns the poet is their human bearing. It was not abnormal for a fourteenth-century Englishman to possess this kind of interest. A recent study of fourteenth-century philosophy remarks that the theologians of the time, in their discussions of freewill and predestination (a favourite topic of Chaucer's) or of nature and grace:

were not pursuing their own private obsessions, remote from the world of reality; for interest in such matters ranged far beyond the Schools, which only reflected a wider concern. Ockham once protested that laymen and old women used to badger university lecturers with their heretical views on necessity and contingency and the limits of God's power. An outstanding example of the interest, even expertise, assumed in the laity is to be found in the text of *Pearl*.[2]

Pearl also indicates the poet's acquaintance with a different aspect of fourteenth-century thought: mystical theology. The fourteenth century in England was a great age of devotional writing, both in Latin and in the vernacular, marked by such names as Richard Rolle, Walter Hilton, Julian of Norwich, and the author of *The Cloud of Unknowing*. *Pearl* has close links with such writings (closer than any that are to be found in Chaucer), and it has recently been pointed out that the Dreamer's definition of his vision of the other world as a 'gostly drem' (790) indicates the poet's familiarity with the classification of visions used by mystical theologians and the mystics themselves.[3] Here again there is no need to suppose any extraordinary learning on the poet's part, for, as their existence in the vernacular and the survival of many manuscripts testifies, most of the devotional writings were by no means esoteric works.

---

[1] Ed. *Pearl*, pp. xxx–xxxi.

[2] J. A. Robson, *Wyclif and the Oxford Schools* (Cambridge, 1961), p. 33.

[3] Edward Wilson, 'The "Gostly Drem" in *Pearl*', *Neuphilologische Mitteilungen*, LXIX (1968), 90–101; see further below, pp. 110–3.

So far as secular Latin writers are concerned, it is difficult to find any definite evidence that the poet shared Chaucer's knowledge of such classical poets as Virgil and Ovid. Recently, however, there have been claims that certain small debts can be detected in *Sir Gawain and the Green Knight* to Virgil and to Seneca the Younger;[1] and in general it is highly likely that he was familiar with the range of Latin literature, classical and medieval, that was current among educated men in the Middle Ages even after scholasticism had brought the triumph of logic over 'grammar'. It is likely enough, too, that he was acquainted in some form with the precepts and examples of the Latin rhetoricians,[2] though they are unlikely to have supplied him with anything more than a formalization of the techniques actually employed in medieval poetry.

If we turn to French, there can be no doubt that the *Gawain*-poet was widely read in courtly literature, which played a crucial part in forming and sustaining the courtly milieu in England. Whether or not the poet was himself responsible for knitting together the various plot-elements of *Sir Gawain and the Green Knight*, this poem owes an enormous debt to the dominant Northern French tradition of courtly romance. To a greater extent, perhaps, than any other Middle English poem, it carries across into English the finest qualities of French romances—elegance, profoundly suggestive fantasy, delicate psychological analysis. Though there is as yet no scholarly agreement about its specific sources,[3] it could certainly have been created only by a man thoroughly soaked in French romance. It is no surprise to find that in *Purity* the poet refers by name to the *Roman de la Rose* and one of its authors (Jean de Meun, also known as Clopinel), since this

---

[1] See Theodore Silverstein, 'The Art of *Sir Gawain and the Green Knight*', *University of Toronto Quarterly*, XXXIII (1964), 258–78, and '*Sir Gawain*, Dear Brutus, and Britain's Fortunate Founding', *MP*, LXII (1964–5), 189–206; a debt to Virgil was earlier suggested by C. O. Chapman, 'Virgil and the *Gawain*-Poet', *PMLA*, LX (1945), 16–23.

[2] See Silverstein (as in note immediately above); and D. A. Pearsall, 'Rhetorical *Descriptio* in *Sir Gawain and the Green Knight*', *MLR*, L (1955), 129–34.

[3] G. V. Smithers, 'What *Sir Gawain and the Green Knight* is About', *Medium Aevum*, XXXII (1963), 171–89, argues in favour of the general influence of the *Queste del Saint Graal*; L. D. Benson, 'The Source of the Beheading Episode in *Sir Gawain and the Green Knight*', *MP*, LIX (1961–2), 1–12, sees a more specific influence from one version of the *Livre de Caradoc*, as does D. D. R. Owen, 'Burlesque Tradition and *Sir Gawain and the Green Knight*', *Forum*, IV (1968), 125–45, from *Le chevalier à l'epée* and *La mule sans frein*.

work was of the greatest importance in disseminating courtly attitudes, especially in matters of love:

> For Clopyngnel in the compas of his clene Rose,
> Ther he expounez a speche, to hym that spede wolde
> Of a lady to be loved: 'Loke to hir sone,
> Of wich bering that ho be, and wych ho best lovyes,
> And be ryght such, in uch a borwe, of body and of dedes'. (1057–61)

The *Gawain*-poet is here using the instructions of the character Ami about the best way to win a lady's favour to suggest by analogy how God's favour can be won. This, and the fact that he refers to Jean de Meun's part of the poem as 'clene', when it was widely regarded as immoral, suggests that he may have been familiar with one of the 'moralized' versions of it, in which the erotic theme was treated as an allegory.[1] There is a further allusion to the *Roman de la Rose* in *Pearl*, where the Dreamer's praise of the Maiden—

> Pymalyon paynted never thy vys,
> Ne Arystotel nawther by hys lettrure
> Of carped the kynde these propertéz (750–52)

—echoes some widely influential lines of Jean de Meun concerning Nature, even while the preceding line—'Thy beauté com never of Nature'—sets the Maiden's beauty above it. The world of *Pearl*, indeed, seems partly inhabited by the ghosts of the personifications who enact the story of the rose:

> To calle hyr Lyste con me enchace,
> Bot Baysment gef myn hert a brunt. (173–4)

Another sign of the poet's acquaintance with French romance material is the sailors' prayers to 'Vernagu' in *Patience* (165), this being the name of a Saracen giant in romances of the Matter of France.

Another French work whose influence can be detected on the *Gawain*-poet is *Mandeville's Travels*. Though this achieved considerable popularity and was translated into English by the end of the fourteenth century, it is a little more off the beaten track than the *Roman de la Rose*. It gives what misleadingly purports to be a first-hand account of travel to the Holy Land and to more distant parts

---

[1] However, it was and is possible to defend Jean's continuation as being literally in accordance with Christian philosophy (see D. W. Robertson, *A Preface to Chaucer* [Princeton, 1963], pp. 361–5), and this may have been the *Gawain*-poet's intention.

of Asia, and the poet uses it in *Purity* to amplify the Biblical descriptions of the Dead Sea and of Belshazzar's palace and its furnishings.[1]

In French and Latin, then, the *Gawain*-poet seems to have been well read, though by no means uniquely well. He is more unusual, however, in apparently sharing with Chaucer some reading in modern Italian poetry. It was the Italian poets of the fourteenth century who first succeeded in giving to a modern vernacular language not merely the fluency, versatility and charm achieved by French, but the gravity and grandeur of a 'high style' comparable with that of classical Latin. This achievement, of which Chaucer gained a knowledge through his visits to Italy and his consequent reading of works by Petrarch, Dante and Boccaccio, was one from which he in turn learned to write an English 'high style'. The new dignity of tone and richness of texture which his verse acquired from *The Parlement of Foules* onwards was of vital importance for the whole subsequent history of English poetry. It has been argued by Father Mathew that a new conception of the poet as opposed to the minstrel, a figure of independent dignity and learning, also came to France and England from Italy, particularly in the work of Boccaccio. Probably few Englishmen before 1400 had read the fourteenth-century Italian poets. Chaucer was one of them, and it seems almost certain that the *Gawain*-poet was another, so that in this respect he was positively *avant-garde* in his tastes. He seems to have known at least the *Divine Comedy* of Dante, and well enough not simply to translate single passages in it, but to take and synthesize hints from a number of different places. In particular it has been argued that the description, and perhaps the whole conception, of the Maiden in *Pearl*, and of the Dreamer's attitude towards her, was influenced by Dante's treatment of Matilda and Beatrice in *Purgatorio* XVIII–XXXI and *Paradiso* I.[2] The poet's knowledge of Dante cannot be regarded as absolutely certain, because the parallels that exist could possibly be accounted for by the fact that both poets drew on a common literary tradition of other-world visions and heavenly instructresses; but it seems highly likely that the relationship was closer than that. It cannot be said that the *Gawain*-poet learned a

---

[1] See I. Gollancz, ed. *Cleanness* (London, 1921), pp. xxvii–xxviii.

[2] Most recently discussed by Kean, pp. 120–33. There are close similarities between the theme of *Pearl* and that of Boccaccio's eclogue *Olympia* (see I. Gollancz, ed. *Pearl*, 2nd edn. [London, 1921]), which is also an elegy on a dead small girl; but these are probably coincidental.

style from Dante, in the way Chaucer did, at least in his later poems; the use he made of Dante may best be compared with that Chaucer made of him in the later parts of *The House of Fame*, where Dantesque material is kept within the bounds of a chatty, octosyllabic medium. *Pearl* is a graver poem than *The House of Fame*, but of both it might be said that 'What is sublime in the *Divina Commedia* is given a much more familiar tone'.[1]

The alliterative tradition

A major influence on the *Gawain*-poet's work was inevitably the native tradition of alliterative poetry in which it was written. This is an ancient tradition, which goes back even in written form to the Anglo Saxon period—much further than any of the social or literary influences we have been considering so far—and it remains the most powerful moulding force on the work of the fourteenth-century poet. Anglo-Saxon alliterative poetry has its roots in an even more ancient oral tradition, whose origins are lost in the pre-history of unlettered tribes, and the surviving Anglo-Saxon poetry, whether or not it was orally composed before being written down, has a traditional form shaped by the necessities of oral composition in the time before writing had been introduced. If poetry is to be composed orally, the poet will need to have available to him a traditional style, which will largely 'compose and think for him', as Goethe said of the Homeric style. There will have to exist a common pool of traditional poetic devices, from which he can select, with such modification as lies within his powers, what he needs for a particular poem on a particular occasion. This traditional style will itself be a kind of communal work of art, shaped and enriched by generations of poets and their audiences; the role of the individual poet will be to use this style, even while being used by it, so as to create his own crystallization out of its continuing flux. Anglo-Saxon alliterative poetry deals with a limited number of units of subject-matter, usually called 'themes' (for example, feasts, journeys, battles, arrivals of messengers, description of certain kinds of landscape and weather, and so on), and new material is often modified, where necessary, so as to be treated in terms of such themes. Moreover, the themes themselves tend to be expressed through systems of traditional words and phrases, of a fixed semantic content and often of a fixed metrical and

[1] Kean, p. 224.

syntactical pattern. These are known as 'formulas'. This is not the place for a detailed study of the poetic style that results—the subject is in any case controversial[1]—but a few small examples may help. The most obvious instance of a system of more or less synonymous words is the group meaning roughly 'man', 'hero', or 'warrior': *æþeling, beorn, ceorl, freca, guma, hæleþ, leod, rinc, scealc, secg, wer, wiga.* There may well have been slight differences in meaning or tone among these words, but they appear to be used almost inter-changeably, and the only essential difference among them, obviously, is that, except for *wer* and *wiga*, each begins with a different sound. Thus one or other of them can be fitted into the alliteration of almost any line. There are similar groups of synonyms for such essential ideas as 'dwelling', 'mind', 'time', 'son', 'blood', and so on. Nothing could be more useful for the oral poet, or for the audience of orally delivered poetry, whether or not orally composed. As an example of the formula, properly speaking, we might take the word *deawigfeðera*, 'dewyfeathered', which by itself exactly makes up a half-line, and which is regularly applied to the eagle, which in turn is regularly mentioned as part of the battle theme: it is one of the birds and beasts of prey that descend on the battlefield once the battle is over. It too has a synonym, identical in its syntactical and metrical form, and entirely interchangeable with it: *urigfeðera*.

Thus Anglo-Saxon alliterative verse possessed a style very different from that of most modern English poetry; and many of its features were transmitted to Middle English alliterative verse. Important changes also occurred: for example, new subject-matter of a courtly and chivalric kind was introduced, so that new themes were gradually developed; while changes in the language itself brought

---

[1] The fundamental modern work on oral poetry was done by Milman Parry, 'Studies in the Epic Technique of Oral Verse-Making', *Harvard Studies in Classical Philology*, XLI (1930), 73–147, and XLIII (1932), 1–50; and by A. B. Lord, 'Homer and Huso', *Transactions and Proceedings of the American Philological Association*, LXVII (1936), 106–13, and LXIX (1938), 439–45, and *The Singer of Tales* (Cambridge, Mass., 1960). This work was applied to Anglo-Saxon alliterative poetry by F. P. Magoun, 'Oral-Formulaic Character of Anglo-Saxon Narrative Poetry', *Spec*, XXVIII (1953), 446–67. For more recent discussion see R. D. Stevick, 'The Oral-Formulaic Analyses of Old English Verse', *Spec*, XXXVII (1962), 382–9; and R. F. Lawrence, 'The Formulaic Theory and Its Application to English Alliterative Poetry', in *Essays on Style and Language*, ed. Roger Fowler (London, 1966), pp. 166–83. The 'dewy-feathered' eagle, mentioned below, is discussed by F. P. Magoun, 'The Theme of the Beasts of Battle in Anglo-Saxon Poetry', *Neuphilologische Mitteilungen*, LVI (1955), 81–90; and A. Bonjour, 'Beowulf and the Beasts of Battle', *PMLA*, LXXII (1957), 563–73.

with them changes in the diction, syntax and even rhythm of poetry. The basic unit of meaning tended to become the complete line rather than the half-line, the line itself lengthened, statements tended to be completed within a single line rather than to link the second half of one line with the first half of the next, alliteration became thicker but less regular, alliteration on the same letter might be continued for several lines. It is true that there is something of a gap in written alliterative verse between about 1100 and about 1340, during which period the only surviving major alliterative poem is Laȝamon's *Brut*, of about 1200. But we may suppose that during this period alliterative verse survived largely by dropping to a popular, orally-transmitted level; those of its characteristics that arise from oral composition might even have been strengthened by such a stage in its development. At all events, when, towards the middle of the fourteenth century, alliterative poetry once more emerges in a court setting and in a written form, it continues to use many of the older methods.

It has, for instance, retained the Anglo-Saxon system of synonyms for man or warrior. *Wer* and *ceorl* have been lost; *hæleþ* and *æþeling* seem to have merged to form a new synonym, *hathel*; one other new word, *tulk*, has been added; otherwise the group remains the same.[1] What is more important, it is used in the same way; there seem to be some differences in dignity among its members as they are used by the *Gawain*-poet, but the words are largely interchangeable. We cannot often find such exact continuity between Anglo-Saxon and Middle English alliterative verse so far as the actual words and phrases used are concerned—the changes in the language over three or four hundred years would make that unlikely—but the techniques of composition remain similar. Certain themes are constantly repeated: the feast, the battle, the sea-voyage, the storm at sea, and so on. And these themes are regularly treated in terms of certain formulas and systems of formulas. A formula is not so easily defined in Middle English as in Anglo-Saxon alliterative verse, partly because the old division into half-line units has broken down. If we attempt to define a Middle English alliterative formula strictly in terms of a metrical-syntactical framework,[2] we tend to be left with something no

---

[1] See Borroff, pp. 53–60.

[2] As is done by R. A. Waldron, 'Oral-Formulaic Technique and Middle English Alliterative Poetry', *Spec*, XXXII (1957), 792–804; compare the recent remarks of Håkon Ringbom about Laȝamon (*Studies in the Narrative Technique of Beowulf and*

more distinctively formulaic than language itself. It seems best to consider it as being essentially a lexical and semantic nexus: an associative tendency among certain words used to express a certain idea, which may be confined to a single line or half-line, but which may also be expanded over several lines. Formulas of this kind would be of less use in oral composition than formulas of the stricter kind found in Anglo-Saxon verse, which follow a specific syntactical pattern and fill a particular gap in the metre; but then there is no reason to suppose that any of the surviving verse of the Alliterative Revival was orally composed.

To give an example: we have seen that feasts are a common theme in *Purity* and *Sir Gawain and the Green Knight*. A common formula used to describe these feasts consists of a line alliterating on *d*, in which at least two of the four words *daynté(s)*, *dece*, *dressed*, and *der(rest)* (*worthly*) are used. Thus:

Purity 38: Abof dukez on dece, wyth dayntys served
      115: The derrest at the hyghe dese that dubbed wer fayrest
   1394: Dere drowen therto and upon des metten
   1399: For non watz dressed upon dece bot the dere selven
Gawain 75: Dressed on the dere des, dubbed al aboute
   114: Thise were dight on the des and derworthly served
   121: Dayntés dryven therwyth of ful dere metes
   445: Toward the derrest on the dece he dressez the face
   483: Of alle dayntyez double, as derrest myght falle.

It is true that here certain metrical-syntactical tendencies are apparent: thus *dece* tends to be the second stress of the first half-line, as part of an adverbial phrase such as *up* (*on*) (*the*) *dece*; but what holds the formula together is not these tendencies (which are not always operative) but the associative link between certain words. We might therefore feel inclined to suppose that we were here faced with an 'image-cluster' of the kind that has been found in Shakespeare's work, and peculiar to the particular author. But in fact the same formula is also found in other alliterative poems. Thus we find in *The Destruction of Troy* 'With al deintés on dese that were dere

---

Lawman's Brut, Acta Academiae Aboensis, Ser. A, vol. 36, no. 2 [Åbo, 1968], p. 76): 'By Lawman's time the inherited body of fixed formulas had apparently disintegrated ...Recurring phrases and expressions abound in the *Brut*, but they have no fixed form... *Formula* in the sense in which the word has been used in Old English scholarship is thus not a suitable term for Lawman's loosely structured, recurrent phrases.'

holden', and in *William of Palerne* 'And derly at that day with deynteyes were thei served'.[1] The formula belongs to a poetic language available to all alliterative poets, and along with the actual words associated in it go certain ideas or attitudes—particularly a regard for hierarchy at the feast, so that the *dere* (noble) are seated on a raised dais, and are served with *dayntés* which may also be described as *dere* (precious, rare).

A similar formula used to express the feast theme is one based on the association *mirth–minstrelsy–melody–meat–(upon) molde*; this too is found in several different alliterative poems, which no-one would wish to attribute to the same author. In such cases, when attempting to arrive at a critical judgment of a particular poem, it would of course be absurd to adopt the assumptions of a later age, and simply blame the poet for using second-hand phraseology or repeating himself. It would be equally absurd to assume that every such repetition within a particular poem is either a deliberate reminiscence of some other specific poem, or in itself an important part of the meaning of the poem under study. Such formulaic repetitions are part of the method of composition available to all these poets; what the critic will be concerned with is the skill with which a particular poet uses the method. This may be illustrated by another example. A formula used to refer to someone kneeling speaks of him as kneeling 'on the cold earth' (*knele* alliterating with *colde*). This is found, for example, at several points in *The Wars of Alexander*, one being 'He knelis doun with his knightis on the cald erthe'.[2] It is also found in *Purity*: 'Ho kneles on the colde erthe, and carpes to hymselven' (1591). But in none of these cases does the poet add anything to the poetic quality of the common phrase; in *Purity*, for example, it refers to Belshazzar's queen kneeling in his banqueting hall, so that she is not literally kneeling on the earth at all, and there is no reason to suppose that the floor was particularly cold. The phrase merely borrows a certain pathos from the tradition, and pays nothing in return. In *Sir Gawain and the Green Knight*, on the other hand, in the line 'And kneled doun on her knes upon the colde erthe' (818), it is used with a more original force, which is conferred by the context rather than by any originality of wording. Here it refers to the people in Sir Bertilak's castle coming out of its warmth and protection in mid-

---

[1] *The Destruction of Troy*, ed. G. A. Panton and D. Donaldson, EETS OS 39 and 56 (London, 1867 and 1874), line 385; *William of Palerne*, ed. W. W. Skeat, line 1421.
[2] *The Wars of Alexander,* ed. W. W. Skeat, EETS ES 47 (London, 1886), line 4928.

winter in order to greet Sir Gawain on his arrival. The earth would indeed be cold, and the seemingly banal repetition 'kneled doun on her knes' serves to emphasize the way their own flesh is brought into contact with the cold Gawain has been suffering on his journey. They show their exemplary courtesy by voluntarily sharing his suffering; and the formula, with its physical sense thus restored, is handed back to the tradition as if newly-minted to be used by the next alliterative poet who needs it. In studying the separate poems of MS Cotton Nero A. x we shall find other examples of how the Gawain-poet shows his skill not by avoiding traditional formulas but by using them with special aptness.

The alliterative tradition involved the handing on not merely of techniques of composition such as those we have been considering but of attitudes towards life. Whatever the nature of the links between the Alliterative Revival and the Anglo-Saxon period, what was passed down to the alliterative poets of the fourteenth century was a tradition of heroic literature. To generalize very broadly, the Anglo-Saxon poets took a somewhat gloomy view of the world: they saw man surrounded by a hostile universe, a warrior fighting against odds, probably defeated, and yet heroic in his defeat. This vision of man and the universe goes back to pagan times: it is built into that pessimistic Northern mythology, which foretells that the forces of light and order will eventually be defeated by those of chaos, and gods and men will go together down into the darkness. In such an imaginative world, heroic conduct has no external incentive in the form of a heavenly reward; its only reward is a fame of which the dead hero can know nothing. Thus loyalty and courage, the virtues that the Anglo-Saxons most admired, could be seen only as values that men created for themselves, for their own sake, as a matter of pure existential choice. And this attitude towards life was retained long after the Anglo-Saxons had been converted to Christianity, with its promise of a heavenly reward for virtuous behaviour on earth. Precisely because the call for heroic action is not felt to be supported by any external sanction (except fame), it is characteristically stated with great explicitness, as a categorical moral imperative, a sceal (ought, must). Thus in Beowulf, undoubtedly a Christian poem, the poet speaks of the hero, confronted with a hideous water-monster impervious to his previously invincible sword, deliberately throwing the sword away and wrestling with the creature—so should a man act!

23

Eft wæs anræd, nalas elnes læt,
mærða gemyndig mæg Hylaces:
wearp ða wundenmæl wrættum gebunden
yrre oretta, þæt hit eorðan læg,
stið ond stylecg; strenge getruwode,
mundgripe mægenes. Swa sceal man don,
þonne he æt guðe gegan þenceð
longsumne lof; na ymb his lif cearað.

Resolute again was Hygelac's kinsman,
Not backward in bravery, mindful of all audacity.
The warrior now infuriated threw down on the ground
The wave-marked sword steel-edged and stubborn
With its bands of rare handiwork; he put faith in strength,
In the handgrip of power. So shall a man act
When in the midst of war he takes heart to win
Long-living praise: careless of his life.[1]

Still more striking, in *The Battle of Maldon,* a poem by a Christian poet of the tenth century about a battle that really occurred between Christian Anglo-Saxons and pagan Vikings, the poet still sees courage in defeat, courage for its own sake, as the ultimate value. The Anglo-Saxons are defeated—if their God is watching, he does not intervene—their leader is killed, and the survivors fight on until they are cut to pieces over his dead body. For this extreme of heroism no religious or even patriotic reasons are given, but the same categorical imperative in the same *sceal,* now emphatically repeated:

Hige sceal þe heardra, heorte þe cenre,
mod sceal þe mare, þe ure mægen lytlað.

Thought shall be the sterner, heart the keener,
Courage the greater, as our strength lessens.[2]

The same attitude, and the same explicit ethic, are handed down with the alliterative tradition to the poets of the Revival. Many of their poems, as we have noted, are translations from Latin or French, but they make their own attitudes felt in their selection of materials for translation, their success in turning various kinds of material into

---

[1] *Beowulf,* ed. F. Klaeber, 3rd edn. (Boston, Mass., 1950), lines 1529–36; trans. Edwin Morgan (Aldington, 1952).
[2] *The Battle of Maldon,* ed. E. V. Gordon (London, 1937), lines 312–13; my translation.

alliterative verse, and, of course, in the additions they make to their sources. A particularly striking example of success with material which is already in keeping with the heroic ethos occurs in *The Destruction of Troy*. Medea has advised Jason to abandon the quest of the Golden Fleece because it is too dangerous and he will certainly be killed. At this he 'wrathit a litill' and spoke as follows:

> A! damsell full dere, with your derffe wordys,
> What lure is of my lyfe and I lyffe here:
> I hope ye found me to fere and my faith breike;
> And if destyny me demys, hit is dere welcum,
> Or it were knowen in my contry and costis aboute,
> That I faintly shuld fle and the fight leve,
> Among knightes accounted coward for ever;
> Me were lever here lefe and my life tyne
> Than as a lurker to lyve in ylke a lond after.
> I wole put me to perell and my payne thole,
> Do my dever yf I dar, and for no dethe wonde.
> For yche wise man of wit, that wilfully hetis
> Any dede for to do, and dernly avowes,
> Shuld chose hym by chaunce to chaunge out of lyve,
> Ere he fayne any faintes and be fals haldyn.[1]

The trappings here are medieval (*damsell, knightes, dever,* and so on), but the feelings are exactly those of *Beowulf* and *Maldon*. As in *Maldon*, a man must perform what he has promised, whatever the cost; as in *Beowulf*, reputation is the only external sanction; as in both, the heroic attitude is transformed into an ethic with a confident *shuld*. Jason is of course a pagan; but it is striking that even with Christian heroes the same attitude may be expressed, and may lie alongside expressions of reliance on God without being essentially modified. This is so in *William of Palerne*, in a speech which the English poet has greatly expanded and indeed transformed. William addresses his men as the Spaniards advance to attack them:

> 'Lo, lordinges,' sede William, 'wich a loveli sight
> Here bifore us of our fon, of ferche men and bold!

---

[1] Ed. Panton and Donaldson, lines 580–94. This speech is very close to its Latin source, which includes both the emphasis on reputation (*gloria*) and the explicit moralizing about the need to perform the deeds one has promised: 'Nam prudentis viri proprium esse debet, ex quo alicuius cepti propositum publicauit in actu, preponere necem uite priusquam a cepto ignominiose desistat' (Guido de Columnis, *Historia Destructionis Troiae*, ed. N. E. Griffin [Cambridge, Mass., 1936], p. 20).

Ther is holli al here ost; now, beth of hertes gode,
And we schul wel this day this werre bring to ende,
Onliche thurh Godes grace and your gode dede.
Though ther be mani mo than ye, dismaie ye nought therfore:
God wol us ay rescue and with the right stonde;
Go we to hem on Godes name, with a god wille.
And I mow come bi the king, bi Crist, as ich hope,
He schal sone therafter to his sone wende,
To sojorne in the cité that he hath seged yore.
Therfor, frendes and felawes, for Him that you bought,
Doth your dede today as doughti men schulle,
And gret worchipe schul ye winne whil this world lasteth.'[1]

In the last two lines particularly, the heroic ethic, with the *schulle* we have come to expect, advances to the foreground from out of a nominally Christian world-view. Earthly fame is the reward for heroic action, and 'whil this world lasteth', which may be intended to qualify it, in fact suggests 'as long as the world endures' quite as much as '*only* as long as *this* world endures'.

Ethically, *William of Palerne* is a somewhat naïve poem; ethics, indeed, is not its concern. There are other poems of the Alliterative Revival in which a fuller and more considered Christianity comes into conflict with the older heroic attitude. By the fourteenth century the world-picture of secular men had become far more completely 'Christianized' than it was in the time of *Beowulf* or *Maldon*. Man was no longer alone in the world, as the Anglo-Saxon poets had often continued to *feel* him to be, long after their conversion to Christianity. Man is surrounded by God's power and God's mercy; they pervade completely the world in which he lives; and in such a world the proper attitude for man is no longer one of heroic defiance, but of humility and obedience. Yet the alliterative tradition remains a heroic tradition. The alliterative style implies by its very nature a heroic view of man; its very stock of words for 'man', its hoard of formulas and the patterns it supplies for creating new formulas, are imbued with heroic feeling; the style and the vision of life cannot be separated. Hence we should expect to find surviving longest in alliterative poetry the tension between heroic and anti-heroic atti-

---

[1] Ed. W. W. Skeat, lines 3795–808. The source has undergone striking modification; the alliterative poet has intensified the religious content, and has himself added the references to fame and duty, thus assimilating it to his native tradition; see *Guillaume de Palerne*, ed. H. Michelant (Paris, 1876), lines 6511–36.

tudes which is common throughout the early medieval literature of north-western Europe. Sometimes this tension is explicit; it is significant that *two* surviving alliterative poems, *Alexander and Dindimus* and *The Wars of Alexander*, deal with the disputation between Alexander, the very type of heroic pagan conqueror, and Dindimus, the king of the peace-loving, contemplative Brahmins. The Brahmins are occupied with the fight against inward foes, and see earthly life as a pilgrimage to heaven; Alexander and his Greeks, with their 'surquitry', their 'bost and...bobans',[1] are fully occupied with earthly conquest. That dispute is left unsettled; but the tension becomes sharper when the expounder and enactor of heroic values is, like King Arthur, a Christian. In the alliterative *Morte Arthure*, the poet himself seems torn between admiration for Arthur's heroic military campaigns, in which he conquers all Europe, and a sense that such heroic energies are radically misdirected. The tone of the poem as a whole is heroic, and, in its emphasis on loyalty and the keeping of promises whatever the cost, it may well remind us of *The Battle of Maldon*.[2] This tone is crystallized, for example, in the speech of Idrous during Arthur's last battle, when he refuses Arthur's command to rescue his father, Ewayne:

> He es my fadire in faithe, forsake sall I never,
> He has me fosterde and fedde and my faire bretheren,
> Bot I forsake this gate, so me God helpe,
> And sothely all sybredyn, bot thy selfe one.
> I breke never his biddynge for beryn one lyfe,
> Bot ever bouxum as beste, blethely to wyrke.
> He commande me kyndly with knyghtly wordes
> That I schulde lelely one the lenge and one noo lede ells;
> I sall hys commandement holde, yif Criste wil me thole.
> He es eldare than I, and ende sall we bothen,
> He sall ferkke before, and I sall come aftyre:

[1] *The Wars of Alexander*, ed. W. W. Skeat, lines 4254, 4252.
[2] Compare the views of its most recent editor: 'The sentiments of our poem are almost purely heroic: the emphasis on the loyalty of his men to Arthur, and of Arthur to them; the attitudes to war and battle, which are almost identical with those in *Beowulf* and the battle of Maldon; the close relationship of Arthur to Gawain, which parallels Charlemagne's relationship to Roland [in the *Chanson de Roland*]; the almost total absence of "love-interest", despite the dominance of courtly love in contemporary literature; the stereotyped laments by Arthur on the death of Gawain, which closely resemble that of Charlemagne for Roland—these are all clear indications that we are in the heroic...world' (*Morte Arthure*, ed. John Finlayson [London, 1967], p. 11).

27

Yiffe him be destaynede to dy todaye one this erthe,
Criste comly with crown take kepe to hys saule![1]

Here there is no clash between heroic and religious attitudes; but in other places we are forcefully reminded that heroic exploits may be directed against both humanity and Christianity. Thus when Arthur's army captures Metz after a siege, they utterly destroy it, an action permitted by the medieval law of arms when a city was taken by assault, and indeed often performed during the Hundred Years War in the poet's own time. But the destruction is described with a humane realism, in which the indiscriminate treatment of houses and churches is felt to be morally significant:

Mynsteris and masondewes they malle to the erthe,
Chirches and chapelles chalke-whitte blawnchede.
Stone stepelles fulle styffe in the strete ligges,
Chawmbyrs with chymnés, and many cheefe inns,
Paysede and pelid downe playsterede walles;
The pyne of the pople was peté for to here.[2]

The critical implications of this description are made explicit shortly afterwards when Arthur has a frightening dream of his overthrow by Fortune, which one of his 'philosophers' interprets as follows:

Thow has schedde myche blode and schalkes distroyede,
Sakeles in cirquytrie in sere kynges landis;
Schryfe the of thy schame and schape for thyn ende.
Thow has a schewynge, sir kynge, take kepe yif the lyke,
For thow sal fersely fall within fyve wynters.
Fownde abbayes in Fraunce, the froytez are theyn awen,
Fore Froill and for Ferawnt and for thir ferse knyghttis
That thowe fremydly in Fraunce has faye belevede.[3]

Though the poet's overall attitude remains favourable to Arthur, we are certainly made to feel that his final defeat and death are in part punishment for the 'cirquytrie' of his conquests (the same vice as the 'surquitry' of which Dindimus accuses Alexander).

In the *Morte Arthure* the tension between admiration and condemnation of the heroic makes the poem richer yet more confused; it is not something the poet has fully under his control, or is even perhaps fully conscious of. In the work of the *Gawain*-poet a similar

---

[1] *Morte Arthure*, ed. J. Finlayson, lines 4142–54.
[2] Ed. E. Brock, EETS OS8, 2nd edn. (London, 1871), lines 3038–43.
[3] Ed. Finlayson, lines 3398–405.

tension exists, but there, I believe, it is under control, and is made a deliberate and crucial part of the meaning of his poems. In each of his four poems we find a situation which is fundamentally the same. In each of them, human beings are shown as living their lives on purely human terms, accepting the values of this world: values which may in themselves be admirable, which range across a spectrum running from common sense to heroism, and which may, at their most elevated and secure, achieve the genuine splendour of an idealized medieval court such as Arthur's. The central figures of the *Gawain*-poet's work are not atheists. Belshazzar indeed comes near to atheism, being an extreme example of an idolatrous pagan who deliberately flouts the true God; but in general the poet shows men as paying a very thorough lipservice to religion, whether that of the Old Testament or that of the New. But the central figures of his poems do not, in the last resort, really *feel* that there are values beyond those of this world that may make some demand on them. And in each of the four poems, human beings living in this state are confronted with some intervention from a world beyond the human, an intervention which acts as a challenging reminder of non-human values and their power. This is most crudely the case with the Old Testament stories re-told in *Purity*: men live in filth, impurity, uncleanness, which directly flouts God, and in consequence they are terribly punished, by flood, fire, and war. The hand suddenly appearing in the middle of Belshazzar's feast to write an ominous message on the wall is a characteristic example from this poem of how directly God intervenes to remind men of the power by which he ensures that his will is done. In *Patience*, Jonah is determined to achieve an independent dignity, first by attempting to evade God's will that he should prophesy in Nineveh, then, when that fails, by insisting that his prophecies of doom ought to come true, even though they have already achieved God's purpose of bringing the Ninevites to repentance. Jonah thinks he can evade the will of God, but God's power impinges again and again on his life, and makes his aspirations absurd. In *Pearl*, the narrator has a vision which carries him out of this world, where he is lost in luxuriant grief for a dead child, into the world beyond death, where the child has become his superior, and he must learn that he has failed to understand, or at least to *realize*, the divine framework of human existence, and that his mourning was based on false assumptions. In *Sir Gawain and the Green Knight*, finally, the cheerful court of King Arthur, in its youthful confidence, is broken in upon at New Year by the mysterious knight, huge in size, green all over, riding a green horse, with his irrational challenge to a game in which heads are at stake. It must be said at once that the Green Knight is a far more ambiguous and problematic figure than the God with whom the *Gawain*-poet's other 'heroes' are confronted. I have no wish to impose a rigid pattern of interpretation on all four poems, but I do think that one can trace a process of development in the *Gawain*-poet's successive treatments of a single fundamental subject. If one accepts provisionally the sequence *Purity, Patience, Pearl, Sir Gawain and the Green Knight* (which I think would be acceptable to most scholars who have worked on the poems), one finds the non-human power with which man is confronted becoming steadily more remote and undefinable. Thus there is a movement from the Old Testament God of *Purity* and *Patience,* who speaks directly to man, to *Pearl,* where God says nothing to the Dreamer, and divine truth is mediated to him partly through vision but largely through the transfigured human shape of the Maiden; and thus to *Sir Gawain and the Green Knight,* where the power by which man is challenged has no defined theological status at all, and has become ambiguous and mysterious, an elusive shape-shifter.

Whether or not this sequence is assumed, it is at least true that we find in the *Gawain*-poet's works this central and repeated subject of a confrontation between man and something more than man. That 'something more' possesses an all-encompassing power, but one whose implications man is unwilling to admit. He is not willing to accept the role of humility and submission that it should impose on him; he wishes to continue to play the heroic role implied by the traditional alliterative style—to be independent, to choose for himself. He struggles to defeat the power with which he is confronted, to evade or outwit it, but his struggle is necessarily vain, and therefore absurd. Thus the hero of the alliterative tradition becomes a hero *manqué,* a would-be hero. His aspirations to heroic or even tragic action are thwarted, and the heroic image of man is undercut and presented ironically. The situation might be called tragi-comic, if one were to bear in mind the classic statement of the tragi-comic view of man given by the Duke in *Measure for Measure*:

> man, proud man,
> Drest in a little brief authority,
> Most ignorant of what he's most assured—

His glassy essence—like an angry ape,
Plays such fantastic tricks before high heaven
As make the angels weep; who, with our spleens,
Would all themselves laugh mortal.[1]

Yet the feeling surrounding this view of man in the *Gawain*-poet's work is less desperate than it is in such plays as *Measure for Measure* and *Troilus and Cressida*. The medieval poet would laugh at him, not weep. At least in *Patience, Pearl,* and *Sir Gawain and the Green Knight,* the main human figures are presented with sympathetic insight, their reactions are studied in detail with knowledge and with kindness: they are not simply dismissed or condemned. The poet does not seem to see himself as superior to his 'heroes', even though he discloses in them an inadequacy to come to terms with the central fact of the human situation: that man lives in a world he did not make, and is at the mercy of non-human powers. For the *Gawain*-poet this view of man can be held charitably, as comic rather than tragi-comic, chiefly because he sees the power with which man is confronted as itself merciful. Even in *Purity,* the most severe of the poems, the anger in which God destroys all mankind except for Noah and his family is preceded by two occasions on which, though he was provoked and dealt out punishment, he did so in moderation and even mercy. First he punished Lucifer, 'In the mesure of his mode, his metz never the lasse' (215); then Adam, and:

Al in mesure and methe watz mad the vengaunce,
And eft amended wyth a mayden that make had never; (247–8)

and only after that did he show 'malys mercyles' (250). In the other poems, the confronting power is above all one which forgives human failings. In *Patience* God forgives first the Ninevites and then Jonah himself; in *Pearl* the Dreamer, for all his almost wilful blindness, is allowed a glimpse of the heavenly city, with his pearl in the train of the Lamb of God; and in *Sir Gawain and the Green Knight* the Green Knight is eventually more lenient towards Gawain's failing than Gawain himself is. It is indeed precisely this forgiving quality of the power man faces that makes it so destructive of human dignity. Thus the *Gawain*-poet's view of life is at once religious and comic. This is a combination characteristic of the Middle Ages: the poet is unusual only in the central image he repeatedly uses to express the

[1] II. ii. 118–24. The idea of a Shakespearean 'tragi-comic view of man' has been explored by A. P. Rossiter, *Angel With Horns* (London, 1961), especially pp. 116–17.

31

view and, of course, in the power and control of his means of expression. But a view of life at once religious and comic has not been at all characteristic of more recent times, and particularly not of the period since the Reformation. For this reason, the modern reader, however much he admires the *Gawain*-poet, may run the risk of misunderstanding him; and indeed it seems to me that much modern criticism of him has been excessively solemn, has not responded to the powerful currents of celebration and forgiveness in his work, and has seen him not only as an exact moralist (which he is), but also as a harsh moralist (which he is not).[1]

The poet

Finally, we must face the question whether we are justified in talking about a single '*Gawain*-poet', the author of all four poems in MS Cotton Nero A. x. One part of the evidence in favour of common authorship will of course be the common view of life and the common central image (of man confronted and baffled by a non-human power) which, in my view, is to be found in the poems. The reader will judge, by measuring my accounts of the separate poems against his own experience of them, whether he finds this convincing; and there can be no point in discussing this kind of evidence in general terms. But there is other evidence of a perhaps more objective kind which is worth mentioning here. Some, indeed, of the evidence which was at one time presented in favour of common authorship can no longer be regarded as valid. Before it was understood that the alliterative style is basically formulaic, similarities in phrasing between different alliterative poems were held to imply common authorship, or at least the imitation of one poet by another. Now that we recognize the existence of a common pool of formulas which was available to all the alliterative poets, we can see that it is extremely difficult to establish authorship on the basis of such similarities, and difficult even to be certain about imitation. The style used by the poets is as anonymous as they were themselves: their names are rarely recorded in their poems,[2] and they must have regarded themselves to some extent as continuators of an ancient tradition of

[1] I include in this censure some aspects of my own earlier study of *Sir Gawain and the Green Knight*, in *Criticism and Medieval Poetry*.

[2] The authors of *William of Palerne* and *Piers Plowman* both name themselves as 'William'; no other names of medieval English alliterative poets are known.

minstrelsy, 'In londe so hatz ben longe' (*Gawain*, 36), rather than as individual creators. The same applies to common units of subject-matter, or 'themes': the fact that, for example, *Patience, The Destruction of Troy*, and *The Siege of Jerusalem* all contain lively descriptions of sea-storms does not mean that they are all by the same poet. This is a convenient place to note that the invalidity of such evidence as a proof of common authorship applies equally to one other alliterative poem, not found in the *Gawain*-manuscript, which has often been attributed to the *Gawain*-poet. This is *Saint Erken-wald*, a poem concerning the finding of a miraculously preserved corpse, found only in a much later manuscript (Harley 2250, dating from 1470–80), in a different dialect from that of the *Gawain*-poems (a mixture of East-Midland and West-Midland forms), closely connected with London by its subject-matter, as none of the *Gawain*-poems is, and not sharing the central image of these other poems. A recent study has shown how weak is the evidence for connecting it with the *Gawain*-poet,[1] and indeed it is difficult to understand why the connection was ever made.

There are more substantial reasons than this for claiming common authorship for the four poems in MS Cotton Nero A. x. For one thing, they do all occur in the same manuscript, in the same dialect, and apparently dating from the same period. Then they possess certain similarities of style and imagery which cannot be accounted for in terms of the common alliterative tradition. One of these is the use of periphrases for God which contain not only such ordinary synonyms for God as lord, father, prince, king as their head-words, but such traditional synonyms for man as *wyy, tulk* and *hathel*.[2] Examples are 'that Wyy that al the world planted' (*Patience*, line 111), 'the Tolke that tyned hem therinne' (*Purity*, 498), and 'the Hathel...That haldez the heven upon hyghe' (*Gawain*, 2056–7). Such phrases belong to a common formulaic system, but the humanizing effect of their head-words is peculiar to the *Gawain*-poet, and as we shall see, this humanizing of God is an important part of his central image of the confrontation of man with a non-human power, especially in *Purity* and *Patience*. Another, and even more telling, similarity is the use of the pearl as an image of purity. This in itself is not uncommon in medieval symbolism, but its recurrence is notable, and it is not only a matter of simple recurrence. The centre

---

[1] L. D. Benson, 'The Authorship of *St Erkenwald*', *JEGP*, LXIV (1965), 393–405.

[2] *Ibid*. pp. 403–4.

of pearl imagery among the poems is of course in *Pearl* itself. There
the pearl that has been lost reappears as a maiden called Pearl, who
is dressed in pearls, is found in a landscape partly composed of
pearls, and wears a great pearl at her breast. The parable of the pearl
of great price is a key argument in the poem, and even the Lamb of
God is described as being as white as pearls. As we shall see, it is
scarcely possible to define the symbolic value of the pearl in terms of
any abstraction, but we may say at least that the pearl is above all
something pure and something *of prys*, precious. In *Sir Gawain and
the Green Knight* it is used in a similar sense at a crucial point in the
poem. At the Green Chapel, when the Green Knight explains to
Gawain how he has been tricked, he assures him that, despite his
fault in accepting and concealing the girdle, he is still the most
perfect of earthly knights:

> As perle bi the quite pese is of prys more,
> So is Gawayn, in god fayth, bi other gay knyghtez. (2364–5)

In *Purity* there is a longer passage comparing the soul purified by
confession to a pearl:

> Thou may schyne thurgh schryfte, thagh thou haf schome served,
> And pure the with penaunce tyl thou a perle worthe.
> Perle praysed is prys ther perré is schewed,
> Thagh hym not derrest be demed to dele for penies.
> Quat may the cause be called bot for hir clene hwes,
> That wynnes worschyp abof alle whyte stones?
> For ho schynes so schyr that is of schap rounde,
> Wythouten faut other fylthe, yif ho fyn were
> And wax ever in the worlde in weryng so olde,
> Yet the perle payres not whyle ho in pyese lasttes;
> And if hit cheve the chaunce uncheryst ho worthe,
> That ho blyndes of ble in bour ther ho lygges,
> Nobot wasch hir wyth worchyp in wyn, as ho askes,
> Ho by kynde schal becom clerer then are.
> So if folk be defowled by unfre chaunce,
> That he be sulped in sawle, seche to schryfte,
> And he may polyce hym at the prest, by penaunce taken,
> Wel bryghter then the beryl other browden perles. (1115–32)

What is striking here is not just the coincidence of image, but the
fact that the thought is so similar. The situation referred to in the
passage from *Purity* is exactly the situation Gawain is in at the moment when the Green Knight compares him to a pearl. He has, at least

in his own eyes, been 'defowled by unfre chaunce', and the Green Knight, acting for the moment as a kind of priest, is about to tell him that, by confession and the penance of the cut in his neck, he has regained his innocence. At this point the Green Knight uses the very image of polishing to mean purification by confession:

> I halde the polysed of that plyght, and pured as clene
> As thou hadez never forfeted sythen thou watz fyrst borne. (2393-4)

This is turn reminds us of another place in *Purity* where polishing is mentioned in connection with the pearl image: the reader is advised:

> Thenne conforme the to Kryst, and the clene make,
> That ever is polyced als playn as the perle selven. (1067-8)

Yet another use of the pearl in *Purity* as an image of purity connects the poem more firmly with *Pearl*. The meaning of the passage in question is somewhat obscure; the text may be corrupt, or we may simply be faced with a sharp anacoluthon. But its gist appears to be: 'Even a tiny speck of sin, in a man otherwise completely pure, is enough to exclude him from the sight of God; in order to gain the Kingdom of Heaven one must be as perfect as the beryl, as spotless as the pearl.'

> For is no segge under sunne so seme of his craftez,
> If he be sulped in synne, that syttez unclene—
> On spec of a spote may spede to mysse
> Of the syghte of the Soverayn that syttez so hyghe;
> For that schewe me schale in tho schyre howsez
> As the beryl bornyst byhovez be clene,
> That is sounde on uche a syde and no sem habes,
> Wythouten maskle other mote as margerye-perle. (549-56)

These lines express a moral rigour such as Gawain applies to himself, in refusing the Green Knight's comfort, and seeing his single fault as an irremediable blot on the perfection he aimed at. Moreover, a passage in *Pearl* expressing the same view, as an amplification of Christ's 'Whosoever shall not receive the kingdom of God as a little child shall not enter into it' (Mark x. 15; Luke xviii. 17), contains a line combining the first halves of lines 550 and 556 of *Purity*, and ends with a reference to the pearl of great price:

> Jesus con calle to hym hys mylde,
> And sayde hys ryche no wyy myght wynne

Bot he com thyder ryght as a chylde,
Other ellez nevermore com therinne.
Harmlez, trwe, and undefylde,
Wythouten mote other mascle of sulpande synne,
Quen such ther cnoken on the bylde,
Tyt schal hem men the yate unpynne.
Ther is the blys that con not blynne
That the jueler soghte thurgh perré pres,
And solde alle hys goud, bothe wolen and lynne,
To bye hym a perle watz mascellez. (721–32)

It is true that this chain of pearl imagery does not take in *Patience*. But, of the four poems, it is perhaps easiest to suppose that *Patience* and *Purity* are by the same author. They are both in long alliterative lines without any form of rhyme, and they are both homilies which treat of a virtue specified in the Beatitudes by giving examples from the Old Testament of the punishment of its opposing vice. It is even possible to imagine quite plausibly what might have led a poet to turn from one subject to the other. It may well be that, as Gollancz put it:

While planning his work [*Purity*], the poet meditated on other Biblical instances of God's anger, and in pondering on the subject of Nineveh he became more interested in the problem of Jonah than in any homiletic exposition as to why the Ninevites escaped from their threatened punishment. Hence, I think, came his decision to treat of the prophet [Jonah] by way of exemplifying the duty of resignation and obedience to the Divine Will.[1]

There is thus evidence of a number of different kinds that links together the four poems in the manuscript. None of this evidence can be held to provide conclusive proof that all four poems are by the same author. It would remain possible to suppose that the manuscript contains the work of a closely linked school of poets, even though one might admit that the four poems taken together form a coherent whole, an *oeuvre*. One might also follow more complicated hypotheses, such as that suggested by Father Mathew: 'possibly the original manuscript was a repertory book composed by the author of *Gawain and the Green Knight*, who included not only his own poem but *Pearl*, a favourite piece of recitation that had influenced his own verse very strongly, and *Patience* and *Cleannesse* which he had inter-

[1] Ed. *Cleanness*, p. xix.

polated and polished'.[1] But ultimately, to establish probabilities in such a case, we can only fall back on the principle of economy, or Ockham's razor. It is easier to believe that towards the end of the fourteenth century, within a certain rather small dialect area, there lived one great poet than to believe that there lived two, or three, or four. For the fact is that the author of each of these poems was a great poet, of a quality rare in any age.

A sense of the *Gawain*-poet's greatness can emerge fully only from the reader's own experience of each of the four poems, each being a unique whole, with its own distinctive virtues. But before I proceed to analyses based on my own responses to each separate poem, there is a little I can say in more general terms about the distinctive merits of his work as a whole. His greatness may be defined partly in terms of his style. The style of alliterative verse in general tends to a greater concreteness and specificity than that of the Chaucerian verse of the same period. Characteristically, it works by juxtaposition and variation, and depends on 'analysis and specification rather than generalization'.[2] The work of the *Gawain*-poet shares in this concreteness; but with him it is a concreteness so heightened as to become a quality of imagination, not merely of style, and one that pervades his poems through and through. For him, every event within his fictions is as fully realized, as fully present to all the senses, as if it were part of everyday reality—more realized, indeed, than reality itself as most of us experience it for most of the time. One way in which he achieves this effect is by imagining the events of his poems as occupying a three-dimensional space. As the early painters of the Italian Renaissance first opened up the picture-space, so the *Gawain*-poet opens up the poem-space, and does so more fully than any of his contemporaries. We have seen that the *Gawain*-poet appears to have been one of the few English writers of his time to have come under Italian literary influences, and this makes it all the more tempting to connect his spatial achievement too with currents flowing from Italy. In his own time there was beginning to take place a gradual penetration of Italian influence into English painting. This shows itself in at least local three-dimensionality in the modelling of faces and figures, and

---

[1] *The Court of Richard II*, p. 116. If one wished to construct such hypotheses, it would surely be easier to postulate that the author of *Pearl*, an original poem if ever there was one, was the redactor and polisher of *Sir Gawain and the Green Knight*, a traditional romance to whose *matiere* he supplied a new, more moralizing *sen*.

[2] Benson, p. 152.

occasionally even in attempts at the realization of a whole picture as a single three-dimensional space. These tendencies reach their culmination around 1400 in the work of one of the illuminators of the Carmelite Missal and in that of two painters whose names we know, Johannes Siferwas and Herman Scheere. One sign of Italian influence in English illumination is an interest in the representation of the human figure in unusual poses and seen from unusual angles. Examples may be found in the kneeling woman seen from behind in a miniature in the M. R. James Memorial Psalter and in the figure with upturned head, also seen from behind, in the Crucifixion miniature in the Lytlington Missal.[1] It is perhaps not by accident that the *Gawain*-poet too shows an intense interest in strange postures, as in the elaborate descriptions of how the Green Knight and Gawain take up their stances, the one to offer the back of his neck to the axe, the other to raise the axe and bring it down with the greatest possible force. The poet is also interested in unusual angles, as when Gawain from his bending position sees the Green Knight's axe coming down on him, and later sees his own blood shooting over his shoulders to the snow.[2]

The *Gawain*-poet, in fact, goes much further than any English artist of the fourteenth century in opening up and entering into the spatial world of his work. In doing this he has, of course, a resource not open to the painter: movement. Not only are the characters and objects in his poems set in motion through a space which the sense of motion makes real (Gawain's axe-blade whirling through the air to chop off the Green Knight's head, the Dreamer of *Pearl* moving towards the river and then along its bank), but the point of view of the narrator of his poems is also in movement, presenting events now from one angle, now from another, now in panorama, now in close-up. Thus he makes use of the technique which distinguishes the cinema from the theatre: the moving 'eye' of the camera, which establishes the solidity of objects and the reality of events by moving freely among and around them.[3] In this way the poet combines the

---

[1] See Margaret Rickert, *Painting in Britain: the Middle Ages* (2nd edn., Harmondsworth, 1965), chapter 7 and plates 154A and 158.

[2] See Borroff, pp. 126–7.

[3] The parallel with the cinema was suggested by Alain Renoir, 'Descriptive Technique in *Sir Gawain and the Green Knight*', *Orbis Litterarum*, XIII (1959), 126–32, and has been elaborated by Borroff, pp. 123–4 and 126–9. My remarks on the means by which the poet realizes the events of his poems are much indebted to both these writers.

vividness of local texture which is so characteristic of the late medieval arts with an exhilarating and much more unusual spatial structure.

A second general aspect of the poet's style to which attention may be directed before we turn to particular poems is this. In his work, to a unique extent among the poets of the Alliterative Revival, the rich concreteness, specificity and spatiality we have been discussing are activated by a powerful and resourceful syntactic energy.[1] One way in which this resourcefulness of syntax shows itself is in the variety of the poet's rhythmic patternings. Alliterative poetry tends to be highly emphatic in rhythm; and the corresponding fault towards which it tends when it is being composed at something less than the highest level of imaginative activity is monotony of rhythm, arising out of the excessive repetition of formulaic phrases with the same syntactical structure. This occurs particularly in the second halves of lines, and may be illustrated with an extract from *The Destruction of Troy*:

> He busket to the banke *with a bolde chere*,
> With his freikes in filde to the fighte on the playne.
> The Grekes hym agayne *with a grym fare*
> Faryn to the fight *with a frike wille*.
> Duke Nestor anon, nobli arayed,
> Countres the kyng *with a a cant pupull*.[2]

Such passages (to put dogmatically what the reader will have to judge for himself) are not found in the *Gawain*-poet's work. On the contrary it is marked by an unfailingly inventive variability of syntax and hence of rhythm. The power of this variability is to make the concreteness of the style, its 'thinginess', not just an accumulation of details, but an organized structure, a unique sequence of tones of voice, which conveys ideas and feelings along with things and events.

In the light of the various considerations just stated, I continue throughout this book to write of 'the *Gawain*-poet', and to mean by that phrase the author of all four poems. My own conviction that we have here the work of a single author arises chiefly from my judgment as to the outstanding literary merit of the poems and from the

---

[1] A beginning to the study of syntax as a means of poetic expression in *Sir Gawain and the Green Knight* has been made by the present author (see p. 12, n1., above) and by Cecily Clark, '*Sir Gawain and the Green Knight*: Characterisation by Syntax', *Essays in Criticism*, XVI (1966), 361–74.

[2] Ed. Panton and Donaldson, lines 1186–91.

interlocking interpretations of them with which the following chapters are concerned. Such matters can, of course, have no claim to scientific objectivity, though I hope that they belong to a field within which rational discussion is possible. What follows is intended primarily as a critical study of four great medieval poems. It would not, I think, be invalidated if it should eventually be proved by objective evidence that the poems were the work not of a single poet but of a school of poets in contact with one another; but that is not my own opinion.

2
Purity

Structure

It has been generally felt that *Purity* is the least unified and the least successful of the *Gawain*-poet's works. Most readers (and those who have read *Purity* with critical attention must be few in number) would perhaps agree with the views expressed by the late Dorothy Everett, in comparing *Purity* with *Patience*:

Patience is simpler in conception than *Purity* and therefore neater and more unified in construction...In *Purity* the homiletic element is more important, for the poet attempts to use the argument as a framework to link together a number of Biblical stories, including the three main ones... This more ambitious scheme is not entirely successful, for, in order to include the story of Belshazzar's Feast, the poet has to juggle with his interpretation of 'uncleanness' and make it cover the defiling of what belongs to God as well as unchastity. Moreover, since he is still mainly interested in narrative, he tends to tell his stories at disproportionate length.[1]

There is a close relationship between the two topics Miss Everett mentions: the poet's interpretation of the vice with which the poem is chiefly concerned, and his management of the poem's structure (in other words, his 'ambitious' attempt 'to use the argument as a framework to link together a number of Biblical stories'). I shall return to the first of these topics later; first, I propose to discuss the structure of *Purity*, to see whether it is really an at least partial failure. From *Sir Gawain and the Green Knight*, we know the *Gawain*-poet as a master of poetic structure, and so it would perhaps be surprising if *Purity* were to be found a total failure in this respect. On the other hand, the principle of structure in *Sir Gawain* is a narrative plot, shaped with exquisite skill to lead us towards the human meaning conceived by the poet's moral imagination, whereas in *Purity* the principle of structure is not a plot but a homiletic purpose, to

[1] Dorothy Everett, *Essays on Middle English Literature* (Oxford, 1955), p. 70.

41

which narrative is subordinate. It is to praise and define the virtue the poet calls *clannesse*, chiefly by giving examples from Scripture of the punishments God has dealt out to its *contrare*, the vice which the poet calls *unclannesse* or, more often and more bluntly, *fylthe*. The intention to praise is suggested in the poem's opening line, along with the naming of the virtue itself (*Patience* and *Pearl* also name their subjects in their very first words): 'Clannesse who so kyndly cowthe comende.' The praise is based on the Beatitudes, where Christ promises to the pure in heart a reward which, taken in a theological sense, is the highest open to mankind, the Beatific Vision: 'Beati mundo corde, quoniam ipsi Deum videbunt' (Matthew v. 8) ('Blessed are the clean of heart; for they shall see God'). The poet paraphrases this promise in his opening section, but immediately turns from the reward for purity to the punishment for impurity:

> The hathel clene of his hert hapenez ful fayre,
> For he schal loke on oure Lorde wyth a bone chere;
> As so saytz, to that syght seche schal he never
> That any unclannesse hatz on, auwhere abowte. (27–30)

Although the heavenly reward for purity is mentioned recurrently in the poem,[1] the main emphasis falls upon the opposite to which the poet so quickly turns. This opposite is exemplified by three main stories taken from the Old Testament—those of the Flood, of Sodom and Gomorrah, and of Belshazzar's Feast—and by the end of the poem the poet clearly acknowledges that these have formed his chief subject, though their purpose is, by the warning they offer, to direct his audience towards virtue and its reward:

> Thus upon thrynne wyses I haf yow thro schewed
> That unclannes tocleves in corage dere
> Of that wynnelych Lorde that wonyes in heven,
> Entyses hym to be tene, teldes up his wrake;
> And clannes is his comfort, and coyntyse he lovyes,
> And those that seme arn and swete schyn se his face.
> That we gon gay in oure gere that grace he uus sende,
> That we may serve in his syght ther solace never blynnez.
>   Amen. (1805–12)

In these closing lines the poet acknowledges a threefold division of his subject—a division in accordance with the methods of medieval preachers, who normally divided the theme of a sermon into three

[1] See lines 176, 178, 552, 576, 595, 1055, 1112, 1804, 1810, 1812.

parts, so as to treat it more amply.[1] This method of the threefold *divisio* would no doubt have been familiar to the poet and his audience, and it is probably the only aspect of the poem's structure that a casual listener would consciously have noticed. But he would have been acted upon unconsciously, I believe, by a considerably more complex structure, and a first stage in understanding how the poem works will be the unravelling of this complexity. The reader may follow more easily if I begin by setting out the poem's structure in skeleton form, and then proceed to examine more closely the contents of each of its sections.[2]

I. Introduction (1–204)
    (*a*) (1–48) General introduction
    (*b*) (49–176) *Exemplum*: parable of the wedding-feast
    (*c*) (177–204) God's anger against sins

II. God's first three punishments of his creatures (205–544)
    (*a*) (205–34) *Exemplum*: Fall of Lucifer
    (*b*) (235–48) *Exemplum*: Fall of Adam
    (*c*) (249–544) *Exemplum*: NOAH AND THE FLOOD

III. Transition (545–600)

IV. *Exemplum*: ABRAHAM, LOT, AND SODOM AND GOMORRAH (601–1048)
    (*a*) (601–780) God's visit to Abraham
    (*b*) (781–1048) The angels' visit to Lot and the destruction of the cities

V. Transition (1049–1148)
    (*a*) (1049–68) We can gain God's love by being like him
    (*b*) (1069–1108) The purity of Christ's life on earth
    (*c*) (1109–48) How man can imitate this purity

[1] On the rhetoric of the sermon, see G. R. Owst, *Preaching in Medieval England* (Cambridge, 1926); Th.-M. Charland, *Artes praedicandi* (Paris and Ottawa, 1936); and E. de Bruyne, *Etudes d'esthétique médiévale*, vol. II (Bruges, 1946).

[2] These sections correspond in only three places (lines 249, 601, 781) with those marked off by decorated initials in the manuscript, which are followed by Menner and Gollancz in their editions. The manuscript has especially large initials at lines 1, 557, and 1157, and it will be seen that the latter two of these come only a few lines after the beginning of my sections III and VI. I think that the scribe used decorated initials with intelligence, but somewhat freely and without making a very close study of the parts into which the poem falls. It must be added, of course, that it is not always certain at exactly which point a line should be drawn between one section and the next. On the use of decorated initials in *Sir Gawain and the Green Knight*, see James W. Tuttleton, 'The Manuscript Divisions of *Sir Gawain and the Green Knight*', *Spec*, XLI (1966), 304–10. Tuttleton seems to me to exaggerate their significance.

VI. *Exemplum*: capture and defilement of the vessels of the Temple (1149–1804)

    (*a*) (1149–1332) Nebuchadnezzar's capture of the vessels

    (*b*) (1333–1804) BELSHAZZAR'S FEAST

VII. Conclusion (1805–12)

From this skeleton it can be seen that the 'thrynne wyses' (here capitalized) in which the poet says he shows God's anger against impurity occupy only 1166 of the poem's 1812 lines, and that they are meshed into a considerably more complicated structure of introductory, connective, illustrative and expository material.

Section I (*a*), as we have seen, names the poem's subject, *clannesse* and its *contrare*. God, here referred to by a kenning or formula as 'the Wyy that wroght alle thinges' (5), is extremely angry with those who are unclean or impure. Thus the poem's opening lines introduce two themes that will run right through it: God's special anger against *fylthe*, and his power (because he created all things, and the world is his) to avenge or punish it. Then the poet turns to consider the special case of 'renkez of relygioun' (7), priests, who daily handle God's body, in the form of the sacrament. If they do so 'in clannes' (12), they receive a great reward, but God is angry with them if they are only outwardly 'honest' (decent) and 'inwith alle fylthes' (14). And the poet refers to this hypocrisy as a lack of *cortaysye* on their part: God is a great king, 'clene in his corte...And honeste in his housholde' (17–18), and the poet, writing for such a court himself, sees the question of purity and impurity as one of manners as well as morals. He quotes the Beatitudes, and the reward they offer to purity is also a theme that runs through the poem. Once more he turns to the opposite, *unclannesse* (30) and its punishment, which he illustrates with a human analogy. If a human lord held a great feast, and a man came to it in torn old clothes, he would be angrily thrown out and banished from the house for ever. So it is with God.

Section I (*b*) consists of an *exemplum* elaborating this point. If an earthly prince would be angered by such behaviour, still more would 'the hyghe Kyng...in heven' (50), as the parable of the wedding feast shows. This parable was already hinted at in the description of God as lord of a great household; now it is retold in greatly expanded form (the usual way in which the poet treats his Scriptural *exempla*). The story, as recounted by Matthew (xxii. 1–14) and Luke (xiv. 16–24), tells of a king who held a great feast for his son's marriage and invited all his friends. They all made excuses for not coming, and so the king sent out his servants to bring in strangers from the street as his guests. Then, as he walked among them at the feast, he found one who was not wearing a wedding-garment, but was in clothes 'fyled with werkkez' (136) (that is, he was uncleanly dressed).[1] The lord was very angry with him, sent him away from the feast, and had him punished with extreme severity. Like the poet's other expansions of Scriptural narratives, the additions he makes to this simple story, to make it fill well over a hundred lines, are nearly all in the direction of increased realism, both of setting and of speech. The realism is of course medieval, that is to say, contemporary, not historical: the feast is treated in terms of the social ritual and traditional formulas we considered in chapter 1, the food includes such medieval delicacies as 'scheldez of wylde swyn, swanez and cronez' (58), and the lord is a medieval great man, as wholehearted in both generosity and anger as the Theseus of *The Knight's Tale*. I shall have more to say about such concrete medievalizings of Scripture later.[2] Then the poet explains the allegorical meaning of the parable. The feast stands for heaven, to which all the baptized are summoned, while the guests' garments are their works on earth. If those garments are not *clene*, they will not be allowed into the presence of the 'Prynce of parage noble' (167), who is of course God.

After this *exemplum* in 1 (*b*), 1 (*c*) is again more discursive. Men, says the poet, may lose the sight of God for many different sins, because all sin is displeasing to God. He mentions a long list of sins, some of the deadly ones and a good many more. But, he says, he has never heard of any sin that displeases God so much as 'fylthe of the flesch' (202). When confronted with that sin, God forgets all his 'fre thewes' (generous qualities) and becomes mad with anger against it, even to vengeance.

In section II, this distinction between the many sins God is displeased by and the one—*fylthe*—which maddens him and incites him to angry vengeance is of crucial importance. The three subsections of II consist of narratives of the first three occasions on which God punished his creatures for their sins: the fall of Lucifer, the fall of Adam, and the Flood. But the poet's aim, however surprising this may seem to us, is to contrast the third of these occasions with the first two. On the first two occasions, God punished Lucifer and his followers, and then Adam and his descendants, but he did so

---

[1] The poet no doubt recognized the etymological connection between *fyled* and *fylthe*.
[2] See pp. 55–65 below.

measurably and without anger. The poet uses similar phrases to define God's attitude in both cases: he punished the rebel angels 'In the mesure of his mode—his metz never the lasse' (215), and he punished Adam 'Al in mesure and methe' (247). In a somewhat obscure passage (230–2) the poet appears to indicate that God failed to take pity on Lucifer only because he showed no repentance; because Adam was repentant, God found a remedy for his sin, through the Blessed Virgin. Lucifer and Adam sinned only in pride and in disobedience; on the occasion of the Flood God punished mankind 'for fylthe upon folde that the folk used' (251). Genesis is vague on this point, but the poet adopts the usual medieval view that the punishment was for sexual promiscuity, one result of which was that women coupled with devils and gave birth to giants. Where he departs from the usual medieval view is in insisting that this *fylthe* made God literally angry. Medieval Biblical commentators usually denied that God was or could be motivated by any feeling analogous to human anger. Thus we find *Cursor Mundi*, a widely read Scriptural version and commentary, which there is some reason to suppose the poet knew, explaining that when God said 'Me *reus* that ever made I man',[1] he was really looking forward to the 'ruth' he was later to show by redeeming man:

> he to pin himselfen did
> For his choslinges on rod-tre;
> Quat was his *reut* than all mai see
> Bi this word that than was said.[2]

The *Gawain*-poet will have none of this ingenious allegorizing. He specifically asserts that God felt 'As wyye' (284), that 'Felle temptande tene towched his hert' (283), and that he showed 'malys mercyles' (250) towards mankind. This third case of God's punishment of his creatures is the poem's first main *exemplum* of the vengeance against impurity. The story of Noah and the Flood is told in the poet's usual elaborately realistic detail.

Section III is a comparatively brief transitional passage. It begins by exhorting any man who desires honour 'In his comlych corte that Kyng is of blysse' (546) to make himself as pure as a pearl. Then the poet turns back to the story of the Flood and explains how God later

---

[1] Cf. Genesis vi. 6: 'Poenituit eum quod hominem fecisset in terra' ('It repented him that he had made man on the earth').

[2] *Cursor Mundi*, ed. Richard Morris, EETS OS 57, 99, 101 (London 1874 and 1893), vol. I, lines 1602, 1608–11 (quoted from the Cotton MS [my italics]).

repented of his anger, returned to *cortaysye, mesure,* and *methe* (564–5), and promised never again to destroy the whole of mankind. Nevertheless, he did on further occasions direct his anger against certain groups of 'wykked men' on account of

> this ilk evel, that unhappen glette,
> The venym and the vylanye and the vycios fylthe
> That bysulpez mannez saule in unsounde hert. (573–5)

The poet warns that such impure men cannot hope to be unseen by God, for it would be absurd to suppose that the very creator of eyes and ears should be deaf and blind (583–90). The lines making this point paraphrase Psalm xciii. 9: 'Qui plantavit aurem non audiet? aut qui finxit oculum non videbit?' ('He that planted the ear, shall he not hear? Or he that formed the eye, doth he not consider?'). The same verse is also paraphrased in *Patience*, 123–4, to the same purpose: to emphasize the controlling power of God over what he has created.

Whether section IV should be subdivided or not I do not feel quite certain. It consists of a single continuous story, taken from Genesis xviii–xix, but the story itself seems to form a kind of diptych, one wing of which corresponds to Genesis xviii and deals with the visit of God to Abraham in the form of three men, while the other wing corresponds to Genesis xix. 1–28 and begins with a parallel visit of two angels to Lot, going on to tell of the destruction of Sodom and Gomorrah. A break between these two parts of the story is indicated by the partial repetition of wording in lines 780–1, suggesting a new beginning—

> Whyl the Soverayn to Sodamas sende to spye.
> His sondes into Sodamas watz sende in that tyme

—and by the fact, for what it is worth, that in the manuscript line 781 begins with a small decorative capital. More important, the two parts of the story seem to exemplify two opposite qualities in God: the mercy he shows by giving ear to Abraham's pleading for the cities in the first part, and the angry vengeance he takes in the second part on all except Lot and his daughters. The whole story, but especially the second part of it, forms the poet's second main *exemplum* of God's punishment of impurity. The kind of impurity punished in it is the 'fylthe of the flesche' usually associated with Sodom, homosexuality.

47

Section v is important, although in a sense merely transitional, because it is the only extended part of the poem in which the poet turns his attention away from the angry God who punishes *fylthe* and towards *clannesse* itself, its presence in God, and his love for it in others. In v (*a*) he carries out a reversal in the opposite direction to that found elsewhere in the poem; that is, not from *clannesse* to its *contrare*, but from *fylthe* to *clannesse*:

> Alle thyse ar teches and tokenes to trow upon yet,
> And wittnesse of that wykked werk, and the wrake after
> That oure Fader forferde for fylthe of those ledes.
> Thenne uch wyye may wel wyt that he the wlonk lovies;
> And if he lovyes clene layk that is oure Lorde ryche,
> And to be couthe in his corte thou coveytes thenne,
> To se that Semly in sete and his swete face,
> Clerrer counseyl con I non, bot that thou clene worthe. (1049–56)

These lines, and those that follow, are argued in a way that for this poem is unusually logical, indeed almost syllogistic. The poet goes on to follow the widespread medieval practice of treating secular love as an exact analogy to divine love, and to suggest following the advice given in the *Roman de la Rose* to the aspiring lover—be as like as you can to the object of your love. In order to 'dele drwrye' with God, try to be as *clene* as he is. Section v (*b*) illustrates the purity of God from Christ's life on earth. Christ was born of a pure virgin; the birth itself was clean and pleasant, not messy; as soon as he was born, the infant Christ was recognized 'by his clannes for Kyng of nature' (1087) by the beasts of the stable; in his life he would never touch impure things, and yet he healed the sick, and made them 'Wel clanner then any crafte cowthe devyse' (1100); and finally (and this is an illustration which we may well feel stretches the meaning of *clannesse* almost to breaking-point), Christ broke bread with his hands more neatly than anyone else could do it with a sharp knife. The point of this last example for the poet is that in the fourteenth century it was good manners to cut bread, not to break it; and so it was regularly argued that when Christ broke bread the result was as neat as if he had cut it.[1] Thus Christ's *norture* (1091) is preserved—the same good breeding that is exemplified in Gawain, 'that fyne fader of nurture' (*Gawain*, 919). Christ's purity involved being *kyryous* (1109), and God is elsewhere in the poem several times

---

[1] This is explained and illustrated by Gollancz, ed. *Cleanness*, pp. xvi–xvii.

described as being *scoymous* (21, 598, 1148)—both words meaning 'particular' or 'fastidious'. In v (*c*) the poet turns back from God to man, and to the question how man can emulate God's *clannesse* and so achieve his love. He says that we are all 'sore and synful and souly' (1111) by nature, but, because God is *mercyable* (1113), we none the less have the chance of attaining his sight, by purifying ourselves and becoming like pearls through confession and absolution. It is here that occurs the long pearl image we examined in chapter 1. The poet goes on that, once you have purified yourself in this way, you must beware of defiling yourself again, because God is doubly angry at the loss of something that was once his,

> Thagh hit be bot a bassyn, a bolle, other a scole,
> A dysche, other a dobler, that Dryghtyn onez served. (1145–6)

These examples, chosen apparently at random, provide an ingenious transition to the poet's last main *exemplum* in section vi. It concerns the capture and defilement by the Babylonians of the sacred vessels of the temple in Jerusalem; and these *were* basins, bowls, cups, and so on, that once served the Lord but were then taken away from him. Like the *exemplum* in section iv, this one is divided into two separate parts, which illustrate opposite points, even though they tell a single continuous story. In vi (*a*) we hear how, as a punishment for the idolatry of Zedekiah, God allowed the Babylonians under their king, Nebuchadnezzar, to capture and sack the temple. Nebuzaradan seized the holy vessels and brought them to Nebuchadnezzar, who placed them in his treasury. But because Nebuchadnezzar treated them carefully and reverently, this is not an example of *unclannesse*, and he was allowed to reign in great prosperity. At last he died, and in vi (*b*) we are told of how his son, Belshazzar, succeeding him, has the vessels taken out of the treasury and uses them to drink from at a feast where he is surrounded by his concubines. This *is* an example of *unclannesse*—'vanyté unclene'—and as a result a mysterious hand appears at the feast and writes a cryptic message on the wall. Daniel interprets the message as meaning that Belshazzar's rule is over, and in fact that very night he is killed and his city is overrun by the Medes and Persians. This is God's punishment for

> the fylthe of the freke that defowled hade
> The ornementes of Goddez hous that holy were maked.
> He watz corsed for his unclannes. (1798–1800)

In the very brief section VII, the poet says that he has shown in three ways how *unclannes* arouses God's anger. *Clannes*, on the contrary, is dear to God; and he neatly ends the poem with an allusion to the opening example of the guest in ragged clothes, by praying that we may 'gon gay in oure gere' (1811) and thus gain the Beatific Vision.

Purpose

We must now ask what purpose underlies and justifies this apparently rambling and yet certainly not random structure of the poem. The principle of connection is obviously the pair of concepts *clannesse* and *unclannesse* (or *fylthe*). But are we to say that the poet uses these concepts as little more than an excuse for bringing in Scriptural narratives he finds attractive, and that, as Dorothy Everett puts it, he 'has to juggle with his interpretation of "uncleanness"' in order to make it cover such disparate material? We must recognize, I think, that the kind of answer we give to this question may depend partly on presuppositions, of which we may not be fully conscious, about the nature of literary structure itself. If we start from Aristotelian presuppositions, and assume that an organic unity embodied in a single unified plot or *mythos* is the ideal structure for a poem, then we shall naturally prefer *Patience* to *Purity*, as Miss Everett does, and, what is more, measure the apparent failure of *Purity* against the success of *Patience*. We shall also find ourselves hard put to it to justify the structure of many other medieval works of literature which are clearly not 'simple in conception...and therefore neat and unified in construction'—*The Parlement of Foules*, for example, or *Piers Plowman*, or the great cycles of Arthurian romance or religious drama. But because *Purity* contains in it so much that is not part of the three main Scriptural episodes, it seems absurd to suppose that the constantly repeated central ideas of *clannesse* and *fylthe* are present only as an excuse for bringing those episodes together; and it also seems absurd to suppose that the poet did not know, or did not care, that he was changing the meaning of these ideas as he went along. It is easier to admit the possibility that the medieval poet had some other, non-Aristotelian idea of literary structure, and that this involved deliberate changes in the meaning of his governing concepts. We have already seen that the purpose of the poem is indicated in its simplest form in the opening lines: to 'comende' *clannesse*, but to do so mainly by showing the hatred in which God holds its 'con-

trare', *fylthe*. The demonstration is carried out chiefly by authoritative examples chosen from sacred history—that is to say, empirically
rather than logically: it is only when the poet is concerned with
clannesse rather than *fylthe* (in section v [a]) that he argues logically
from the evidence of the *tokenes* his Scriptural *exempla* provide.

The great bulk of the poem is made up of the *exempla* or *tokenes*.
From it we learn not abstractly but concretely what *clannesse* is, how
desirable and how dear to God (because part of himself), and, still
more, we learn what *fylthe* is and how God shows his abhorrence of
it. To describe the poet as 'juggling with his interpretation of "uncleanness"'' is to suggest that 'uncleanness' has a single right meaning on which the poet is performing a frivolous feat of ingenuity.
But in fact moral abstractions such as *clannesse* and *fylthe* have no
meanings except in so far as they are embodied in actual human
situations; and the purpose of the poem is to create or re-create
meanings for them by juxtaposing situations to which they can be
applied. This is true of all moral abstractions—how can we know
what loyalty, generosity, truthfulness, and so on actually are except
from real or fictional examples?—but it is particularly true of terms
such as *clannesse* and *fylthe* which have living physical senses as well
as moral senses. I say 'living' physical senses because no doubt many
or even all of our terms of moral appraisal derive from dead metaphors
relating moral to physical qualities, as, for example, 'generosity' may
be traced back to a root concerned with a man's birth or race. But
clene and *foule* have a living sense of physical cleanness and dirtiness
as well as their more strictly moral senses. The *Gawain*-poet's purpose involves making use of this survival of the physical sense: not,
as we might suppose, by distinguishing the moral sense from it, but
by running the two together so that the moral qualities can arouse in
us a physical response of delight or disgust. In acting thus, the poet
is not doing something illegitimate or deceptive, not 'juggling' like
Macbeth's 'juggling fiends...That palter with us in a double sense'.
He is restoring to us the primitive force of response which is often
lost when a term such as 'purity' is used in a religious context, but
which still in the twentieth century underlies such usages as 'a dirty
thing to do' or 'a dirty book'. Perhaps indeed such instinctive
responses towards good and evil, by which they attract or repel us
as if they were physically wholesome or filthy, form the fundamental
basis of the whole elaborate structure of ethics. Such at least seems
to be the lesson of Plato's dialogue *Gorgias*, in which what finally

restrains Callicles in his argument that whatever gives pleasure is
good is not any theoretical answer but his shudder of disgust at
Socrates' introduction of a concrete example of pleasure—sodomy.[1]
This is also, of course, one of the *Gawain*-poet's examples of *fylthe*.
And the *Gawain*-poet conceives of God himself as responding to
fylthe in just this instinctive way, with fastidious revulsion (that is
why he is described as *kyryous* and *scoymous*) and ultimately with
violent anger, mad anger even (see *wod* in line 204), against behaviour
which is most fittingly described in such physical terms as *glette*
or *ordure*.

The re-creation of concrete meanings for moral *clannesse* and
moral *fylthe* is thus supported by linguistic usage and by psychological fact; but it remains work that has to be done in a particular
piece of literature. It is not an event that has already taken place
when the poem begins; it is a process which occurs in the course of
the poem, as we move through the concrete *exempla* the poet chooses.
The detailed nature of their concreteness is something we shall
examine shortly; here we must consider the nature of the general
process of re-creation or redefinition by which they are linked. The
poet begins with the parable of the wedding-feast, prepared for by
the example of the real-life feast. In both of these *fylthe* has its most
physical sense, slovenliness of outward appearance:

> Wyth rent cokrez at the kne, and his clutte traschez,
> And his tabarde totorne, and his totez oute (40–1)

> In on so ratted a robe and rent at the sydez (144)

Then at the end of the parable comes the interpretation, by which
these physical garments are given a moral meaning (human works),
without however losing their physicality:

> That tho be frely and fresch fonde in thy lyve,
> And fetyse of a fayr forme, to fote and to honde,
> And sythen alle thyn other lymez lapped ful clene. (173–5)

The major *exempla*, in sections II, IV and VI, take this development
further by stages. Those in sections II and IV extend the sense of
fylthe to include moral depravity, but the two kinds exemplified
there, sexual promiscuity and homosexuality, both have a physical
basis, in being sins of the flesh. Finally, in section VI, comes the last

---

[1] *Gorgias*, 494.

and most daring development in the meaning of *fylthe*, to mean defilement of what is holy, sacrilege, in a more general and less physical sense. Yet even here the physical is by no means left behind. The defilement of the sacred vessels takes place in a setting of fleshly sinfulness: Belshazzar's feast, where gluttony, drunkenness and sexual licence are rife. Moreover, to end the poem with this *exemplum* is to frame it between two feasts, the wedding-feast of the Lord and Belshazzar's. The latter is a profane parody of the former, which is why its mirth, as at Macbeth's banquet, is 'displaced'.

The poet's purpose is by no means to distinguish one variety of *fylthe* from another, the physical from the moral. On the contrary, his whole method involves running the two together. He defines not by analysis but by synthesis, mapping out an area of meaning common to a number of superficially different situations from human life. We shall find the *Gawain*-poet using the same method to create the meaning of the central image in *Pearl*; and it is a method used by other poets of his time too.[1] In *Purity* it is a technique he applies to *clannesse* as well as to *fylthe*, though, since *clannesse* is not the central focus of the poem, we see the technique applied to it on a smaller scale. This is so especially in section v (*b*), on the life of Christ. We saw how *clannesse* was found in Christ's conception, his birth, his *cortays* and fastidious life, his miracles of healing, and his breaking of bread. Menner, in his edition of *Purity*, has a revealing note on the summarizing statement 'Thus is he kyryous and clene' with which this survey of Christ's life ends:

The lines on Christ's cutting the bread have, of course, little to do with Christ's purity, and the passage is introduced only by means of a kind of play on words. *Clene* means at once 'pure,' and, with reference to cutting, 'smooth, sharp, without ragged edges'. So *kyryous* in this line='skilful' as far as the cutting of the bread is concerned, but='particular' in connection with Christ's abhorrence of everything vile.[2]

Menner here describes very well the nature of what is happening in the passage, but, writing half a century ago, he was not able to see its significance. Nowadays we are more prepared to see in puns something beyond frivolous ingenuity, and we can recognize that when the poet extends the sense of *clene* in this way he is doing something more than connecting quite different ideas that just happen, by some

---

[1] I have argued that it is used by Langland (*Criticism and Medieval Poetry*, pp. 90–5).
[2] Ed. *Purity*, p. 103.

freak of language, to have the same name. He is getting back to a substantial identity of ideas and feelings that underlies and has sustained the identity of words (we still speak of a 'clean cut'). He is finding behind the pun a large primitive node of meaning which is not verbal but experiential.

If the poet is not concerned to distinguish the various senses of *fylthe* and *clannesse* but to identify them, he is, of course, concerned to distinguish *fylthe* from other sins, as being the sin most remote from God's own nature, and therefore the one he hates most and punishes most severely. There is thus a strict limit to the merging process; synthesis and analysis lie alongside each other in the poem, and it is this combination which causes the unusual difficulty of its structure. Each of the three main Old Testament *exempla* of *fylthe* and its punishment is preceded by other exemplary material which is both linked with it and contrasted with it: linked as part of a historical and causal or semi-causal sequence, contrasted as showing some opposite to God's extreme anger against *fylthe*. The first main *exemplum*, of the Flood, is preceded by the punishments of Lucifer and Adam. All three are examples of God's punishment of sin, and they are linked in sequence: Adam was created in order to inherit 'that home that aungelez forgart' (240) when Lucifer fell, while the people of Noah's time were in turn

> the forme-foster that the folde bred,
> The athel aunceterez sunez that Adam watz called. (257-8)

But Lucifer and Adam were not punished for *fylthe* in anger, but, as we have seen, for different sins in *mesure*. The second main *exemplum*, of Sodom and Gomorrah, is preceded, as we have also seen, by God's visit to Abraham, in which he comes not as an avenger, but as a bringer of good news (the forthcoming birth of a child to Sarah) and as a merciful Lord, who listens with forbearance to Abraham's pleas for the righteous inhabitants of Sodom and Gomorrah. Finally, the *exemplum* of Belshazzar's feast is also preceded by an episode historically continuous with it but opposite in meaning: though Nebuchadnezzar receives the sacred vessels, he treats them reverently, and is therefore allowed to die a natural death after a prosperous life. As we discover from Daniel's speech in the Belshazzar episode, Nebuchadnezzar too had been a blasphemer, and had received a terrible warning from God (his seven years in the wilderness), but he, unlike Belshazzar, had learned his lesson, had 'com to knawlach and kenned hymselven' (1702), and thus avoided destruction. The pattern of relationships between the different parts of the poem is thus extremely complex. This complexity is in accordance with the medieval taste for a continuously and intricately interwoven surface, whether in literature or the visual arts. A distinguished scholar, comparing the structure of the thirteenth-century cycles of Arthurian romance with that of the decorated initials in illuminated manuscripts, has recently written:

The fascination of tracing a theme through all its phases, of waiting for its return while following other themes, of experiencing the constant sense of their simultaneous presence, depends upon our grasp of the entire structure—the most elusive that has ever been devised.[1]

The remark would apply equally well to *Purity*. But the emphasis I wish to make finally in considering the poem's structure is that, for all its formal ingenuity, it is not merely decorative, but is the direct expression of the poem's meaning. Structure and purpose are one.

Realization of scripture

We can now turn from the more general considerations of structure and purpose to examine the texture of *Purity* in greater detail. We have seen that the poet's main sources in his narrative sections are Biblical, and that his habit is greatly to expand these sources. Expansion is the normal tendency of any medieval re-creation of sources, but one way in which we can come to appreciate this particular poet's art is to examine the *nature* of his expansions: what features of his original does he amplify, and what does he add? (The question of omission does not usually arise.) He expands most fully in sections IV and VI, and there, by comparing his work with the Vulgate, we can often take the opportunity of watching his imagination at work in great detail. I do not of course mean to assert that his *only* source for the stories of Abraham and Lot and of Nebuchadnezzar and Belshazzar was the Vulgate Bible: we know for example that he used details from Mandeville to amplify the description of Belshazzar's feast. But the Vulgate was certainly his basic source, and the simplicity of its narrative makes the elaborated detail of the *Gawain*-poet's work stand out vividly by contrast. In Genesis especially that

---

[1] Eugène Vinaver, 'Form and Meaning in Medieval Romance', *Presidential Address of the Modern Humanities Research Association* (1966), p. 16.

simplicity is of a special kind, fraught with the implication of significance, and I therefore begin by quoting part of the best account I know of the narrative style of Genesis, considered as a literary phenomenon. It is from Erich Auerbach's brilliant study *Mimesis*, and concerns the story of Abraham and Isaac from Genesis xxii: an example chosen from slightly later in Genesis than the story of Abraham and Lot, but dealing with the same favourite subject of the *Gawain*-poet, the confrontation between man and the supernatural. Auerbach writes:

God appears without bodily form (yet he 'appears'), coming from some unspecified place—we only hear his voice, and that utters nothing but a name, a name without an adjective, without a descriptive epithet for the person spoken to...and of Abraham too nothing is made perceptible except the words in which he answers God: *Hinne-ni*, Behold me here—with which, to be sure, a most touching gesture expressive of obedience and readiness is suggested, but it is left to the reader to visualize it. Moreover the two speakers are not on the same level: if we conceive of Abraham in the foreground, where it might be possible to picture him as prostrate or kneeling or bowing with outspread arms or gazing upward, God is not there too: Abraham's words and gestures are directed toward the depths of the picture or upward, but in any case the undetermined, dark place from which the voice comes to him is not in the foreground.

After this opening, God gives his command, and the story itself begins: everyone knows it; it unrolls with no episodes in a few independent sentences whose syntactical connection is of the most rudimentary sort. In this atmosphere it is unthinkable that an implement, a landscape through which the travelers passed, the serving-men, or the ass, should be described, that their origin or descent or material or appearance or usefulness should be set forth in terms of praise; they do not even admit an adjective: they are serving-men, ass, wood, and knife, and nothing else, without an epithet; they are there to serve the end which God has commanded; what in other respects they were, are, or will be, remains in darkness...

The personages speak in the Bible story... but their speech does not serve, as does speech in Homer, to manifest, to externalize thoughts—on the contrary, it serves to indicate thoughts which remain unexpressed. God gives his command in direct discourse, but he leaves his motives and his purpose unexpressed; Abraham, receiving the command, says nothing and does what he has been told to do.[1]

---

[1] Erich Auerbach, *Mimesis*, trans. Willard Trask (Princeton, 1953), pp. 9–11. Auerbach has in mind throughout a comparison with the narrative methods of Homer.

If I now quote the opening verses of Genesis xviii it will be seen that Auerbach's remarks about chapter xxii, though generally true, do not apply in every detail:

Apparuit autem et Dominus in convalle Mambre, sedenti in ostio tabernaculi sui in ipso fervore diei.

Cumque elevasset oculos, apparuerunt ei tres viri stantes prope eum. Quos cum vidisset, cucurrit in occursum eorum de ostio tabernaculi, et adoravit in terram,

Et dixit: Domine, si inveni gratiam in oculis tuis, ne transeas servum tuum;

Sed afferam pauxillum aquae, et lavate pedes vestros, et requiescite sub arbore.

Ponamque buccellam panis, et confortate cor vestrum, postea transibitis; idcirco enim declinastis ad servum vestrum. Qui dixerunt: Fac ut locutus es.

Festinavit Abraham in tabernaculum ad Saram, dixitque ei: Accelera, tria sata similae commisce, et fac subcinericios panes.

Ipse vero ad armentum cucurrit, et tulit inde vitulum tenerrimum et optimum, deditque puero; qui festinavit et coxit illum.

Tulit quoque butyrum et lac, et vitulum quem coxerat, et posuit coram eis. Ipse vero stabat iuxta eos sub arbore.

Cumque comedissent, dixerunt ad eum: Ubi est Sara uxor tua? Ille respondit: Ecce in tabernaculo est.

Cui dixit: Revertens veniam ad te tempore isto, vita comite, et habebit filium Sara uxor tua. Quo audito, Sara risit post ostium tabernaculi.

(And the Lord appeared to him in the vale of Mambre as he was sitting at the door of his tent, in the very heat of the day.

And when he had lifted up his eyes, there appeared to him three men standing near him: and as soon as he saw them he ran to meet them from the door of his tent, and adored down to the ground.

And he said: Lord, if I have found favour in thy sight, pass not away from thy servant:

But I will fetch a little water; and wash ye your feet, and rest ye under the tree.

And I will set a morsel of bread, and strengthen ye your heart; afterwards you shall pass on: for therefore are you come aside to your servant. And they said: Do as thou has spoken.

Abraham made haste into the tent to Sara, and said to her: Make haste, temper together three measures of flour, and make cakes upon the hearth.

And he himself ran to the herd, and took from thence a calf, very tender and very good: and gave it to a young man, who made haste and boiled it.

He took also butter and milk, and the calf which he had boiled; and set before them. But he stood by them under the tree.

And when they had eaten, they said to him: Where is Sara thy wife? He answered: Lo, she is in the tent.

And he said to him: I will return and come to thee at this time, life accompanying; and Sara thy wife shall have a son. Which when Sara heard, she laughed behind the door of the tent.)

This is a meeting between God and man in which God, though he mysteriously appears out of nowhere as Abraham raises his eyes, takes on the bodily form of three men. There is a strange equivocation between singular and plural in the nouns and verbs, and this passage was taken in the Middle Ages as an Old Testament prefiguration of the doctrine of the Trinity, by which God is both one and three. The *Gawain*-poet was fully aware of the theological implications of the narrative, and he makes them explicit, by explaining Abraham's addressing of the three as 'Lord' on the grounds that he greeted them as God:

> And as to God the good mon gos hem agaynez,
> And haylsed hem in onhede, and sayde: 'Hende Lorde'. (611–12)

But the poet's main interest in the narrative was not, as it was likely to be in the Middle Ages, for its theological significance, but for its literal significance as a human and social document. He was attracted by just those elements of material detail in the setting by which this passage differs from the one studied by Auerbach. It is a hot day, the meeting is an occasion for hospitality to be given and received, the domestic arrangements are specified in some detail, and so is the preparation of the food (the cakes are to be made of 'three measures of flour', the chosen calf is 'very tender and very good', and it is boiled and served with milk and butter). Then Sarah's overhearing of the conversation is explained by our being told that she was standing out of sight 'behind the door of the tent'. In a later verse she is given a sceptical comment ('After I am grown old, and my lord is an old man, shall I give myself to pleasure?' [12]), made under her breath (*occulte*), which is eminently natural on a simple human level as the externalization of thought. It is details of this kind that the poet seizes on, and he draws them out and weaves them together to form a thoroughly realistic presentation of an event which in itself is mysterious and even portentous. The dark background Auerbach finds in Genesis is flooded with a clear light, which reveals every detail and articulates space so as to make it intelligible and even intimate.

For example, in Genesis Abraham invites his visitors to 'rest ye under the tree'; in *Purity* this tree becomes an important stage-property. At the very beginning the poet tells us that Abraham was sitting 'under an oke grene' (602). Immediately the setting becomes English, and of course 'the door of his tent', which would remind us of the desert, becomes 'his hous-dore' (602). The poet mentions the scene again to explain that Abraham 'watz schunt to the schadow under schyre levez' (605), because 'Bryght blykked the bem of the brode heven' (603)—just the kind of explanatory detail that is only vaguely implied by Genesis, but is made explicit by the medieval poet. Such detail articulates both the spatial and the psychological dimension: the sun is blazing in the sky, below it are the green leaves, shining in its light, below them is Abraham enjoying the cool shade. We see the tree in closer detail when Abraham begs the visitors not to leave till they have 'under bowe restted' (616), and it becomes more solid still when he invites them, 'Resttez here on this rote' (619). Clearly, for the *Gawain*-poet, something mentioned in only a single word of his source (*sub arbore*) is as completely present in every detail as it would be in reality. If it is an oak tree, mature enough to give shade on a really hot day, then it will obviously have roots large enough to sit on. The same thing happens with the calf the servant is told to prepare for supper. In Genesis he simply boils it, but in *Purity* Abraham reminds him to skin it first, and then to boil it 'faste' (630–1). The desert meal becomes an English picnic when the poet explains that Abraham 'Clechez to a clene clothe and kestez on the grene' (634). For his imagination, the different items of food that Abraham 'set before them' inevitably assume a specific spatial arrangement on the cloth, and two kinds of soup are added to them, contained in a decent dish:

> Thrwe thryftyly theron tho thre therve kakez,
> And bryngez butter wythal, and by the bred settez;
> Mete messez of mylke he merkkez bytwene,
> Sythen potage and polment in a plater honest. (635–8)

(It may be added that, besides their material solidity, the '*clene* clothe' and the 'plater *honest*' have appropriate symbolic overtones.) The Bible's remark that Abraham 'stood by' the visitors while they ate is another signal for the poet to imagine the scene in full detail, and we are told that he stood there with his hat politely removed, and his arms folded (643).

I have mentioned only a selection of the authenticating details the poet has added to a single brief scene in Genesis. They show how completely pictorial is his imagination, how fully it enters into the shadowy spaces suggested by his original and fills them with objects and events. But the pictorial detail often suggests psychological detail of a kind which renders the scene fully human. This humanizing process is also applied to God, as we see from a slightly later moment in the story. After Sarah has laughed at what she has overheard, God asks why she did so. She denies having laughed, 'For she was afraid' (15), and God contradicts her denial with the simple statement, 'Nay; but thou didst laugh'. In *Purity* this remark of God's is expanded:

> 'Now innoghe, hit is not so,' thenne nurned the Dryghtyn,
> 'For thou laghed alow—bot let we hit one'. (669–70)

The phrasing here captures exactly a certain human situation, in God's firmness and certainty in cutting short any further denial, combined with the fatherly tolerance with which he declines to pursue the matter: 'let we hit one'. It is extraordinarily charming, and one cannot help responding sympathetically to the confidence with which the poet has transformed a remote and shadowy situation into something familiar, intimate, and almost domestic. And yet I think one might reasonably have doubts about the wisdom of his treatment of this particular moment, because the gain in realism surely involves a loss in suggestiveness—suggestiveness about what cannot be fully stated, the nature of the divine as it impinges on the human. In the speech just quoted, it seems to me that God has become man all too completely for the purposes of this particular story. God's power has lost some of its essential mystery, and it is symptomatic, I think, that the almost chillingly bald explanation in Genesis, 'For she was afraid' (*timore perterrita*), has been simply omitted by the *Gawain*-poet. In this scene, his God has no power to arouse fear. The realizing imagination which we shall again and again have cause to admire in the *Gawain*-poet's work does sometimes run out of control, and particularly in *Purity*, which is in this respect his least mature work.

The *Gawain*-poet's power to imagine plausible speech is perhaps his most brilliant and most dangerous gift. For any situation he can find the right words, words that define an attitude of mind so exactly that they seem to be the very voice of thought. We seem to catch this imaginative power in the very midst of its operation at a later moment in the same *exemplum* from Genesis. When the two angels visit Lot in Sodom, he presses them to stay the night with him, and when they finally agree, 'he made them a feast, and baked unleavened bread; and they ate' (Genesis xix. 3). Now the poet adopts a Hebrew story that the reason why Lot's wife was later turned into a pillar of salt was not only that she had disobeyed the angels' orders in looking behind her at the burning city, but that she had also disobeyed her husband's orders to bake unleavened bread for the angels. Instead, she baked bread with salt in it, and we find the poet in the very act of imagining what she muttered to herself as she vigorously sprinkled salt into the cooking. She heard Lot's order,

> Bot yet I wene that the wyf hit wroth to dyspyt,
> And sayde softely to hirself: 'This unsavere hyne
> Lovez no salt in her sauce; yet hit no skyl were
> That other burne be boute, thagh bothe be nyse.'
> Thenne ho saverez wyth salt her seuez uch one. (821–5)

What the poet here supposes (without of course any Scriptural warrant) is irresistibly persuasive: it has just the right note of grumbling obstinacy. Yet is it perhaps so right as to have the effect almost of parody, an effect at least too delightfully comic for the mysterious import of the situation? I certainly find that this is true of the speech the poet later invents for Lot, when he tries to persuade the Sodomites not to make improper advances to his angel guests. The angels have been introduced, solidly placed among the other strollers in the streets, with a visual detail quite lacking from Genesis:

> As he stared into the strete ther stout men played,
> He syghe ther swey in asent swete men tweyne;
> Bolde burnez were thay bothe, wyth berdles chynnez,
> Royl rollande fax, to raw sylk lyke,
> Of ble as the brere-flor where so the bare schewed;
> Ful clene watz the countenaunce of her cler yyen;
> Wlonk whit watz her wede, and wel hit hem semed. (787–3)

These are angels from a late medieval painting, depicted with a loving exactitude of colour and texture; and the passage both suggests how the Sodomites can have known of their presence (in Genesis there is no mention that anyone else was present when they appeared to Lot) and makes us understand why the Sodomites found them so attractive. And so at night the Sodomites come and clamour outside Lot's house, demanding that they should have a chance to 'know' his guests (xix. 5). The first part of Lot's answer is simply as follows in Genesis: 'Nolite, quaeso, fratres mei, nolite malum hoc facere' (xix. 7) ('Do not so, I beseech you, my brethren; do not commit this evil'). The *Gawain*-poet expands these words into a comically persuasive bit of rhetoric, in which every social nuance of this highly embarrassing situation is brought out. His method has clearly been to imagine himself inside the situation, supposing that it were from real life. What would one say, to try to smoothe the whole thing over, if one happened to be entertaining a pair of angels, and a party of one's fellow-citizens came along and started making indecent proposals outside the house?

> Oo, my frendez so fre, yor fare is to strange!
> Dotz away yor derf dyn, and derez never my gestes.
> Avoy! hit is yor vylaynye, ye vylen yorselven;
> And ye are jolyf gentylmen, yor japez ar ille. (861–4)

That surely is exactly what a fourteenth-century gentleman would say: emphasizing not, as the Lot of Genesis does, the simple wickedness of what they propose, but its social unsuitability, both to the angels, who ought as guests to be respected, and, even more emphatically, to the Sodomites themselves—how can it be in the nature of *gentylmen* to commit *vylaynye*? It is a marvellously dramatic speech, and one that no reader would willingly give up; but surely, when we consider the purpose of the episode as a whole, and the terrifying violence with which it concludes, we must agree that the poet has been carried away by the vividness of his imagination.

A full analysis of how in *Purity* the *Gawain*-poet 'realizes' his Scriptural sources in terms of the life of his own society would be very extensive; but it would in any case be unnecessary. Given a hint or two, the modern reader will wish to read the poem for himself, not to have it read for him. There can be no doubt that it is realization rather than allegorization that mainly concerns the poet. He may acknowledge the allegorical sense of the visit of the three men to Abraham, which was so well known as to be scarcely avoidable, but it is noticeable that there seems to be no suggestion that Noah is a type of Christ (a normal interpretation). Again, while the poet gives his own allegorical reading of the parable of the wedding feast, it is kept as simple as possible, and there are none of the detailed allegorical interpretations of the 'beeves and fatlings' (Matthew xxii. 4) that were common in the Middle Ages.[1] No allegorical or typological interpretation at all is suggested for the story of Nebuchadnezzar and Belshazzar, though there are occasional discreet hints of a general moral meaning, as when Belshazzar's palace is described as 'a palayce of pryde' (1389). We have earlier been told,

> Thus in pryde and olipraunce his empyre he haldes,
> In lust and in lecherye, and lothelych werkkes. (1349–50)

We have already seen how his feast is presented in medieval terms. His pride is crystallized with the *Gawain*-poet's usual mastery of dramatic speech in his splendidly drunken command to bring in the holy vessels and use them for drinking:

> Bryng hem now to my borde, of beverage hem fylles,
> Let thise ladyes of hem lape—I luf hem in hert!
> That schal I cortaysly kythe, and thay schin knawe sone
> Ther is no bounté in burne lyk Baltazar thewes. (1433–6)

'Thise ladyes' are his concubines (we have earlier been told that his feudal inferiors have been summoned to the feast 'To loke on his lemanes and ladis hem calle' [1370]), and they are mentioned recurrently in the description of the feast, like an ominous theme in music. Belshazzar's use of the gross word 'lape' undermines his pretensions to *cortaysye*, quite apart from the sacrilege he is ordering. But what seem to a modern reader certain signs of strain make themselves apparent when the poet comes to describe the vessels themselves. They are described in some detail in Jeremiah lii. 17–23, but the poet greatly augments this description, partly with details taken from Mandeville's accounts of the palace of the Great Chan and of the land of Prester John. The result is a formal *descriptio* of fifty lines (1439–88), in the course of which the poem comes almost to a halt. If we compare a passage from Jeremiah with its parallel in *Purity*, we shall see that the *Gawain*-poet is doing his best to introduce movement and life within something essentially static: 'and network and pomegranates were upon the chapiters round about, all of brass' (Jeremiah lii. 22).

---

[1] E.g. *Piers Plowman*, ed. W. W. Skeat (1886), B. xv. lines 454 ff.

And all bolled abof wyth braunches and leves,
Pyes and papejayes purtayed withinne,
As thay prudly hade piked of pomgarnades;
For all the blomes of the bowes were blyknande perles,
And alle the fruyt in tho formes of flaumbeande gemmes. (1464–8)

but this then degenerates into a mere catalogue:

Ande safyres, and sardiners, and semely topace,
Alabaundarynes, and amaraunz, and amaffised stones,
Casydoynes, and crysolytes, and clere rubies,
Penitotes, and pynkardines, ay perles bitwene. (1469–72)

The poet has found no method other than the usual medieval enumerative *descriptio* to emphasize the importance of the sacred vessels; and this is unfortunate, because they are his central symbol of purity.

I must give one last example of the realization of Scripture in the *exemplum* of Nebuchadnezzar and Belshazzar. This too seems to me not to produce quite the effect required, though in its own way it is certainly a complete success. In the description of Belshazzar's feast in the Book of Daniel, the appearance of the hand writing the message on the wall has a real effect of mystery and terror, largely because it is given baldly, with almost no detail. It is contained in a single verse:

In the same hour there appeared fingers, as it were of the hand of a man, writing over against the candlestick upon the surface of the wall of the king's palace: and the king beheld the joints of the hand that wrote (Daniel v. 5).

That single detail ('et rex aspiciebat articulos manus scribentis') is well calculated to authenticate the experience without offering any explanation. But the *Gawain*-poet, with his irresistible urge to make every event fully solid, fully present to the senses, naturally cannot leave it at that. He knows exactly what the mystery looked like, and he tells us:

In the palays pryncipale upon the playn wowe,
In contrary of the candelstik that clerest hit schyned,
Ther apered a paume, wyth poyntel in fyngres,
That watz grysly and gret, and grymly he wrytes;
Non other forme bot a fust faylande the wryste,
Pared on the parget, purtrayed lettres...

And rasped on the rogh wowe runisch sauez.
When hit the scrypture hade scraped wyth a scrof penne,
As a coltor in clay cerves tho forwes,
Thenne hit vanist verayly and voyded of syght;
Bot the lettres bileved ful large upon plaster. (1531–6, 1545–9)

This is utterly convincing, but now the mystery has vanished, and
we are left with a stage-managed marvel, a sort of clever conjuring
trick. We are less frightened than Belshazzar and his court, just as in
Sir Gawain and the Green Knight we are less frightened of the Green
Knight when he first appears than Arthur and his court. In *Gawain*
that is the effect intended: there is a hint of contrivance, by which
we become partial accomplices with the poet in the attempt to terrify
the courtiers. In *Purity* it is difficult to believe that we ought to be
sharing the poet's relish in his *ferly* quite as fully as we do.

Divine power

We have seen how the *Gawain*-poet realizes and humanizes his
Scriptural sources in *Purity*, and how the humanization sometimes
includes God in his intercourse with man, and the realization, in the
last example mentioned, includes the display of God's power. But
the God of *Purity* is shown above all as angry and destructive: longsuffering in his endurance of human sin, merciful in his warnings
and his acceptance of a repentance such as Nebuchadnezzar's, but
ultimately terrible in his destruction of persistent *fylthe*. In our study
of the poem, we have so far seen little of this terrible aspect of God,
and the time has now come to rectify this omission, for it is perhaps
the crucial part of the poem's meaning. What each of the main
exempla shows is an angry God reminding men by a display of his
punitive power that he is the ruler of earth as well as of heaven.
Moreover, divine vengeance is a feature even of those *exempla* which
are not concerned with the punishment of *fylthe*. Thus the poet gives
a detailed account of the fall of Lucifer, not derived from any
Biblical source. The punishment of Nebuchadnezzar for his pride,
narrated as a retrospective episode in the *exemplum* of Belshazzar's
feast (lines 1642–1708) is another case of divine vengeance. What
Nebuchadnezzar is warned by the voice from heaven when he is
exulting in his earthly power is what is taught by the whole poem:
'scias quod dominetur Excelsus in regno hominum' (Daniel iv. 29)
('know that the most High ruleth in the kingdom of men'). It is

striking that this phrase, or one similar to it, is repeated four times
in Daniel iv and v: it is, I believe, the crucial fact about the world
for the *Gawain*-poet, that it is ruled by a power higher than the
human. In the parable of the wedding feast, God's anger and his
power are shown allegorically in human form, and the lord of the
feast, as a recent critic has put it, 'changes his mood terrifyingly,
like a fiercely jovial sergeant-major who finds an improperly dressed
soldier'[1] and has the wretched 'harlot' thrown

> Depe in my doungoun ther doel ever dwellez,
> Greving and gretyng and gryspyng harde
> Of tethe tenfully togeder. (158–60)

That dungeon is of course Hell. In the *exempla* of the fall of Lucifer,
of the Flood, and of Sodom and Gomorrah, God manifests his
kingship over the world he has created directly *through* that world:
through disaster on a cosmic scale, of the kind that fascinated the
imagination of Leonardo da Vinci. The *Gawain*-poet's skill is hardly
less than that Leonardo shows in his drawings of such subjects as
the Flood. What is almost unimaginable—the fall through space of a
horde of angels—is seen by the poet with extraordinary precision.
His lines have the violence of sound that alliterative poetry has such
a gift for, but the scene is also seen as if from an immense distance,
through a series of precisely chosen similes from every day life:

> Thikke thowsandez thro thrwen theroute,
> Fellen fro the fyrmament fendez ful blake,
> Sweved at the fyrst swap as the snawe thikke,
> Hurled into helle-hole as the hyve swarmez.
> Fylter fenden folk forty dayez lencthe,
> Er that styngande storme stynt ne myght;
> Bot as smylt mele under smal sive smokez forthikke,
> So fro heven to helle that hatel schor laste,
> On uche syde of the worlde aywhere ilyche. (220–8)

The three similes, of falling snow, of a swarming hive of bees, and,
most ingenious and evocative of all, of meal seeming to smoke as it
is sieved, move us step by step further away from the fall, until
finally, in a panoramic shot, we can see the whole world at once.

In the description of the Flood, it is the world itself that seems to
be breaking up, and the lines are bursting with verbs of violent

---

[1] Brewer, 'Courtesy and the Gawain-Poet', p. 59.

action: swelled, burst out, reared up, tore to rags, ripped to pieces, rushed:

> Then bolned the abyme, and bonkez con ryse,
> Waltes out uch welle-heved in ful wode stremez,
> Watz no brymme that abod unbrosten bylyve;
> The mukel lavande loghe to the lyfte rered.
> Mony clustered clowde clef alle in clowtez,
> Torent uch a rayn-ryfte and rusched to the urthe. (363–8)

This vision of destruction has its origin, stylistically, in the frequent descriptions of storms found in poems of the Alliterative Revival, where the same verbs, and the same formulaic clusters, are often found, though never with quite such concentration on the effect of something being torn or burst to pieces. The Flood, unlike the casting out of Lucifer, is directed against human beings, and the poet imagines its consequences to them, and to animals, with a compassion that seems almost a reproach to God. He imagines the animals staring at the heavens, roaring in fear and bewilderment, and human friends and lovers coming together, determined to endure their terrible fate in each others' company:

> Frendez fellen in fere and fathmed togeder,
> To drygh her delful deystyné and dyyen alle samen;
> Luf lokez to luf and his leve takez,
> For to ende alle at onez and for ever twynne. (399–402)

There is an odd contradiction of feeling here: we have been told just before that God's

> mercy watz passed,
> And alle his pyté departed fro peple that he hated, (395–6)

yet it seems clear that the poet's pity has not departed, and he feels the force of that bond that joins people together in the face of death. The poet certainly enjoys his own re-creation of God's destructive power: there is nothing half-hearted about his storm (of which Genesis says nothing). But, because he imagines its actual consequences in detail rather than in the generalizations of Genesis— 'And all flesh was destroyed that moved upon the earth, both of fowl, and of cattle, and of beasts, and of all creeping things that creep upon the earth: and all men' (vii. 21)—he cannot be neutral about them. Because the whirlwind that destroys the cities of the plain is less indiscriminate, he does not have the same mixed feelings

about it. In this description there is the same enactment of violence
through verbs of vigorous action, now with an appropriate sense of
whirling confusion as elemental forces are hurled in opposite directions and struggle against each other. The clouds are thrown up into
towers, the rain pelts down, the winds wrestle together and strive
against each other:

> The grete God in his greme bygynnez on lofte;
> To wakan wederez so wylde the wyndez he callez,
> And thay wrothely upwafte and wrastled togeder,
> Fro fawre half of the folde flytande loude.
> Clowdez clustered bytwene, kesten up torres,
> That the thik thunder-thrast thirled hem ofte.
> The rayn rueled adoun, ridlande thikke,
> Of felle flaunkes of fyr and flakes of soufre,
> Alle in smolderande smoke smachande ful ille. (947–55)

Here every phrase does its work: 'And thay wrothely upwafte', for
example, conveys in its tongue-twisting sequence of sounds a brief
struggle followed by a sudden release of fierce forces, while 'ridlande
thikke' both recalls the smoky visual effect of sieving used in the
description of the angels' fall and, through its sound, evokes the
drumming of the rain. The description continues with the same
effects of violent fission that we found in the Flood description, and
once again an unexpectedly precise simile from everyday life helps
us to stand outside the violence and see it as a whole:

> For when that the helle herde the houndez of heven,
> He watz ferlyly fayn, unfolded bylyve;
> The grete barrez of the abyme he barst up at onez,
> That alle the regioun torof in riftes ful grete,
> And cloven alle in lyttel cloutes the clyffez aywhere,
> As lance levez of the boke that lepes in twynne. (961–6)

To read the passage is to be battered and torn, and, having read it,
we may need to remind ourselves that the author lived six hundred
years before the invention of nuclear weapons. For him, such destruction coming from within the elements themselves could only be
imagined. Imagined too, though with the aid of Mandeville's sup-
posedly first-hand evidence, is the description of the waste landscape,
the Dead Sea, that is produced by such tampering with the frame of
nature—a landscape of perverse contradictions, where lead floats,
feathers sink, and delicious fruit turns to ashes.

The poem's final manifestation of divine power through violent destruction is somewhat different from the others, because the destruction is wrought not by natural forces but by men. Belshazzar and his court are destroyed in a surprise night-time attack by their enemies, but the violence is no less authentic or terrifying. Here there is no *amplificatio*: only the silence in which the city is entered, broken suddenly by trumpet-blasts so loud that they seem to come from the heavens—as in a sense they do. There follows a business-like savagery, tersely conveyed, and, in the murder of Belshazzar, a crystallization of human helplessness:

> Wythinne an oure of the nyght an entré thay hade,
> Yet afrayed thay no freke; fyrre thay passen
> And to the palays pryncipal thay aproched ful stylle.
> Thenne ran thay in on a res, on rowtes ful grete;
> Blastes out of bryght brasse brestes so hyghe,
> Ascry scarred on the scue that scomfyted mony.
> Segges slepande were slayne er thay slyppe myght,
> Uche hous heyred watz wythinne a hondewhyle;
> Baltazar in his bed watz beten to dethe,
> That bothe his blod and his brayn blende on the clothes;
> The kyng in his cortyn watz kaght bi the heles,
> Feryed out bi the fete, and fowle dispysed,
> That watz so doghty that day and drank of the vessayl;
> Now is a dogge also dere that in a dych lygges. (1779–92)

What is so effective here is the combination of concreteness with economy. The death-scene is reduced to its bare essentials, each hideously physical, the whole profoundly suggestive: the blood and brains on the bedclothes, the curtain used as a rough shroud (the richly fitted bed being almost a symbol of luxury in medieval courtly literature,[1] now put to a very different purpose), the contempt with which the body is treated ('I'll lug the guts into the neighbour room'),[2] and the horribly sudden passage from drinking to death and from being a king to being like a dead dog in a ditch. The focus is unflinchingly sharp, and the message clear.

The last two lines of the last passage quoted lead us on to another way in which the power of God is expressed in *Purity*. They make up a neat pattern of reversal, in which past and present are juxtaposed and contrasted. Section VI of the poem is full of such patternings:

---

[1] Cf. Gawain's bed at Sir Bertilak's castle.   [2] *Hamlet*, III. iv. 212.

the very texture of the narrative evokes a world in which sudden reversals of fortune are the common order of things. Such reversals are ultimately the work of God, the manifestation of his power. Thus, in a passage concerning the Jews under the Babylonian captivity, imposed on them because of the idolatry of Zedekiah, the reversal pattern occurs twice, and is itself reversed so as to form a chiasmus (*sumtyme-now*; *now-sumtyme*):

> So sytte in servage and syte that sumtyme wer gentyle;
> Now ar chaunged to chorles, and charged wyth werkkes,
> Bothe to cayre at the kart and the kuy mylke,
> That sumtyme sete in her sale syres and burdes. (1257–60)

Nebuchadnezzar's madness, also a punishment sent by God, is summarized in a sentence whose syntax has a kind of plot, conveying an ironic reversal in its turn on the relative pronoun: 'Thus he countes hym a kow that watz a kyng ryche' (1685).[1] It must be admitted, though, that men are also allowed to bring about such reversals, by putting what is God's at the service of the Devil. This is what happens to the vessels of the temple, and the reversal is several times brought out in sentence-patterns. The past of the 'gay coroun of golde' (1444) is contrasted with its present; what had been blessed and anointed:

> Bifore the Lorde of the lyfte in lovyng hymselven,
> Now is sette for to serve Satanas the blake,
> Bifore the bolde Baltazar wyth bost and wyth pryde. (1448–50)

Of the vessels in general:

> Soberly in his sacrafyce summe wer anoynted,
> Thurgh the somones of Himselfe that syttes so hyghe;
> Now a boster on bench bibbes therof,
> Tyl he be dronkken as the devel, and dotes ther he syttes.
> (1497–1500)

Daniel points out the same reversal to Belshazzar, saying that he has:

> his vessayles avyled in vanyté unclene,
> That in his hows hym to honor were hevened of fyrst (1713–14)

> Bifore thy borde hatz thou broght beverage in thede
> That blythely were fyrst blest wyth bischopes hondes. (1717–18)

---

[1] For a discussion of how sentences can have plots, see Donald Davie, *Articulate Energy* (London, 1955), pp. 79 ff.

Here there are further examples of an ironic turn on the relative pronoun. But the final reversal is God's, and the author of these blasphemies is its victim. God can overturn earthly kings, because he is the true king of the earth. This is something of which we are frequently reminded in section VI by the very formulaic phrases used to refer to God. These phrases are scattered particularly thickly through the story of Nebuchadnezzar and Belshazzar. They remind of God's constant presence and his high power: he is 'Hym that in heven wonies' (1340), 'the Lorde of the lyfte' (1356 and 1448), 'the Lorde that the lyfte yemes' (1493), 'Himselfe that syttes so hyghe' (1498), 'the Soverayn of heven' (1643), and 'that wynnelych Lorde that wonyes in heven' (1807). But, besides these references to God as the ruler of heaven, there are a number of others that remind us of how 'the most High ruleth in the kingdom of men' also. This indeed had been asserted in the opening lines of the poem, in an allusion to God as the universal Creator, 'the Wyy that wroght alle thinges' (5). It is repeated in 'the Worcher of this worlde' (1501), 'Hym that alle goudes gives' (1528), 'God that gyes alle sothes' (1598), and 'Goddes gost...that gyes alle thynges' (1627). These formulas are clearly used by the *Gawain*-poet not indiscriminately, as they might be used by a primitive oral poet for whom they were a mere necessity of composition, but as a means of keeping before our minds the sovereignty of God over a world that men try to treat as their own.

Purity, as we have seen, is concerned mainly with impurity, and therefore with the punitive aspect of God's power, with his justice rather than mercy. But it would be wrong to leave this as an unqualified final impression of the poem. God's own *clannesse*, as we have seen, is treated in section V (*b*), and, particularly in the vignette of the Nativity, it is presented with a winning gaiety and strength. Here too the characteristic reversal-patterns are found, in three parallel lines, but the reversal is now from bad to good, from *fylthe* and sickness to *clannesse* and health:

> For ther watz seknesse al sounde that sarrest is halden,
> And ther watz rose reflayr where rote hatz ben ever,
> And ther watz solace and songe wher sorw hatz ay cryed;
> For aungelles wyth instrumentes of organes and pypes,
> And rial ryngande rotes, and the reken fythel,
> And alle hende that honestly moght an hert glade,
> Aboutte my Lady watz lent, quen ho delyver were. (1078–84)

It was the fall of Adam, brought about by the temptation of the fallen
Lucifer, that was ultimately responsible for all the examples of
fylthe punished in the poem; this is a further reason why the
exemplum of the Flood is preceded by *exempla* of the falls of Lucifer
and of Adam. But God's mercy was to find a remedy for Adam's fall;
it was to be 'amended wyth a mayden that make had never' (248). In
the passage just quoted, the nature of the remedy is presented with
the poet's usual concreteness, rottenness being replaced by the scent
of roses (for the Blessed Virgin is the 'plantatio rosae in Jericho' of
Ecclesiasticus xxiv. 18), and lamentation by that music which is a
common medieval symbol of the divine harmony. It is against the
background of this promise and fulfilment that the Old Testament
stories of divine vengeance against *fylthe* are to be seen, and the poet
gives us just enough stimulus to keep this in mind, without confusing
the main theme of his poem. The central reminder is in the section
on God's own *clannesse*, which we have just been discussing, but
mention should also be made of the subsequent elaboration of the
pearl image,[1] and finally of a striking speech made by God himself
to Abraham in section IV (*a*). Here God is condemning the unnatural
love of the Sodomites, but he does so by contrasting it not with
chastity (which is one meaning of *clannesse*) but with lawful love
between man and woman. God commends natural human love in
terminology that would have been familiar and acceptable to a
courtly audience—*drwry, paramorez, luf-lowe*—and with exactly the
comparison with paradise that is common in secular love poetry in
the tradition of the *Roman de la Rose*.[2] The passage has a relish
(*play, myriest, merthe, lasched*) such as is rarely found in medieval
religious poetry, and such as could certainly never have been pre-
dicted as representing the word of God in a medieval poem on the
subject of purity and impurity:

> I compast hem a kynde crafte and kende hit hem derne,
> And amed hit in myn ordenaunce oddely dere,
> And dyght drwry therinne, doole altherswettest,
> And the play of paramorez I portrayed myselven;
> And made therto a maner myriest of other,
> When two true togeder had tyyed hemselven,
> Bytwene a male and his make such merthe schulde come,
> Wel nyghe pure paradys moght preve no better,

---

[1] Discussed above, pp. 34-5.   [2] See below, pp. 118-19.

Ellez thay moght honestly ayther other welde;
At a stylle stollen steven, unstered wyth syght,
Luf-lowe hem bytwene lasched so hote,
That alle the meschefez on mold moght hit not sleke. (697–708)

Thus God himself is made responsible for and seems almost to participate in the delightful secrecy of *fine amour*, so long as it is between those who are truly joined. This a kind of *clannesse* that is open to all, and this is the firmly stated positive that lies behind the poem's fierce negatives.

3

Patience

Structure and purpose

Patience is a simpler, less ambitious, and more perfect poem than *Purity*. It is the shortest of the four poems in the manuscript, and it presents the poet's central subject, the confrontation between the human and the more than human, in its simplest possible form: through a single *exemplum*, admirably chosen for the poet's purpose. The story of Jonah, told in one of the shortest books of the Old Testament, offers a complete and ready-made image of man in futile rebellion against God. The poet is not faced with any problems of selection or modification, and the result is a small masterpiece, a poem which makes its point swiftly and confidently, and with little complication in its treatment of the relationship between man and God. Its straightforwardness will be apparent from a summary of its structure:

- I.   Introduction (1–60)
- II. *Exemplum:* the story of Jonah (61–527)
  - (*a*) (61–408) The whale and the Ninevites
  - (*b*) (409–527) The aftermath: Jonah and God
- III. Conclusion (528–31).[1]

The introduction commends patience on the ground of its profitability, and indeed necessity:

> For quoso suffer cowthe syt, sele wolde folwe;
> And quo for thro may noght thole, the thikker he suffres. (5–6)

There is a kind of pun here on *suffer* that may remind us of the poet's flexible treatment of *clannesse* in *Purity*: by longsuffering we achieve happiness; resistance brings suffering. It then turns to the Beatitudes, which were also the source of the praise of *clannesse*. Patience is seen as the subject of the last Beatitude: 'Beati qui persecutionem

---

[1] The manuscript has decorated initials at lines, 1, 61, 245, 305 and 409, thus dividing the poem according to the four chapters of the Book of Jonah.

74

patiuntur propter iustitiam' (Matthew v. 10) ('Blessed are they that
suffer persecution for justice' sake'). The whole series of Beatitudes
is recited, along with their promised rewards, as the narrator says
that he himself heard them 'on a halyday at a hyghe masse' (9). This
personal note is struck again when he adds that one would be most
blessed if one possessed all these virtues,

> Bot syn I am put to a poynt that Poverte hatte,
> I schal me porvay Pacyence, and play me with bothe. (35-6)

This at least partially personal presentation of the narrator is not
found in *Purity*, and there has been some doubt as to what is meant
by this reference to the narrator's poverty. One scholar has argued
that it is the 'poverty of spirit, humility' of the first Beatitude that
the narrator is attributing to himself.[1] He is of course alluding to
'Beati pauperes spiritu', but what he mentions is simply *poverte*. By
this he must surely mean material poverty, for to claim humility for
oneself is necessarily to lack it. He is making a wry joke: he may have
no other virtues, but at least he has poverty, and so he had better
take up patience too. There is no reason to suppose that this is
literally autobiographical, and that the poet was really poor, either
voluntarily (through having taken religious vows) or involuntarily,
though of course this may have been the case. He may well be
adopting the conventional guise of the minstrel, who mentions his
own poverty in order to beg for a reward from his patrons; though
in this case he would perhaps be more likely to refer to his poverty
near the end of the poem than near the beginning. But in any case, I
believe that the main purpose of this characterization of the narrator
is not to point to something outside the poem, but to play a part
within it. The narrator is himself an example of patience, in the
sense of putting up with what is ordained for one; he is thus an exact
opposite to Jonah, the poem's *exemplum* of impatience. The narrator
takes sides in the poem, enters into it as a partisan, and thus makes
the case against Jonah more forcefully than a neutral narrator could.
He is an integral part of the poem, in the same way, though not to
the same extent, as Chaucer's Merchant is part of *The Merchant's
Tale*.[2] The remainder of the introduction is largely in personal

---

[1] Charles Moorman, 'The Role of the Narrator in *Patience*', *MP*, LXI (1963-4), 90-5;
p. 92.
[2] Moorman suggests a comparison with *The Pardoner's Tale*, and notes that the
narrator of *Patience* is 'actively present in the poem, and the reader is from time to

terms: it concerns the narrator's own situation so much as to look forward to the completely autobiographical fiction of *Pearl*, whose narrator has to learn in the course of the poem the patience that the narrator of this poem has already achieved.

A word more must be said about an additional, and interestingly odd, reason the narrator gives for linking poverty with patience. He remarks, with reference to the Beatitudes:

> For in the tyxte there thyse two arn in teme layde,
> Hit arn fettled in on forme, the forme and the laste,
> And by quest of her quoyntyse enquylen on mede. (37–9)

The Beatitudes promise to both the poor in spirit and those who suffer persecution the reward of the kingdom of heaven; but for the narrator it is obviously important that they are also the first and the last in the list. For him, formal arrangement is clearly part of a statement's meaning; and here he surely speaks for the poet who is such a master of significant structure, and who, in three of his four poems, is so careful to make the end agree verbally with the beginning.[1]

Section II of *Patience*, which forms the main bulk of the poem, tells the story of Jonah as an *exemplum* of the folly and pointlessness of impatience—that is, of failing to play willingly the role God has laid down for one. I believe that from the *Gawain*-poet's point of view this story fell into two parts, and a brief summary will make clear why this should be so. In the first part the goal of the action is the conversion of the Ninevites. God speaks to Jonah and orders him to go and preach against the wickedness of the Ninevites, but instead Jonah runs away and takes a boat to Tarshish. God therefore sends a great storm; Jonah manages to sleep through it, but the sailors are terrified and, by drawing lots, they determine that Jonah is responsible for it. He confesses that he is running away from his god, and agrees that they should throw him overboard. They do so; the storm immediately stops, and Jonah is swallowed up by a great fish (in the poem, and traditionally, though not in the Bible, a whale).

---

time made aware that he is listening not to an impersonal and omniscient author but to a narrator who, although not strongly individualized, is nevertheless a man of firm opinion' (*ibid.* p. 90). So far as Jonah's motives are concerned, however, the narrator surely *is* omniscient—more so than his counterpart in the Book of Jonah.

[1] I have this point from Benson, who points out (p. 166) how this passage shows the poet's 'keen awareness of the semantic function of form'.

Jonah prays to God from inside the fish, and begs for mercy, and after three days and nights he is vomited up on dry land—the shore of Nineveh. God again tells him to preach in Nineveh. It appears that he has learned his lesson; he does so, and prophesies to the Ninevites that their city will be destroyed if they do not repent and reform. Unlike the inhabitants of Sodom in *Purity*, they do repent; and their king, unlike Belshazzar, 'radly upros and ran fro his chayer' (378), takes to sackcloth and ashes for himself, and orders a general fast. The Ninevites are thus converted, and God does not destroy them. Here the story might end, its initial goal having been achieved. But in fact it passes into a second phase, one more closely concerned with Jonah himself, and with his understanding of God's purposes. Jonah sees the mercy that God has shown towards Nineveh as spoiling his own reputation as a prophet, because he had said that God would destroy it. In his anger he rebukes God and asks him to kill him. God answers simply, 'Putasne bene irasceris tu'? (Jonah iv. 4) ('Dost thou think thou hast reason to be angry?'). Then Jonah goes off in a huff to the desert, and makes himself a 'booth' from which to watch what happens to Nineveh. God makes a gourd grow up to shade it, and Jonah is very pleased. Next day, however, God sends a worm and an east wind to make the gourd wither; Jonah faints in the heat, and becomes angry all over again. God, in answer, points a moral which relates as much to his own nature as to Jonah's behaviour. Jonah was angry about the destruction of a gourd, which he had not made himself, and yet he expected God not to care about the destruction of a city of six score thousand persons, including many people innocent through ignorance, and dumb beasts. Here the Book of Jonah ends, but the poet makes God go on to contrast more explicitly his own mercy and longsuffering with Jonah's impatience. Since the manuscript has no punctuation to indicate speech, it is not clear at what point these remarks of God's pass into the brief conclusion, in which the poet points the moral of the need for patience, as it applies to himself and to men in general.

The purpose of this poem is clear enough: to commend patience by an *exemplum* which first shows God's thwarting of impatience in a human being, and then expounds his own patience by contrast. The term 'patience', for which the poet's word is the same as ours, has a somewhat wider sense than it commonly possesses nowadays. It means both putting up with one's lot and being longsuffering towards folly and wickedness, rather than hasty to take vengeance on them. The first sense applies especially to man, the second especially to God. There is no question in *Patience*, as there is in *Purity*, of running together physical and moral senses of the term, or (at least to anything like the same extent) of re-creating its meaning by juxtaposing a whole range of different situations to which it applies. But the poet does make use of the process of his poem—its movement through time, both its own and ours—to bring about a gradual shift in focus. In the first part of the story, the emphasis is largely on Jonah's impatience and the means by which it is corrected; later, the emphasis moves towards God's patience, as a fulness against which Jonah's lack can be measured. How would it be if God were like Jonah? And then, as we look back over the poem from its end, we see its earlier stages in a somewhat different perspective, the emphasis falling now less on Jonah's impatience and more on the merciful patience that God showed towards him as well as towards Nineveh. In this respect, the *Gawain*-poet has found a story better suited to his purpose than the *exempla* of *Purity* were. There, God's *clannesse* did not quite emerge from the stories of man's *fylthe* and God's punishment of it; instead, it had to be brought out in discursive connecting passages such as those of section v. In *Patience*, human impatience and divine patience are shown simultaneously, and since divine patience is brought out especially towards the end of the story, this positive emerges more emphatically than *clannesse* does in *Purity*. It is for this rather than for more strictly structural reasons that I call *Patience* more perfect than *Purity*.

Another reason is connected with the same facts. The God of *Patience* is more merciful than the God of *Purity*; this indeed is implied by the very subjects of the poems. The God of *Purity*, based on the fierce and jealous God of Genesis, destroys with the Flood all living things except those in the ark, and, as we saw, there seemed to be a certain tension between his indiscriminate vengeance and the poet's compassion for his victims—the friends and lovers taking leave of one another, and the uncomprehending animals that

> alle cryed for care to the Kyng of heven,
> Recoverer of the Creator thay cryed uchone. (*Purity*, 393-4)

But the God of *Patience*, in determining the fate of Nineveh, tells Jonah that he had in mind precisely such facts: that it contained innocent women and children, and 'doumbe bestez...That may not synne in no syt hemselven to greve' (516-17). The *Gawain*-poet clearly had more sympathy, if one may so put it, for the God of Jonah than he had for the God of Genesis. Jonah, from the whale's belly, confidently puts his trust in God's mercy rather than in the avenging justice displayed against Sodom or Belshazzar:

> Thou schal releve me, renk, whil thy ryght slepez,
> Thurgh myght of thy mercy that mukel is to tryste. (323-4)

And this emphasis on God's mercy conduces to a greater certainty of tone throughout the poem than in *Purity*. The *Gawain*-poet's ' realization' of human beings always tends towards comedy, as indeed medieval realism generally does, and in *Patience* his 'hero' can be an essentially comic figure, almost an anti-hero, precisely because God is not going to destroy him, but to forgive him. In this poem, patience is the highest virtue to which human beings can aspire— it is the only course open to them—and this gives their futile strivings against God's merciful omnipotence a certain absurdity, a lack of dignity which is entirely in keeping with the poet's humour. The result is a work of masterly ease, less richly complex than *Pearl* or *Sir Gawain and the Green Knight*, but indisputably a masterpiece, and one which, if it were from a later period or even in a less difficult dialect, would have had widespread recognition as such.

Human comedy

The narrative of *Patience* follows closely that of the Book of Jonah, and the method I shall follow in analysing it will again be to characterize the *Gawain*-poet's methods and attitudes by contrasting them with those of the Biblical narrator. As with *Purity*, it is possible that the poet used other sources than the Vulgate text of the Bible, such as the poem *De Jona et Ninive* attributed to Tertullian; but even if he did so, our purposes will best be served by considering what he made of his Scriptural source, with or without other help. The Book of Jonah has many of the same literary qualities as Auerbach points to in Genesis. It shows a direct confrontation between God and man, and focuses very sharply and fiercely on that single relationship: the vertical relationship between man and God is far more important than the horizontal relationship between man and his social and natural environment. As a result, there is very little local detail in the Biblical story. Nearly everything that is included is pared down to bare necessities, and, while we are told what the characters say, we are usually told little or nothing of the motives that cause them to speak as they do. It is true that there are some indications of locality and mundane detail:

et invenit navem euntem in Tharsis, et dedit naulem eius, et descendit in eam ut iret cum eis in Tharsis a facie Domini (Jonah i. 3)

(and [he] found a ship going to Tharsis. And he paid the fare thereof and went down into it, to go with them to Tharsis from the face of the Lord.)

There are some hints of characterization, in the hurried questions of the sailors in the storm:

Et dixerunt ad eum: Indica nobis cuius causa malum istud sit nobis. Quod est opus tuum? quae terra tua, et quo vadis, vel ex quo populo es tu? (i. 8)

(And they said to him: Tell us for what cause this evil is upon us. What is thy business? Of what country art thou and whither goest thou? Or of what people art thou?)

There is some interpretation by the narrator of the characters' thoughts:

Et timuerunt viri timore magno, et dixerunt ad eum: Quid hoc fecisti? Cognoverunt enim quod a facie Domini fugeret, quia indicaverat eis. (i. 10)

(And the men were greatly afraid, and they said to him: Why hast thou done this? (For the men knew that he fled from the face of the Lord: because he had told them).)

Even God is not entirely a voice speaking out of darkness; though he never, as in his visits to Abraham and Lot, takes on human or angelic form, he is humanized sufficiently to be provided with comprehensible motives:

Et vidit Deus opera eorum, quia conversi sunt de via sua mala; et misertus est Deus super malitiam quam locutus fuerat ut faceret eis, et non fecit. (iii. 10)

(And God saw their works, that they were turned from their evil way: and God had mercy with regard to the evil which he had said that he would do to them, and he did it not.)

In these ways, the Book of Jonah is somewhat less granite-hewn and challenging than Genesis xxii as described by Auerbach, though not less than Genesis vi–viii and xviii–xix or the other Scriptural sources of *Purity*. The Book of Jonah remains challenging to a very considerable degree, because so much in it is left unexplained, and what is unexplained is often what is most suggestive and provokes most curiosity. In particular, there is no hint of any reply by Jonah to God's original command to preach in Nineveh: no interpretation whatever of the reaction on his part that led him to escape to Tarshish. We are told simply:

Et factum est verbum Domini ad Ionam filium Amathi, dicens:
Surge, et vade in Niniven civitatem grandem, et praedica in ea, quia ascendit malitia eius coram me.
Et surrexit Ionas, ut fugeret in Tharsis a facie Domini (i. 1–3)

(Now the word of the Lord came to Jonas the son of Amathi, saying:
Arise, and go to Ninive the great city and preach in it: for the wickedness thereof is come up before me.
And Jonas rose up to flee into Tharsis from the face of the Lord.)

And there is no information whatever about what must have been for Jonah himself the most extraordinary experience of his life: being swallowed by a great fish. The Bible does not enter into Jonah's experience at all. For the Biblical narrative, his three days and nights in the fish's belly exist solely as a means of producing a spiritual conversion, and so we are told simply:

Et praeparavit Dominus piscem grandem ut deglutiret Ionam; et erat Ionas in ventre piscis tribus diebus et tribus noctibus. (ii. 1)

(Now the Lord prepared a great fish to swallow up Jonas: and Jonas was in the belly of the fish three days and three nights.)

Then follows Jonah's magnificent prayer from the fish's belly, and, immediately at the end of it, 'dixit Dominus pisci; et evomuit Ionam in aridam' (ii. 11) ('the Lord spoke to the fish: and it vomited out Jonas upon the dry land').

Much of the *Gawain*-poet's realization of this bare and economical Scriptural narrative consists of the same kind of filling in of material detail that we found throughout *Purity*. Departure on a sea-voyage is a common theme in the alliterative tradition, and so it comes naturally to the poet to linger over the departure of Jonah's ship from Joppa, an event which the Bible does not even mention. But the poet supplies far more nautical detail than is common in alliterative poems: he is passionately interested in everything that is contained in the physical world of the poem, and so he tells us how the sailors

> her tramme ruchen,
> Cachen up the crossayl, cables thay fasten,
> Wight at the wyndas weghen her ankres,
> Sprude spak to the sprete the spare bawe-lyne,
> Gederen to the gyde-ropes,—the grete-cloth falles;
> Thay layden in on ladde-borde and the lofe wynnes.
> The blythe brethe at her bak the bosum he fyndes;
> He swenges me thys swete schip swefte fro the haven. (101–8)

Or, to take another smaller example, when the storm hits the ship, the Bible tells us that the sailors 'cast forth the wares that were in the ship into the sea, to lighten it of them' (i. 5). For the *Gawain*-poet, these generalized 'wares' (*vasa*) immediately take on concrete and varied shapes, of all the things that would really have been thrown from a medieval ship:

> Her bagges, and her fether-beddes, and her bryght wedes,
> Her kysttes, and her coferes, her caraldes alle. (158–9)

As in *Purity*, this realizing activity of the imagination extends beyond the merely pictorial to take in actions and words, so that almost every moment of the narrative is not left as a suggestive outline, but is developed into a little dramatic scene, with its own internal dynamic. For example, while the sailors are throwing things overboard, Jonah is sleeping. This sleep was commonly interpreted in the Middle Ages as standing for the obliviousness of the sinner, insensible of the impending danger of divine judgment, and such an interpretation was possible precisely because the Biblical narrative is so bare: 'Ionas...dormiebat sopore gravi' (i. 5) ('Jonas...fell into a deep sleep'). But for the *Gawain*-poet it was in the first place a literal sleep, in which Jonah (as a man might when uncomfortably placed in the hold of a tossing ship) was slavering and snoring, and from which he had to be aroused with a kick and a curse: he

> Slypped upon a sloumbe-slepe, and sloberande[1] he routes.
> The freke hym frunt with his fot, and bede hym ferk up:
> Ther Raguel in his rakentes hym rere of his dremes! (186–8)

I do not suggest that for the *Gawain*-poet and his readers the traditional allegorization of the Book of Jonah was completely absent; on

---

[1] *Sloberande* is the manuscript reading. Both Bateson and Gollancz suggest that it ought to be *slôberande*, i.e. *slomberande*. This would be more conventional, but it would be entirely in keeping with the *Gawain*-poet's usual method to add an unexpected and undignified but realistic detail.

the contrary, the shipmaster's curse, with its reference to the devil, positively encourages a wider perspective of significance; but this is present, not as a hidden, unexpressed layer of meaning, but as part of the implication of an engrossing literal meaning.

Unlike *Purity*, *Patience* tells a story which centres in a single character, and the *Gawain*-poet's imaginative realization of the story focuses in Jonah's own experience. That experience is presented with a delicate balance of sympathy and detachment: we share in Jonah's experience of his adventures, yet there tends to be a certain irony holding us back from accepting his own view of them. Evidence of this may be found if we turn to the poem at the point where Jonah is vomited out by the whale:

> The whal wendez at his wylle and a warthe fyndez,
> And ther he brakez up the buyrne, as bede hym oure Lorde.
> Thenne he swepe to the sonde in sluchchede clothes,—
> Hit may wel be that mester were his mantyle to wasche. (339–42)

The state of the prophet's clothes at this point is not mentioned by Scripture, and in the supposition of the last sentence we seem to catch the *Gawain*-poet's imagination in the very act of re-creating the Scriptural account, just as we did in *Purity* when, with an 'I wene', he guessed what Lot's wife said to herself as she sprinkled salt on the angels' food. Yet the 'hit may wel be' also has the effect of ironic understatement; after three days in the filth of the whale's belly, Jonah's clothes certainly would be soiled and in need of a wash. Moreover, in the light of the normal medieval use of garments as a symbol of the wearer's spiritual state,[1] and especially in the light of the *Gawain*-poet's interpretation of the guests' garments in the parable of the wedding feast as standing for their works and dispositions, we would surely be right to find a hint of allegory here: Jonah is soiled inwardly as well as outwardly. This adds to the irony, for it is the narrator who is dropping the hint; Jonah is unaware of it.

Before this, the narrator on our behalf has entered with extraordinary completeness into Jonah's physical and psychological experience first of being swallowed by a fish, and then of staying inside it. Yet even in that sequence there is no question of our completely losing our independence of judgment. Jonah is seized by the fish with a rapidity that is wittily defined in a single line of

---

[1] Mentioned by Bateson in his note on line 342; he compares the soiled cloak of Hawkyn in *Piers Plowman* (B. XIII. 272 ff.).

graphic imagination and packed action: 'The folk yet haldande his fete, the fysch hym tyd hentes' (251). Incidentally, this moment is illustrated in the manuscript with delightful literalism: we actually see Jonah's head entering the whale's jaws while the sailors still have a grip on his feet, as if the illuminator had for once responded to the poem itself, not just to the story. Then Jonah's descent to the fish's belly is not immediate: the poet imagines it as a lengthy process, past the gills, through guts that seem as large as roads, and finally, staggering, into the darkness, slime and stench of the belly itself (the *fylthe* of *Purity* in its most physical sense):

> Lorde! colde watz his cumfort, and his care huge,
> For he knew uche a cace and kark that hym lymped:
> How fro the bot into the blober watz with a best lachched,
> And thrwe in at hit throte withouten thret more,
> As mote in at a munster dor, so mukel wern his chawlez!
> He glydes in by the giles thurgh glaym ande glette,
> Relande in by a rop, a rode that hym thoght,
> Ay hele over hed, hourlande aboute,
> Til he blunt in a blok as brod as a halle;
> And ther he festnes the fete and fathmez aboute,
> And stod up in his stomak, that stank as the devel.
> Ther in saym and in saur that savoured as helle,
> Ther watz bylded his bour, that wyl no bale suffer;
> And thenne he lurkkes and laytes where watz le best,
> In uche a nok of his navel, bot nowhere he fyndez
> No rest ne recoverer, bot ramel and myre
> In wych gut so ever he gotz; bot ever is God swete. (264–80)

The poet has gone with Jonah inside the fish, and we follow with him the headlong, uncontrolled journey, coming to a sudden stumbling halt in the fish's belly. Sound, rhythm and syntax work together to produce an astonishingly complete enactment of the experience, as, for example, when the liquid and verbless confusion of 'Ay hele over hede, hourlande aboute' is jarringly cut short by the past tense and plosives of 'Til he blunt in a blok'. Submitted to all these indignities, realized with such grotesque vigour, Jonah becomes an absurd figure, the butt of a monstrous farce; and yet the passage contains signs of a greater subtlety of approach than this farcical quality might suggest. There is, for instance, the odd precision of the simile 'as mote in at a munster dore', reminiscent of similes from *Purity* such as 'as smylt mele under smal sive smokez forthikke'

(*Purity*, 226), and hinting, too, that the terrible experience may have a spiritual purpose. There is the quiet and exact irony of 'Ther watz bylded his bour, that wyl no bale suffer', the point lying in the contrast between a whale's belly and the usual implications of 'bour', and between Jonah's wish to avoid trouble and the trouble he finds himself in as a consequence. Again, there is the quietness of 'bot ever is God swete', where, after the stench of the whale, an almost sensible fragrance seems to be attributed to God, in a way that may remind us of *Purity*'s 'ther watz rose reflayr where rote hatz ben ever' (*Purity*, 1079). Finally, we may note that the references to the devil and hell do not merely intensify the physically revolting quality of the description, but remind us of its symbolic sense, for Jonah's three days in the whale were, by a tradition going back to the New Testament, interpreted as a type of Christ's descent into hell after the crucifixion:

Sicut enim fuit Ionas in ventre ceti tribus diebus et tribus noctibus, sic erit Filius hominis in corde terrae tribus diebus et tribus noctibus. (Matthew xii. 40)

(For, as Jonas was in the whale's belly three days and three nights; so shall the Son of man be in the heart of the earth three days and three nights.)

(The typological interpretation gives a further layer of significance to the simile of the cathedral door.)[1] These notes alien to simple farce make it clear that the poet is far from being naïve in his realistic treatment of Jonah's time in the whale—a point that would not need making, but for the persistence of patronizing remarks such as Gollancz's that 'the poet...transformed and amplified in characteristic fashion the terse Biblical narrative, so that the story might vividly appeal to simple folk',[2] and Normand Berlin's that 'the poet's primary purpose was to make the Jonah story appeal vividly to the English folk of the fourteenth century...His description [of the whale] is bold and vivid, undoubtedly appealing to a popular circle'.[3]

I shall return to this point later, but first I want to examine the poet's treatment of the other Biblical passage which I mentioned as being left mysterious: Jonah's reaction to God's original command to

---

[1] And the momentary identification of hell with a cathedral is paralleled in Gawain's fear that he will find the Devil at the Green Chapel (*Gawain*, 2191–6).

[2] Ed. *Patience*, 2nd edn. (London, 1924), p. 8.

[3] Normand Berlin, '*Patience*: A Study in Poetic Elaboration', *Studia Neophilologica*, XXXIII (1961), 80–5; pp. 80, 82.

prophesy in Nineveh. The Bible tells us nothing of Jonah's motives, but the medieval poet enters into his very consciousness, and follows out the flow of thought and feeling in a detail that is convincing and devastating. He imagines vividly what his fate will be if he goes to Nineveh:

> He telles me those traytoures arn typpede schrewes;
> I com wyth those tythynges, thay ta me bylyve,
> Pynez me in a prysoun, put me in stokkes,
> Wrythe me in a warlok, wrast out myn yyen.
> This is a mervayl message a man for to preche,
> Amonge enmyes so mony and mansed fendes! (77–82)

Here the poet's power of instant realization is attributed to Jonah himself; and again a farcical quality can be felt in the eagerness with which Jonah's imagination leaps forward in time to call up the scene, one detail suggesting another, and the whole nightmare seen as present rather than future (the ambiguity of the verbs is put to good effect). Soliloquy for the *Gawain*-poet is not, as it tends to be in Elizabethan drama, a form of conscious self-dramatization, the acting out of a chosen role, but a form of unconscious self-exposure, over-heard by the audience, or an uncensored transcript of the workings of the character's mind. Jonah works himself up to the point of setting out for the port on the spot. As he sets off, moving into the three-dimensional poem-space, he seems to draw away from us, and his mutterings are turned from direct into reported speech:

> Thenne he ryses radly, and raykes bylyve
> Jonas toward port Japh, ay janglande for tene,
> That he nolde thole, for nothyng, non of those pynes. (89–91)

The emphatic triple negative of the last line, while not an uncommon feature of Middle English syntax, here seems to be used expressively, to give an effect of childish petulance. Then the reported speech turns back into direct, as if we were following Jonah and had now caught up with him, and so were able to hear his very words (or thoughts) again:

> 'Oure syre syttes', he says, 'on sege so hyghe
> In his glowande glorye, and gloumbes ful lyttel
> Thagh I be nummen in Nunive and naked dispoyled,
> On rode rwly torent, with rybaudes mony.' (93–6)

This catches the very note of a personal grudge against God, whose apparent remoteness from human suffering Jonah holds as a reproach against him, as if he were a brass-hat leading his army of prophets and martyrs from the rear. Yet the last line and a half contains a clear allusion to Christ's sufferings, of which Jonah's are a type, and, in the context of this tone, it is almost shocking. Jonah was a type of Christ in being a prophet as well as in the 'three days and three nights' in hell:

Nam sicut fuit Ionas signum Ninivitis, ita erit et Filius hominis generationi isti. (Luke xi. 30)

(For as Jonas was a sign to the Ninivites; so shall the Son of man also be to this generation.)

By reminding us of the standard of which Jonah is so miserably falling short, the allusion serves to belittle him still further. In the Bible he is a type of Christ; in the poem, an antitype. The silence of the Bible at this point, which allows Jonah's motives for flight to retain a certain dignity, is shattered in the poem by his own voice, grumbling incessantly, and reducing him to absurdity.

From here it will be revealing to turn to a later point in *Patience*, in the second phase of the story. Jonah has finally obeyed God's command to preach in Nineveh, and God, taking pity on the repentant Ninevites, has 'withhelde his vengaunce' (408). As in the Biblical account, Jonah is deeply offended at God's mercy, and the poet follows the Bible in making him say that he knew all along that God would not punish the Ninevites, and that was why he fled to Tarshish in the first place:

Obsecro, Domine, numquid non hoc est verbum meum, cum adhuc essem in terra mea; propter hoc praeoccupavi ut fugerem in Tharsis. Scio enim quia tu Deus clemens et misericors es, patiens et multae miserationis, et ignoscens super malitia. (Jonah iv. 2)

(I beseech thee, O Lord, is not this what I said, when I was yet in my own country? Therefore I went before to flee into Tharsis: for I know that thou art a gracious and merciful God, patient and of much compassion and easy to forgive evil.)

But we have just seen that, unlike the Biblical narrator, the poet has earlier made Jonah admit to a quite different motive for his flight, namely that he was being instructed to preach a doctrine that would make him exceedingly unpopular. Thus the medieval Jonah convicts himself of a childish inconsistency, quite apart from the way in which his repeated emphasis on God's patient mercy (expanded from the verse just quoted) tells against him:

Wel knew I thi cortaysye, thi quoynt soffraunce,
Thy bounté of debonerté and thy bene grace,
Thy longe abydyng wyth lur, thy late vengaunce;
And ay thy mercy is mete, be mysse never so huge.[1] (417-20)

Jonah intends all this as a reproach of God—he would rather be prophet to the avenging God of *Purity*—but for us, of course, it has just the opposite effect.

In this second phase of the story, Jonah becomes almost a symbol of man in rebellion against God. This is a theme which in other ages has been treated, however ambiguously, as potentially heroic and glamorous: witness Marlowe's Faustus or Milton's Satan, and later Byron's Cain or Shelley's Prometheus. But for the medieval poet it can only be comic. Jonah wishes to die, and challenges God to kill him, rather than make him 'lede lenger thi lore, that thus me les makez' (428). But in saying this he is seeing the situation back-to-front. He takes it that God's mercy or punishment of the Ninevites is only a means to the end of giving himself a reputation as a true prophet; the reverse is the case. Jonah's death-wish seems childish, particularly in the note of exaggerated self-dramatization the poet adds to his relatively dignified original: 'Et nunc, Domine, tolle quaeso animam meam a me' (Jonah iv. 3) ('And now, O Lord, I beseech thee take my life from me').

Now, Lorde, lach out my lyf, hit lastes to longe;
Bed me bilyve my bale-stour, and bryng me on ende. (425-6)

The added reference to death-pangs, with its patent self-pity, tips the balance towards the comic. One is often reminded of a child's behaviour in this second phase of the story. As God speaks to him, he flees again, *janglande* (433) as he did on his first flight. (Compare line 90: *janglande* conveniently alliterates with *Jonas*, but so do many other words.) While he sleeps, God makes a *wod-bynde* (Vulgate *hedera*; Douay 'ivy') grow up to shelter him, and Jonah when he sees it changes with a child's rapidity from extreme dejection to equally extreme delight. He sees it as a house:

For hit watz brod at the bothem, boghted on lofte,
Happed upon ayther half, a hous as hit were. (449-50)

It is the *Gawain*-poet, of course, who supplies all these details. Jonah

---

[1] D. S. Brewer ('Courtesy and the *Gawain*-Poet', p. 57) notes that the terms used here are 'part synonyms [of *cortaysye*], part members of the associative field of the word'.

looks at the many amenities of this desirable residence, the green leaves, the cool breeze playing in them, the shade. And

> Thenne watz the gome so glad of his gay logge,
> Lys loltrande therinne lokande to toune;
> So blythe of his wod-bynde he balteres therunder,
> That of no diete that day the-devel-haf he roght. (457–60)

His childish pleasure and engrossment are exactly caught in the gestures of the verbs, *loltrande* and *balteres*, and it is just like a child to be so pleased with a new plaything that he cannot be bothered to eat. He laughs with delight every time he looks at it, and immediately starts thinking of it as his own possession, and wishing that he could take it home with him to live in. This possessiveness too is childish.

Now God sends the worm to destroy the *wod-bynde*, and Jonah quickly reverts to anger and depression. It is still *his*—'His wod-bynde watz away, he weped for sorwe' (480)—and he immediately accuses God of deliberately tormenting him. Once more he over-dramatizes his situation, inflating his loss of a mere *wod-bynde* to a tragedy:

> I kevered me a cumfort that now is caght fro me,
> My wod-bynde so wlonk that wered my heved;
> Bot now I se thou art sette my solace to reve.
> Why ne dyghttez thou me to diye? I dure to longe. (485–8)

The next exchange captures the very note of the father-child relationship, with an attempt at comfort on one side, and petulant rejection on the other, culminating in a complete huff:

> 'Why art thou so waymot, wyye, for so lyttle?'
> 'Hit is *not* lyttel,' quoth the lede, 'bot lykker to ryght;
> I wolde I were of this worlde wrapped in moldez.' (492–4)

How vivid, and in a sense how pleasing, the prospect of his own death always is to Jonah! In his reply, God at first humours him by referring to the plant as '*thy* wod-bynde' (497), but in the next line this condescension turns to irony with the reminder that Jonah had done nothing to make it grow in the first place:

> Thou art waxen so wroth for thy wod-bynde,
> And travayledez never to tent hit the tyme of an howre. (497–8)

God draws the moral, and this, as we have seen, passes without a break into the poet's brief conclusion. The tone of both is the same:

a charitable wisdom which, without being patronizing—perhaps indeed because it is not patronizing—makes its recipient feel and seem very small:

> Be noght so gryndel, godman, bot go forth thy wayes. (524)

Divine power

Jonah, then, a man set against God, is presented in *Patience* as absurd, childish, a would-be hero, whose successive attempts at self-assertion are successively deflated. This element of deflating comedy is far more marked than in *Purity*; and in the case of *Patience* one might feel more strongly tempted to wonder how conscious this treatment of the subject was. Could it not be that the vividly realizing and humanizing energy of the poet's imagination led him unawares towards the comic, and that his work, though lively, is what medieval art has so often been found—quaint? Certainly one might be encouraged towards this view by comments such as those I have quoted from Bateson ('naïve charm of happy primitive faith'), Gollancz ('appeal to simple folk'), and Berlin ('undoubtedly appealing to a popular circle'). I have tried to show, however, that the *Gawain*-poet wrote not for 'simple folk' but for a highly sophisticated aristocratic society; and we have just seen how Jonah himself attributes to his God a collection of courtly virtues centring in the quintessential courtly virtue of *cortaysye*. And in fact, in *Patience* as a whole, the comedy of human impotence is all the more effective because it is set against the grandeur of divine omnipotence; and this is not by any means made absurd or quaint. Sometimes, it is true, God is humanized, and becomes a father to the childish Jonah, but he is never so fully humanized as in some parts of *Purity*, and in general he remains the voice without place and without expressed motives that Auerbach found in Genesis xxii. His commands to Jonah are somewhat amplified from the Biblical version, but they retain an unimpeded imperative quality:

> Goddes glam to hym glod that hym unglad made,
> With a roghlych rurd rowned in his ere:
> 'Rys radly,' he says, 'and rayke forth even,
> Nym the way to Nynyve, wythouten other speche.' (63–6)

And the power of God is centrally displayed as we found it was most effectively in *Purity*: not in a human way, but through description of the dark, violent aspect of his handiwork, the natural world. In *Patience* this means the storm which causes Jonah to be thrown overboard. It is described twice, once directly by the poet when it actually occurs, and a second time when Jonah recalls it in his prayer from the fish's belly. These two passages form the imaginative core of the whole poem, and there is nothing funny about them.

In the first storm-description, which is largely the invention of the poet, the emphasis falls at once on the storm as the manifestation of God's power. The winds blow in answer to God's command, their obedience as prompt as that which accompanied the *dixit* of the Creation:

> 'Ewrus and Aquiloun that on Est sittes,
> Blowes bothe at my bode upon blo watteres.'
> Thenne watz no tom ther bytwene his tale and her dede,
> So bayn wer thay bothe two, his bone for to wyrk. (133-6)

The verse enacts this obedience, by leaving no gap between 'his tale' and 'her dede', but only an 'and'. The storm begins, conceived largely as a structure of noise and movement, but with a single vivid glimpse of the visual effect, a sinister red glare beneath the storm-clouds. As in the destruction of Sodom and Gomorrah, natural forces are thrown against each other: the winds wrestle,[1] and the waves are mountainous in one line, and then plunge sickeningly down in the next:

> Rogh rakkes ther ros, with rudnyng anunder;
> The see soughed ful sore, gret selly to here;
> The wyndes on the wonne water so wrastel togeder
> That the wawes ful wode waltered so highe
> And eft busched to the abyme. (139-43)

Then, with striking originality, as if a film of a storm were suddenly to include a shot taken underwater, we are shown the fish themselves being hurled about in their own element:

> that breed fysches
> Durst nowhere for rogh arest at the bothem. (143-4)

Then our attention is directed to Jonah's ship being tossed and battered, its tackle breaking, and finally seeming about to go under; at which the cry of the men on it penetrates faintly through the roaring of the storm:

---

[1] Compare *Purity*, line 949, and *Gawain*, line 525.

91

The sayl sweyed on the see, thenne suppe bihoved
The coge of the colde water, and thenne the cry ryses. (151–2)

At last, moving in for a close-up, the poet shows us the sailors throwing goods overboard, in a passage we have already examined. They pray to their various gods, and now we can hear their voices distinctly as they decide to draw lots. The cine-camera-like movement of the narrator's eye, culminating in the prolonged closing-in effect, is a good example of the *Gawain*-poet's skill in manipulating perspective, so as to convey economically both the large-scale and the small-scale effects of the storm.

Throughout the subsequent scene, we are not allowed to forget the continuing storm. The sailors, having lost their sail, take to rowing, but to no avail: 'In bluber of the blo flod bursten her ores' (221) —a splendidly onomatopoeic line. At last, when they are rid of Jonah, calm comes; but now the poet turns to a second, even more striking description of the storm, as recalled in Jonah's prayer when he has reached the fish's belly. It is based on a passage already superb in the Vulgate:

Circumdederunt me aquae usque ad animam; abyssus vallavit me, pelagus operuit caput meum.

Ad extrema montium descendi; terrae vectes concluserunt me in aeternum, et sublevabis de corruptione vitam meam, Domine Deus meus! (Jonah ii. 6–7)

(The waters compassed me about even to the soul: the deep hath closed me round about: the sea hath covered my head.

I went down to the lowest parts of the mountains: the bars of the earth have shut me up for ever: and thou wilt bring up my life from corruption, O Lord my God.)

The poet has not lost the grandeur of this rhetoric. He has indeed enriched it, re-creating the storm as sound and movement, and at the same time bringing out the double implication of the 'compassing about' by the sea and the earth that Jonah undergoes. 'Flumen circumdedit me...circumdederunt me aquae...terrae vectes concluserunt me' (ii. 4, 6, 7): the effect is at once threatening and protective. The result is a poetic conception of the sea extraordinarily similar to that of the later Shakespeare, in *Pericles* or *The Tempest*:[1] it is powerful with a power that may be either destructive or pro-

---

[1] Bateson (p. xli) mentions *Pericles* in connection with the storm.

vidential, or both at once. This double effect is one way in which the second storm-description in *Patience* differs from the various evocations of destructive natural forces in *Purity*: they are destructive only, because God's mercy does not work through them as well as his avenging justice. From the beginning of the passage in *Patience*, the sea is presented as enveloping Jonah in a way that might be protective, enfolding: 'The grete flem of thy flod folded me umbe' (309). Then the same event is seen as a convergence of separate mighty forces into a single onslaught, in which all the various dangers of the sea conspire to break over Jonah:

> Alle the gotes of thy guferes, and groundelez powlez,
> And thy stryvande stremez of stryndes so mony,
> In on daschande dam dryvez me over. (310–12)

In the very midst of this assault, however, God's mercy also manifests itself to Jonah. Separated from God, he is yet surrounded by his power:

> And yet I sayde as I seet in the se-bothem,
> 'Careful am I, kest out fro thy cler yyen
> And desevered fro thy syght; yet surely I hope
> Efte to trede on thy temple and teme to thyselven.' (313–16)

The image of envelopment is now repeated: this time the word is 'wrap'. It passes into one of simple power—from 'wrapping' to 'binding'—and then Jonah, buried in the whale, is submerged beneath the whirlpool:

> I am wrapped in water to my wo-stoundez;
> The abyme byndes the body that I byde inne;
> The pure poplande hourle playes on my heved. (317–19)

This last line is worth more detailed comment. It was long ago pointed out that its first half also occurs in another poem of the Alliterative Revival, *The Wars of Alexander*: 'The pure populande hurle passis it umby'.[1] It is likely then that this beautifully expressive half-line was a formula belonging to the common style of alliterative poetry rather than to any one poet. But it is noticeable how the *Gawain*-poet has brought out its bubbling quality to best effect by the liquid sound of *playes* in his second half-line, while in *The Wars of Alexander* the second half-line gives no such help to the first. It is differences of

---

[1] Ed. W. W. Skeat, line 1154, noted by O. F. Emerson, reviewing the first edition of Bateson's *Patience*, *Modern Language Notes*, XXVIII (1913), 171–80; p. 174.

this kind, each one minute in itself, that mark the distinction between more and less successful uses of a traditional formulaic style.

Throughout this second storm-description the texture of sound is extraordinarily rich, and co-operates so closely with the sense that it can scarcely be analysed in abstraction from it. Similarly with rhythm and syntax; all these features collaborate to produce a passage which, in the alternate advance and recession of its enactment of power, seems to re-create the energy of the sea itself.

God's power is most strikingly present, then, in these two sea-passages, but it is also, as we found to be the case in *Purity*, a fact that pervades the whole world of the poem. Along with the comic treatment of Jonah, this fact makes us see him not as a heroic challenger, but as one who foolishly sets himself against the very nature of the world he lives in. The divine power is pervasively present in reminders of the divine creativity, which are found everywhere in *Patience*. The poet comments sardonically on Jonah's first flight:

> He wende wel that that Wyy that al the world planted
> Hade no maght in that mere no man for to greve. (111–12)

This is similar to the use of formulaic phrases for God in *Purity*, and another such phrase occurs in:

> For the Welder of wyt, that wot alle thynges,
> That ay wakes and waytes, at wylle hatz he slyghtes. (129–30)

Another similarity to *Purity* occurs, as we have already noted, when the poet quotes Psalm xciii. 9:

> Hope ye that he heres not that eres alle made?
> Hit may not be that he is blynde that bigged uche yye. (123–4)

Jonah himself knows, when he comes to consider the matter, that he cannot escape from the God he worships, who created the only world available for escaping into. So he tells the sailors, in a passage closely following Scripture:

> That Wyye I worchyp, Iwysse, that wroght alle thynges,
> Alle the worlde with the welkyn, the wynde and the sternes,
> And alle that wonez ther withinne, at a worde one. (206–8)

This statement consists in effect of an unusually expanded formula for God. The poet points out how God's power preserved Jonah inside the whale, quite against the course of nature:

> nade the hyghe heven-Kyng, thurgh his honde-myght,
> Warded this wrech man in Warlowes guttez,
> What lede moght lyve bi lawe of any kynde
> That any lyf myght be lent so long hym withinne? (257–60)

Jonah calls on God to prove himself 'a lorde in londe and in water' (288) by saving him. The king of Nineveh praises God's power, and sees his very capacity for mercy as evidence of it:

> I wot his myght is so much, thagh he be mysse-payed,
> That in his mylde amesyng he mercy may fynde. (399–400)

God shows his power by creating the *wod-bynde* of course, but also, as the poet's formulaic description of dawn reminds us, by creating the daylight which enables Jonah to see it:

> When the dawande day Dryghtyn con sende,
> Then wakened the wyy under wod-bynde,
> Loked alofte on the lef that lylled grene. (445–7)

Having created it, God shows his power further by destroying the *wod-bynde*, in a kind of miniature parallel to the storm, using this time not the north and east winds, but the west:

> God wayned a worme that wrot upe the rote,
> And wyddered watz the wod-bynde bi that the wyye wakned;
> And sythen he warnez the West waken ful softe,
> And sayez unto Zeferus that he syfle warme,
> That ther quikken no cloude bifore the cler sunne. (467–71)

And finally he explains to Jonah that he cannot take vengeance on the Ninevites because he created them 'of materes myn one' (503), out of the *materia prima* which he had also created himself, and which is the basis of all created things.

Thus there is no escaping from the power of God the creator—it is present everywhere within the world of the poem—and this very power is the source of God's mercy, his 'patience'. Jonah sets himself against the power and the mercy, and it is the mercy even more than the power that defeats him, not by destroying him like Belshazzar or the Sodomites, but by reducing him to absurdity. He is not overwhelmed by the storm, but protected in the midst of it; he is not even allowed to die defiantly. Towards such a God, an unheroic patience is the only viable attitude.

4

Pearl

Pearl, Purity and Patience

Pearl has the reputation of being an exceptionally difficult poem. Much discussion of it begins by asking 'What does it mean?' or 'What is it about?'—questions we should have no need to ask of *Purity* or *Patience*. I shall eventually come to give a kind of answer to questions like this, but for the moment I want to avoid doing so. Questions of this sort may seem to imply that the poem is a kind of cryptogram, difficult to solve, but offering a single definite solution to the skilled cryptologist. I do not believe that this is so with *Pearl*, and I believe that critics and scholars have often obscured the poem by coming too quickly to such crucial questions. I therefore prefer to begin more obliquely by considering what *kind* of poem it is. This will involve discussing its affinities with other literary works and literary traditions. I begin by considering some of the ways in which *Pearl* is similar to and different from the two works by the *Gawain*-poet that we have already examined.

Purity and *Patience* are alike, we have seen, in consisting largely of amplifications of Old Testament stories set in the framework of a homily, in which the stories function as *exempla*. The main source of *Pearl*, however, belongs not to the Old Testament but to the New— it is the Apocalypse or Revelation of St John—and this Biblical part of the poem is present not as an *exemplum* but as a direct part of the experience of the narrator. He has been carried into Paradise, and he has seen what St John saw. He is careful to remind us of his distinguished predecessor in these realms, whose unimpeachable vision authenticates his own:

> In the Apokalypce is the fasoun preved,
> As devysez hit the apostel Jhon. (983–4)

In *Purity* and *Patience* the Biblical stories are told in the third person, so that such central figures as Abraham, Lot, Belshazzar, or Jonah are always 'he'. The narrator of these poems is present only in the opening, closing and transitional sections, and occasionally as a commentator who mediates between his sources and his audience by offering speculation about the detail or significance of his stories (as when he guesses at what Lot's wife felt and said on being told to bake saltless bread). But in *Pearl* the narrator ceases to be a discreet master of ceremonies and, moving into the foreground, becomes his own hero or anti-hero. The poem tells us of an experience of his own, and there is no part of it of which he is not an eyewitness—the poem's 'eye' as well as its 'I'. This method of narration would in itself produce a quite different effect if applied to the same Old Testament material as is used in the other two poems. *Patience*, for example, would become an entirely different poem if Jonah's adventures were told by Jonah himself. And the difference is made more marked by the fact that the source-material of *Pearl* is different in its nature from that of *Purity* and *Patience*. Those two poems are set in an Old Testament past which is conceived as largely identical with the medieval present. It is, as we have seen, a familiar world, a world which, even under the impact of extraordinary events of supernatural origin, is one of detailed and recognizable verisimilitude: it is *this* world, *our* world. *Pearl* is set in the present, in the narrator's own lifetime, but for the main part of the poem it is a visionary present, set outside time and outside this world. It is set in the 'other world' of Christian eschatology, a world of harsh glittering light, containing trees with blue trunks and leaves like burnished silver (very different from the homely 'oke grene' of *Purity*), a city made of precious stones, and a bleeding Lamb worshipped by virgins adorned with pearls.

These differences in subject-matter and manner of presentation are matched by differences in literary form. *Purity* and *Patience* are both written continuously in unrhymed long alliterative lines, and, though their form and style are certainly the product of a complex art, that art is used mainly, with whatever virtuosity, as a means of presenting reality. *Pearl*, on the other hand, is composed in twelve-line stanzas, in which the difficulty of the rhyme-scheme (*ababababbcbc*) is compounded by the shortness of the lines, the fact that they are none the less thickly alliterative, and the linking of the stanzas in groups of five, each stanza in a group ending with a variant of the same line (so that all the *c* rhymes in a group must be the same), and each stanza also repeating in its first line a phrase from the last line of the previous stanza. The consequence of all this is an art which displays itself, not, as we shall see, irresponsibly, but certainly proudly, to produce a verbal effect as bejewelled as the other world it describes. Over an insistent metrical pattern of four heavy stresses to the line plays an elaborate music of alliteration, repetition, rhythmic variation and rhyme—a showpiece of virtuosity, in striking contrast to the comparative sobriety of *Purity* and *Patience*. In *Pearl*, indeed, we seem to have a kind of verbal equivalent to the latest Gothic styles in art and architecture of the period in which it was written. On purely formal grounds, it would appeal to the same kind of taste as the ostentatiously detailed ingenuity of the castle described in *Sir Gawain and the Green Knight*. It is closer still to the religious architecture of the fourteenth century, in the way its repeated overcoming of apparently insuperable difficulties expresses an excitement touching on ecstasy. Professor Pevsner, for example, writing of the Lady Chapel at Ely Cathedral, which he dates 1335–53, remarks how the unknown designer 'has set the flat surfaces in an undulating motion, and it is from this that the great fascination of the room derives'. As in *Pearl*, richly detailed variables play like flames over a rigid framework—in the case of *Pearl*, the twelve-line stanza of four-beat lines, in the case of the Ely Lady Chapel the 'plain parallelogram' which is the basic shape of the room. At Ely, seats are placed round the walls, and (Pevsner continues):

Each seat is treated as a deep niche and has a canopy with that most characteristic Dec[orated] motif, the nodding ogee arch or three-dimensional ogee arch. The arches are cusped, gabled, and thickly crocketed. Underneath them and half hidden by them, the niches on the N and S sides...have each a double arch against their back walls. This increases the complexity of the design considerably. Moreover, at intervals...is a wider niche projecting in its arch further forward. In addition the corners are veiled by niches placed diagonally. By these various means the designer gives the vivid impression of a movement swinging and rocking forward and upward...The windows [originally]...had stained glass and the architectural details...were all painted. So there was not the clarity of today, but a rather hotter and more exciting effect.[1]

The parallel between the *Gawain*-poet's work and the 'Decorated' art-style of the fourteenth century has been noted;[2] it applies far more exactly to *Pearl* than to the poet's other works.

---

[1] Nikolaus Pevsner, *Cambridgeshire* (Harmondsworth, 1954), pp. 285–6.
[2] Elizabeth Salter, 'The Alliterative Revival', p. 236.

However, beneath the differences we have been discussing between *Pearl* and the two Old Testament poems there lie important similarities, which the initial contrast must not be allowed to obscure. We have seen that *Purity* and *Patience*, in praising their respective virtues, relate them to the heavenly rewards promised to them by the Beatitudes: the pure in heart shall see God and the patient shall possess the kingdom of heaven. In *Pearl*, similarly, the central part of the poem is occupied with demonstrating that a heavenly reward is promised for another virtue, though this time not one mentioned in the Beatitudes: innocence. Between lines 421 and 728, the Pearl Maiden is concerned to prove to the Dreamer that innocent children, even though they have no knowledge of God or of good and evil, have a right to the kingdom of heaven, won by Christ's sacrifice; indeed, they have a right to be kings and queens there, just as much as those who won the heavenly reward for themselves with good works. This promise of heaven for a particular virtue is clearly a central preoccupation of the *Gawain*-poet's, and though in *Pearl* he cannot ground it in the Beatitudes he does base his argument on Scriptural texts of a similar kind. The Maiden refers to two texts, one from the Old Testament and one from the New. The first is from the Psalter, and is used to show that entrance to heaven is promised to two classes of men, the righteous and the innocent:

> The Sauter hyt satz thus in a pace:
> 'Lorde, quo schal klymbe thy hygh hylle,
> Other rest wythinne thy holy place?'
> Hymself to onsware he is not dylle:
> 'Hondelyngez harme that dyt not ille,
> That is of hert bothe clene and lyght,
> Ther schal hys step stable stylle'—
> The innosent is ay saf by ryght.
>
> The ryghtwys man also sertayn
> Aproche he schal that proper pyle:—
> 'That takez not her lyf in vayne,
> Ne glaverez her nieghbor wyth no gyle.' (677–88)

This is based on Psalm xxiii. 3–4:

Quis ascendet in montem Domini, aut quis stabit in loco sancto eius?

Innocens manibus et mundo corde, qui non accepit in vano animam suam, nec iuravit in dolo proximo suo.

99

(Who shall ascend into the mountain of the Lord: or who shall stand in his holy place?

The innocent in hands, and clean of heart, who hath not taken his soul in vain, nor sworn deceitfully to his neighbour.)

The poet has evidently taken verse 4 as offering a twofold answer to the twofold questions of verse 3,[1] and thus distinguishes between 'innocens in manibus et mundo corde' (the innocent) and 'qui non accepit in vano animam suam, nec iuravit in dolo proximo suo' (the righteous).[2] The second text quoted by the Maiden to prove the salvation of the innocent is a saying of Jesus which parallels in its wording those Beatitudes—the first and the last—on which *Patience* is based:

> Do way, let chylder unto me tyght.
> To suche is hevenryche arayed. (718–19)

Sinite parvulos, et nolite eos prohibere ad me venire: talium est enim regnum caelorum. (Matthew xix.14)

(Suffer the little children and forbid them not to come to me; for the kingdom of heaven is for such.)

This argument in *Pearl* about the nature of the heavenly reward promised to innocence brings home the fact that *Pearl* is not concerned with an area of experience unrelated to those of *Patience* and *Purity*, but that it rather complements and completes the themes of those poems. They are concerned chiefly with the kingdom of men, and with how God intervenes in it in order to enforce his hatred of certain vices; *Pearl* is concerned with the kingdom of heaven, which is the promised reward for the corresponding virtues. Because of the close interrelatedness of purity and innocence, *Pearl* is to be seen in particular as the complement to *Purity*. It is a study of the true nature of the vision of God which is the reward for the *mundo corde*, of which the Pearl Maiden is an extreme case.

In the course of her argument in this central section of the poem that innocent children are promised the kingdom of heaven, the Maiden repeats and amplifies one part of the New Testament in a way that reminds one strongly of the treatment of Old Testament material in *Purity* and *Patience*. This is the parable of the vineyard,

---

[1] I have modified Gordon's punctuation accordingly.
[2] The fact that the innocent soul is here described as *clene* (682) provides a further link with *Purity*.

which she uses to prove to the Dreamer that it is in accordance with
God's justice that she, who performed no good works, should receive
an equal reward in heaven to those who had lived longer in the world
and suffered more. In Matthew this is one of the longest of the
parables of the kingdom, and the *Gawain*-poet does not amplify it
as fully as he does the Scriptural sources of *Purity* and *Patience*—not
so fully, for example, as the other parable of the kingdom that he
repeats in *Purity*, that of the wedding-feast. But his attitude towards
it is clearly similar. Although the story is a parable, told to convey a
meaning which is not part of its literal sense, it already possesses in
the Gospel a fairly fully realized material setting and human content.
It is a vivid and concrete story of everyday life, as applicable to the
agricultural society of fourteenth-century England as to that of first-
century Palestine. The poet responds to these aspects of the parable
in ways we have found to be characteristic of *Purity* and *Patience*.
For example, where Matthew says simply that the hired labourers
went into the vineyard, the *Gawain*-poet is more specific about the
various kinds of work they had to do there, and the effort they put
into it:

> forth thay gotz,
> Wrythen and worchen and don gret pyne,
> Kerven and caggen and man hit clos. (510–12)

Again, the indications of time given by Matthew, though exact, are
minimal: the lord hired his last group of labourers 'about the
eleventh hour' and paid all the labourers off 'when evening was
come' (Matthew xx. 6, 8). The *Gawain*-poet elaborates these indications so as to make them more atmospheric, as though he were casting an evocative light over a whole picture. The last workmen are
taken on:

> At the date of day of evensonge,
> On oure byfore the sonne go doun, (529–30)

and then:

> Sone the worlde bycom wel broun;
> The sunne watz doun and hit wex late.
> To take her hyre he mad sumoun;
> The day watz al apassed date. (537–40)

As usual, the poet conceives his characters as occupying physical
space and as spatially related to each other. Thus whereas in Matthew
the lord tells his steward, 'Call the labourers and pay them their hire,

beginning from the last even to the first' (xx. 8), in *Pearl* he adds the instruction to 'Set hem alle upon a rawe' (545). Most striking of all, just as we found in *Purity* and *Patience*, speech is imagined for the characters in which tones of voice are so exactly suggested as to give the effect of mimicry, or even of comic parody. An ample cue for this is given in the Gospel when the first-hired labourers are dissatisfied with their wages:

Venientes autem et primi, arbitrati sunt quod plus essent accepturi: acceperunt autem et ipsi singulos denarios.

Et accipientes murmurabant adversus patremfamilias,

Dicentes: Hi novissimi una hora fecerunt, et pares illos nobis fecisti, qui portavimus pondus diei, et aestus. (xx. 10–12)

(But, when the first also came, they thought that they should receive more; and they also received every man a penny.

And, receiving it, they murmured against the master of the house,

Saying: These last have worked but one hour; and thou hast made them equal to us that have borne the burden of the day and the heats.)

The *Gawain*-poet takes the cue, and elaborates the complaint in convincingly colloquial terms:

> And thenne the fyrst bygonne to pleny
> And sayden that thay hade travayled sore:
> 'These bot on oure hem con streny;
> Uus thynk uus oghe to take more.
>
> More haf we served, uus thynk so,
> That suffred han the dayez hete,
> Thenn thyse that wroght not hourez two,
> And thou dotz hem uus to counterfete.' (549–56)

This speech of discontent seems to catch the authentic note of the fourteenth-century equivalent of the trade-unionist: the journeyman protesting, let us say, against an over-strict interpretation of the Statute of Labourers. The grumbling note, the hint of not entirely confident truculence, is particularly convincingly captured in the parenthetic 'uus thynk so', repeating the earlier 'uus thynk'. Such imitation of tones of voice must have been much more difficult to achieve in the short-lined stanzas of *Pearl* than in the unrhymed long lines of *Purity* and *Patience*. It may be added that, just as with the parable of the wedding-feast in *Purity*, the parable of the vineyard is given a full and explicit exegesis by the poet. In neither case can

there be any question of the poet's relying on his audience's knowledge of current exegesis to interpret the text for him, because in
both cases he is offering his own individual interpretation of it,
which is not necessarily in line with tradition.

The poet cannot be said to treat his main Scriptural source, the
Apocalypse of St John, in the same way as he treats this parable,
largely because the part he uses is not susceptible of such treatment.
In particular he uses Apocalypse xxi. 10–23 as the basis for his
description of the heavenly Jerusalem, and there is no possibility
here of any systematic 'realization'. The passage is already descriptive, not narrative, so that there can be no question of supplying
material background or tones of voice, and it is descriptive in a
minute way typified in the fact that St John knows that the city forms
a twelve-thousand-furlong cube because he sees his angel-guide
measuring it with a measuring rod. The *Gawain*-poet indeed wisely
leaves the measuring rod to be used by Wordsworth in *The Thorn*,
and, whether by accident or design, reduces the size of the city from
twelve thousand furlongs to twelve furlongs. He contents himself
with adding various details designed to heighten the visual effect.
Thus St John simply lists the twelve precious stones with which the
foundations of the city are adorned, but the *Gawain*-poet tells us
more of what some of them looked like, taking his material presumably from a contemporary enyclopaedia or lapidary. The jasper 'glente
grene' (1001); the chalcedony was 'wythouten wemme' and 'con
purly pale' (1003–4); the emerald was 'grene of scale' (1005); the
beryl was 'cler and quyt' (1011); the topaz was 'twynne-hew' (1012);
and the amethyst was 'purpre wyth ynde blente' (1016). The effect
of multi-coloured glitter is far more striking than in the Scriptural
source, though we can scarcely speak of verisimilitude; the point
being that the New Jerusalem is *not* like everyday life, and the poet
was wise, in this one attempt of his to describe something outside the
bounds of the material world, not to attempt to make it so. His model
was not the life of his time but the art of his time. The thirteenth,
fourteenth and fifteenth centuries saw the production in England of
many illuminated Apocalypse books, of which nearly a hundred still
survive. Typically, they are brilliantly coloured, and make much use
of gold leaf, the purpose of which is not to imitate a possible reality,
but to impress and dazzle, by reflecting that light which is the most
common medieval symbol of God himself. It is suggestive that a few
lines beyond the passage I have been quoting, the poet writes that

the jasper walls of the city 'glent as glayre' (1026), egg-white being
'the normal fixative for gold leaf' in medieval manuscripts.[1] The
influence of manuscript illumination, a small-scale art, might even
account for the poet's reduction in size of the heavenly city, and for
the lack of verisimilitude by which he represents the Dreamer as
being able to see from the other side of the river what is going on
inside the city. (Characteristically, however, he adds the explanatory
detail that the walls were transparent:

> Thurgh wowe and won my lokyng yede,
> For sotyle cler noght lette no lyght. [1049–50])

But there is no need to describe what the poet is doing in terms of
influences. In abandoning for his description of the Dreamer's
vision of the heavenly city the methods of verisimilitude which he
uses elsewhere in his work, he is doing what is proper for this special
subject. He is describing, through the eyes of a human being, something that men cannot normally see, and for which the only parallel
is to be found in records of the visions of saints. In this part of the
poem he repeatedly refers to St John, and he once alludes to St Paul,
in claiming that the mere fact of his survival proves that he must have
been 'out of the body', and therefore not experiencing the radiance of
heaven through his bodily senses—the senses to which most of the
poet's work appeals.[2] When he does use an earthly comparison, it is
chosen from the unearthliest field of human experience: the sudden
appearance of the procession of virgins in the city is compared to the
mysterious emergence of the moon in the evening sky, when its
rising has taken place earlier under cover of daylight:

> Ryght as the maynful mon con rys
> Er thenne the day-glem dryve al doun,
> So sodanly on a wonder wyse
> I watz war of a prosessyoun. (1093–6)

Most importantly, beneath these features of presentation which
relate it to *Purity* and *Patience*, *Pearl* shares with them the same
fundamental subject. This, as we have seen, concerns the relation
between the human and the more-than-human, the latter being con-

---

[1] Elizabeth Salter, 'The Alliterative Revival', p. 149 n. 24. Mrs Salter remarks on the
availability of such manuscripts to a poet of the West Midlands: an Apocalypse was
among the books given to Bordesley Abbey by Guy of Warwick in 1305. On medieval
Apocalypse books in general, see M. R. James, *The Apocalypse in Art* (London, 1931).
[2] See lines 1081–92, discussed below, pp. 111–12.

ceived in terms of Christian theology. In *Purity* and *Patience* we saw human beings attempting to establish a purely human order in their lives, whether personal or social. That order was then shattered by the intervention of divine power, with the reminder that 'the most High ruleth in the kingdom of men' as well as in that kingdom of heaven which is the promised reward for human virtue. By this demonstration of the dependence of the human on the divine, man, though usually treated with charitable sympathy, was diminished in stature and made the object of comedy. *Pearl* still treats of the relationship between man and the divine order, but now the situation is reversed. Instead of God intervening into the human world, a human being is thrust into the divine world, into the kingdom of heaven. That at least is the situation through the bulk of the poem —man in heaven, not God on earth—but, if we also take into account the beginning of *Pearl* and its end, we shall see that its action is essentially the same as that of *Purity* or, more especially, of *Patience*. Like Jonah, the 'hero' of *Pearl* suffers an intervention into his life by an irresistible divine power, which plucks him from his normal earthly setting and, when he attempts to circumvent its purposes, rudely brings home to him his powerlessness. When the intervention is over, the Dreamer of *Pearl*, like Jonah, has been taught the necessity of patience:

> Lorde, mad hit arn that agayn the stryven,
> Other proferen the oght agayn thy paye. (1199–1200)

During the intervention, the Dreamer is brought into contact with the divine, and particularly with the divine purity which is the *datum* of *Purity*; and, being merely human, not, like the Maiden, transmuted into an aspect of that purity, he cannot be anything but inadequate to the role he is called on to play. He is no John the Divine, no Paul: like Dante faced with the task of entering the world beyond death while still alive, he might protest, 'Io non Enea, io non Paolo sono'.[1] He is not indeed comparable to either the pagan or the Christian hero who explored the other world; but, unlike the narrator of Dante's poem, he does not at first even recognize this. Part of his inadequacy is not to recognize his inadequacy. At the beginning of his vision he finds himself propelled, like a knight in medieval romance, 'In aventure ther mervaylez meven' (64), and by

---

[1] *Inferno* ii. 32. For further comment, see below, pp. 107–9.

its end he has still not lost the conviction that he can make an independent and heroic way towards his goal, by leaping into the
river and swimming across it, even at the cost of his life:

> I thoght that nothyng myght me dere
> To fech me bur and take me halte,
> And to start in the strem schulde non me stere,
> To swymme the remnaunt, thagh I ther swalte. (1157–60)

It would be right for the hero of a chivalric romance to risk his life
in this way in order to gain his lady; it is not right in a poem set in
the Christian other world, where the barrier has been ordained by
God. And the Dreamer in *Pearl* sees himself not only as a hero but
also, more absurdly, as a scholar. He is always ready to bandy arguments and texts against the Maiden's explanations of her situation
and his, forgetting that she is one of those who 'thurghoutly haven
cnawyng' (859). In consequence, the Dreamer, like Jonah, becomes
a comic figure, struggling in vain to dominate a world which is not
his and which he does not understand. Yet the situation is more
poignant than in *Patience*, for a reason we have already glanced at:
that the would-be hero is also 'I'. Two states of consciousness are
presented to us in an alternation so rapid that it feels like simultaneity:
that of the Dreamer who naïvely experiences the successive phases of
his adventure, and that of the narrator who has already learned the
lesson of the vision, and who is telling the story with the benefit of
that wisdom. Thus, in the very arrogance and egoism of the Dreamer,
because these qualities are defined and placed by the narrator, who
is also 'I', there is often a most moving effect of humility. He seems
to stand both inside and outside himself as he undergoes astonishment and incomprehension in the strange world of his vision and yet
can himself present to us the comic aspect of his reactions as they
would be visible to a detached observer.[1] For example, when he first
sees the Maiden on the other side of the river, he tells us that:

> Wyth yyen open and mouth ful clos,
> I stod as hende as hawk in halle. (183–4)

And similarly, when he first sees the heavenly city, he says that 'I

---

[1] The effect of 'duality in unity' has been noted by D. S. Brewer, 'Courtesy and the
Gawain-Poet', p. 65 n. 1, and by M. P. Hamilton, 'The Meaning of the Middle
English *Pearl*', *PMLA*, LXX (1955), 805–24, p. 811. Hamilton quotes an interesting
passage from Francis Fergusson, *Dante's Drama of the Mind*, on the similar relation
between Dante as author and Dante as pilgrim.

stod as stylle as dased quayle' (1085). Both these bird images suggest
bewilderment of a completely undignified kind.

Religious visions

So far I have been arguing that *Pearl* can reasonably be seen as a
natural development out of *Purity* and *Patience*, or at the very least
as being intelligibly related to those poems. But what we find in
Pearl is certainly not the product solely of the poet's autonomous
development. His achievement was modified by the availability to
him of already existing literary traditions of great complexity. To the
main influences on the Old Testament poems—the Old Testament
itself and commentaries on it, the alliterative tradition, and perhaps
the tradition of sermon writing—*Pearl* adds the traditions of
visionary literature, both religious and secular. To study the history
of these traditions in any detail would be a task for a separate book,
but I must attempt a brief sketch of it here, because the poet undoubtedly made the traditions part of the meaning of his poem.
Purity and *Patience* have no parallels outside the work of the
Gawain-poet, but close parallels to some important aspects of *Pearl*
are to be found not so much in his work as in other vision poems of
the fourteenth century and in the traditions which lie behind them.

Something of these traditions is hinted at in the line quoted just
now from another fourteenth-century poet: 'Io non Enea, io non
Paolo sono'. Though *The Divine Comedy* is not in the form of a
dream or vision in which, as in *Pearl*, the poet's soul is ravished from
his body for a time, the narrator describes a visit to the world after
death, and he mentions as his predecessors on such a journey Aeneas
and St Paul. Our own period has virtually no literature set in the
other world; its place has been taken by visions of the future, just
as our political theories have ceased to point towards the salvation of
souls, and direct themselves instead to the achievement of social
justice at some future period of time. The parallel, though imperfect,
may be helpful: the modern reader of *Pearl* might do well to bear in
mind Zamyatin's *We* or Orwell's *1984*, or still more those many
science fiction stories of the type of Wells's *The Time Machine*, in
which a man from the present pays a visit to the future.[1] But in the

[1] A striking difference between modern visions of the future and older visions of
eternity lies in the almost unrelieved pessimism of the former. Though governments
may continue to see the future as the home of desirable goals, the imaginations of their
subjects are occupied with visions of the future conceived not as paradise but as hell.

past the theatre of literature was very frequently not this world but the next. In primitive societies the role of the poet is indistinguishable from that of the prophet or seer, who 'sees' things unknown to other men: he has visions of heaven, of the underworld, of the past, the future, and the distant.[1] Signs of this visionary role for the poet are still to be seen in the invocations with which the Homeric poems open: the inspired poet begs the Muse to disclose to him, to bring back from oblivion, events distant in time and place. A more remarkable sign is found in the account in *Odyssey* XI of Odysseus's descent to Tartarus, the world of the dead, where he interrogates the spirit of the dead seer Teiresias and learns about his own future. That episode is imitated by Virgil in *Aeneid* VI, and it is to this that Dante is referring in the line quoted. Aeneas goes down to the underworld, where he sees the damned souls undergoing appropriate torments, but he also sees the homes of the blest, where:

> largior hic campos aether et lumine vestit
> purpureo, solemque suum, sua sidera norunt

('an ampler air clothes the plains with brilliant light, and always they see a sun and stars which are theirs alone').[2] This is a recurrent feature of otherworld visions: in *Pearl*, similarly, the heavenly city is lit not by our sun and moon but by the light emanating from the Lamb of God himself:

> Of sunne ne mone had thay no nede;
> The self God watz her lombe-lyght,
> The Lombe her lantyrne, wythouten drede;
> Thurgh hym blysned the borw al bryght. (1045–8)

There is no reason, however, to suppose any direct influence from the *Aeneid* on *Pearl*. We have to deal not with specific influences but with a great and complex stream of tradition of visions of the other world, in which certain features recur again and again, and it is difficult to be sure whether the recurrences depend on literary influences or on psychological archetypes. In the case of *Pearl*, the lines just quoted stem directly from the Apocalypse of St John:

Et civitas non eget sole neque luna, ut luceant in ea: nam claritas Dei illuminavit eam, et lucerna eius est Agnus ...

Et nox ultra non erit, et non egebunt lumine lucernae, neque lumine solis; quoniam Dominus Deus illuminabit illos. (xxi. 23, xxii. 5)

---

[1] See N. K. Chadwick, *Poetry and Prophecy* (Cambridge, 1942).
[2] *Aeneid* VI. 640–1, translated by W. F. J. Knight (Harmondsworth, 1956).

(And the city hath no need of the sun, nor of the moon, to shine in it; for the glory of God hath enlightened it, and the Lamb is the lamp thereof...

And night shall be no more; and they shall not need the light of the lamp, nor the light of the sun, because the Lord God shall enlighten them.)

The existing tradition of otherworld visions was given a powerful new impetus by Christianity, with its otherworldly emphasis. The Biblical Apocalypse is an early example of this. The typical visionary is now not the epic hero completing his experience of life by seeing the other world as well as this, but the saint or holy man for whom the other world is not one of wailing ghosts and unreality, but is more real than this world. St John sees heaven, with God in it in the form both of the Father and of the Lamb. The future of the world is revealed to him, down to the end of all things and the resurrection of the dead, and finally he sees the heavenly Jerusalem, a paradisal scene that in part derives from the garden of Eden as described in Genesis. In imitation of St John's vision there were composed various other apocalypses attributed to the various apostles. One of these, which right down to the fourteenth century was widely read and held to have canonical status, was the Apocalypse of St Paul.[1] Its third-century author (not really St Paul, of course) begins with the passage from II Corinthians xii in which the saint tells of his visit to 'the third heaven' and to 'paradise', where he heard 'secret words which it is not granted to man to utter' (2–4). The author of the Apocalypse does not imitate the saint's reticence, but gives a detailed description of how he was carried up 'in the spirit' into heaven by an angel. What he sees there is an odd and confused mixture of apocalyptic and paradisal fantasies, partly based on the earthly paradise (Eden) of Genesis and the heavenly paradise of the Apocalypse of St John. He sees too the various destinations and fates of the souls of the good and the wicked. Sinners are undergoing appropriate torments, but the general effect is of glittering brilliance: bright light, a flowing river, fruit-trees, a city of gold. This vision is what Dante has in mind in pairing Paul with Aeneas, and there can be little doubt that the *Gawain*-poet also knew and made use of it.

While such early Christian writers as these continued to be read down to the Middle Ages, new visions of the other world were constantly being written. Once Christian doctrine had been syste-

[1] For an English translation, see M. R. James, *The Apocryphal New Testament* (Oxford, 1924), pp. 525–55.

matized into theology, a vision of the other world could provide not simply an exciting and edifying experience, but also apparently authoritative backing for certain doctrinal views. As one example from among many of this use of the vision one may mention the ninth-century *De visione Bernoldi presbyteri* of Hincmar, archbishop of Rheims.[1] Bernoldus, while lying ill, is carried to the other world, where he meets various dead people who explain to him in what way the prayers of the living could assist them. He sees with his own eyes how the prayers have the desired effect, and then returns to the living to tell his story. Hincmar's work was a contribution to a contemporary controversy on this very doctrinal point of the influence upon the souls of the dead of the prayers of the living. As literature, the work is nothing like *Pearl*, but in both a man is carried in spirit to the other world, meets there a dead person whom he has known while alive, and is instructed on points of theological doctrine in such a way that what he sees for himself is as important as what he is told. The connection between vision and doctrinal instruction was already present in the tradition long before it reached the *Gawain*-poet, and the audience of *Pearl* would have been less surprised than we may be to find a vision of the other world framing a discussion of the salvation of the innocent and the equality of heavenly rewards.

The vision of Bernoldus was of a simple and materialistic kind—he saw the dead being eaten by actual worms—but minds more sophisticated and spiritually inclined than Hincmar's also addressed themselves to the question of visions, their content and reliability. Among the Christian Fathers, St Augustine had already surveyed the numerous cases of vision mentioned in Scripture, and had developed distinctions between different varieties of this general kind of experience. Beginning from the doubt St Paul expressed as to whether or not he was 'in the body' when he had his vision of paradise, Augustine distinguishes between three kinds of religious vision: 'bodily vision' in which experience is received directly through the natural senses of the body; 'spiritual vision' in which spiritual forces affect the imagination *as if* they were sensory images; and 'intellectual vision' in which God communicates directly with the human intellect in a way which is speechless and imageless and therefore ineffable.[2] (St Paul's vision, as described by himself, though not as elaborated in the Apocalypse of St Paul, belongs to this last kind, for its crucial

[1] Latin text in *PL*, CXXV, cols. 1115–20.
[2] *De Genesi ad litteram*, *PL*, XXXIV, cols. 458 ff.

content is incommunicable: 'secret words which it is not granted to man to utter'.) It has recently been pointed out that when this classification was repeated in fourteenth-century England by the unknown author of *The Chastising of God's Children*, the Apocalypse of St John was included in the second category, and that when the Dreamer in *Pearl* refers to St John's vision as a 'gostly drem' (790) he is using that phrase as an equivalent to Augustine's 'spiritual vision'.[1] On the other hand, the *Pearl* Dreamer elsewhere seems to be obliquely comparing his experience with St Paul's 'intellectual vision'. St Paul writes that his visionary experience came to him 'whether in the body, I know not, or out of the body, I know not: God knoweth' (II Corinthians xii. 2); and the Dreamer remarks, when he first sees the heavenly Jerusalem:

> Anunder mone so great merwayle
> No fleschly hert ne myght endeure
> As quen I blusched upon that bayle...
> For I dar say wyth conciens sure,
> Hade bodyly burne abiden that bone,
> Thagh alle clerkez hym hade in cure,
> His lyf were loste anunder mone. (1081–92)

The Dreamer is thus claiming to be even more certain than St Paul that he was 'out of the body' during his vision, and indeed we know from the opening of the vision that during it his body was left behind in the garden:

> Fro spot my spyryt ther sprang in space;
> My body on balke ther bod; in sweven
> My goste is gon in Godez grace
> In aventure ther mervaylez meven.[2] (61–4)

---

[1] Edward Wilson, 'The "Gostly Drem" in *Pearl*'.

[2] Punctuation of line 62 suggested by Kean, p. 29. For the separation of spirit and body as preliminary to a literary presentation of a mystical experience, compare Carleton Brown, *Religious Lyrics of the Fifteenth Century* (Oxford, 1939), p. 70:

> my spirit was ravysshed, my boody abood,
> Than sawh I my Makere in his manhood.

This is from a poem about the coronation of the Blessed Virgin. As Wilson points out ('The "Gostly Drem" in *Pearl*'), the word *ravish*, which is used by mystical writers to refer to the detachment of the spirit from the body, also occurs in *Pearl* ('So watz I ravyste wyth glymme pure' [1088]). This is in keeping with the treatment of the vision in *Pearl* as a genuine religious experience.

It may not be possible to fit the dream in *Pearl* exactly into one of Augustine's categories (there were in any case many different ways of classifying dreams and visions current in the poet's time), but it is clear that it is intended to represent a genuine spiritual experience, giving access to religious truth. After it is over, the narrator acknowledges that he has enjoyed a 'veray avysyoun' (1184).

It need not surprise us that this spiritual experience is presented in the form of a dream occurring during natural slumber. Several influential devotional writers of the Middle Ages comment on 'dreams' occurring in Scripture in such a way as to make it clear that sleeping and dreaming are used as images referring to mystical states. Richard of St-Victor, for example, discussing the dream of Nebuchadnezzar interpreted by Daniel (and referred to, incidentally, in *Purity* [1622 ff.]), writes as follows:

We fall asleep before seeing a dream. Since by a dream of the body the bodily senses are quieted, we rightly understand by a dream of the mind a separation by which the memory of all outward things is completely cut off. Thus to see a dream is to pass over in the mind into the secret place of divine contemplation. Hence he sleeps and sees a dream who through ecstasy of the mind rises into the contemplation of divine things.[1]

This describes precisely what happens in *Pearl:* the Dreamer's experience is a 'gostly drem', or what Richard calls *somnium mentis*, not a *somnium corporis* or bodily dream, and it leads the Dreamer into a contemplation of divine mysteries. What Richard and other medieval mystics mean by 'ecstasy' (*excessus*) is explained by a modern scholar:

The slumbering of the external senses is accompanied, in the mystic slumber, by an 'abduction' of the internal sense. By that must be understood that without falling asleep, but on the contrary remaining watchful, the internal sense is carried away by God, who illumines it. This state therefore has all the appearance of a sleep, but it is quite the opposite of a torpor.[2]

The paradoxical watchfulness in slumber of the contemplative experience is also noted by St Bernard, in commenting on the 'sleep' of the Bride of Christ in the Song of Songs, from which she is not

[1] *De eruditione hominis interioris*, lib. II, cap. ii, *PL*, CXCVI, cols. 1299–1300. Cf. cols. 1261 and 1304.
[2] E. Gilson, *The Mystical Theology of St Bernard*, trans. A. H. C. Downes (London, 1940), p. 105, n. 149.

to be wakened: 'I adjure you, O ye daughters of Jerusalem...that you stir not up, nor make the beloved to awake, till she please' (ii. 7). He distinguishes this desirable sleep from bodily sleep, the sleep of death, and the sleep of sin, and claims that: 'This may, on the contrary, be called a sleep of life, and even a wakefulness, which illuminates the inward sense, banishing death and contributing to eternal life.'[1] Another text from the Song of Songs, 'Ego dormio et cor meum vigilat' (v. 2) ('I sleep, and my heart watcheth'), was commonly taken to exemplify the same paradox of contemplation. This can be found, for example, in an English contemporary of the *Gawain*-poet, Walter Hilton, who writes:

And this is also the wakeful sleep of the spouse, of the which Holy Writ saith thus: *Ego dormio, et cor meum vigilat*. I sleep and my heart waketh... The more I sleep from outward things, the more wakeful am I in knowing of Jhesu and of inward things. I may not wake to Jhesu but if I sleep to the world. And therefore, the grace of the Holy Ghost shutting the fleshly eyes, doth the soul sleep from worldly vanity, and opening the ghostly eyes waketh into the sight of God's majesty hid under cloud of His precious manhood.[2]

An anthology of quotations from medieval mystics, such as I have just been giving, goes a long way towards helping us to understand the peculiar nature of the sleep and dream that are represented in *Pearl*. Dreaming, in this poem, does not indicate an abdication of responsibility on the poet's part, an escape into a world less demanding and less serious than that of everyday waking life. This *is* what dreaming tends to indicate in secular dream-poems such as Chaucer's, where dreaming itself is mentioned with depreciatory tentativeness, and nothing more is claimed for the poetic dream than that it is 'wonderful'.[3] Even in *Piers Plowman*, which in most respects is more similar to *Pearl* than it is to dream-poems of the Chaucerian kind, the conclusion to a discussion of the significance of dreams is not that they lead us to religious truth, but something much more ambiguous: 'Al this maketh me on meteles to studie.'[4] In *Piers Plowman*, too, as in *The Book of the Duchess* or *The House of Fame*,

---

[1] *Sermones in Cantica Canticorum*, LII. 3; *PL*, CLXXXIII, col. 1031.
[2] *The Scale of Perfection*, ed. Evelyn Underhill (London, 1923), pp. 424–5. The relevance of this passage to *Piers Plowman* and, by implication, to *Pearl* is noted by Elizabeth Salter, *Piers Plowman—An Introduction* (Oxford, 1962), p. 61.
[3] See *The Book of the Duchess*, line 277, and *The House of Fame*, line 62.
[4] Ed. W. W. Skeat (1886), C. x. 317.

what is seen in the dream is often seen with something like the indistinctness of actual bodily dreams, and things and settings have a tendency to dissolve or disappear without warning. In *Pearl*, on the contrary, the dream-landscape is seen with extraordinary sharpness, and it is a harder and more permanent landscape than that of the garden in which the narrator falls asleep. There it is harvest-time, 'Quen corne is corven wyth crokez kene' (40), the season when ripeness and perfection fade or are cut down; in the dream-world there is a constant brilliance, and even the leaves on the trees and the normally shifting banks of rivers have about them suggestions of the durability of precious metals:

> As bornyst sylver the lef on slydez (77)
>
> rych reverez—
> As fyldor fyn her bonkes brent. (105–6)

As the Maiden explains to the Dreamer, what he lost in the world to which the garden belongs was a fading rose; what he has found in the unchangeable world of the dream is a lasting pearl:

> For that thou lestez watz bot a rose
> That flowred and fayled as kynde hyt gef.
> Now thurgh kynde of the kyste that hyt con close
> To a perle of prys hit is put in pref. (269–72)

In this wakeful sleep, in which the internal senses operate with such fineness that he can see every detail of the heavenly city despite its distance from him, the Dreamer achieves too something of the mystic's 'contemplation of divine things'. The heavenly city of Jerusalem is itself the peace of God, which can be fully possessed only after death; and in telling the Dreamer this, the Maiden is repeating the common doctrine of medieval devotional writers. Her words are that there are two Jerusalems, one the earthly 'ceté of God' (952) in which Christ was crucified, the other the heavenly 'syght of pes', and:

> In that other is noght bot pes to glene
> That ay schal laste wythouten reles.
> That is the borw that we to pres
> Fro that oure flesch be layd to rote. (955–8)

Walter Hilton similarly uses the journey to Jerusalem as an image of contemplative activity: 'Ghostly to our purpose, Jerusalem is as mickle for to say as sight of peace, and betokeneth contemplation in perfect love of God. For contemplation is not else but a sight of Jhesu, which is very peace.'[1] The Dreamer has a 'sight of God's majesty', not 'hid under cloud of His precious manhood', but in the form of the wounded Lamb, who arouses his strong compassion:

> Alas, thoght I, who did that spyt?
> Ani breste for bale aght haf forbrent
> Er he therto hade had delyt. (1138-40)

This sight, however, is only momentary, and does not involve any deeper penetration into the divine mysteries: there can be no question of the Dreamer achieving the highest kind of mystical experience. In one sense the reason for this is that the *Gawain*-poet is not truly a mystic, nor does he suppose that he is; and, in any case, even if he were, the highest kind of mystical experience is not capable of being conveyed in literary form. But this incapacity is in fact made a strength of the poem, for, within the poem, it is the Dreamer's fault, not the poet's, that his contemplative experience is not more complete. The Dreamer himself brings his 'dream of the spirit' to an end by his attempt to leap across the river to join the Maiden, and thus, as he ruefully acknowledges afterwards, he loses the chance of coming into the very presence of God and achieving a communion with him that goes even deeper than compassion:

> To that Pryncez paye hade I ay bente,
> And yerned no more then watz me gyven,
> And halden me ther in trwe entent,
> As the perle me prayed that watz so thryven,
> As helde, drawen to Goddez present,
> To mo of his mysterys I hade ben dryven.[2] (1189-94)

True contemplation can be achieved only by a 'sleep' which involves not only the bodily senses, but all memories and feelings regarding this world. We have seen this stated by Richard of St-Victor, in his reference to 'a separation [*alienatio*] by which the memory of all outward things is completely cut off.' It is repeated by Hilton as a continuation of the image of the journey to Jerusalem: 'Right as a true pilgrim going to Jerusalem leaveth behind him house and land, wife and child, and maketh himself poor and bare from all that he hath, that he might go lightly without letting: right so if thou wilt

---

[1] *The Scale of Perfection*, p. 305.
[2] For further comment on these lost 'mysterys', see below, pp. 169-70.

be a ghostly pilgrim, thou shalt make thyself naked from all that thou hast.'[1] The same point is made by another English contemporary of the *Gawain*-poet, perhaps indeed the most distinguished devotional writer of his time, the anonymous author of *The Cloud of Unknowing*. In *The Book of Privy Counselling* he makes the usual comparison of contemplative activity to sleep:

And wel is this werk licnyd to a slepe. For as in the slepe the use of the bodely wittys is cesid, that the body may take his ful rest in fedyng and in strengthing of the bodyly kynde; right so in this goostly sleep the wantoun questyons of the wilde goostly wittys, ymaginatyve resons, ben fast bounden and utterly voidid, so that the sely soule may softly sleep and rest in the lovely beholdyng of God as He is, in ful fedyng and strengthing of the goostly kynde.[2]

In all these respects the narrator of *Pearl* is unfit to achieve contemplation. He has not undergone the necessary *alienatio* from earthly memories: on the contrary, throughout the poem he is preoccupied with his recollection of the Pearl Maiden as she was, and this hinders him from seeing even her as she is, still more from seeing God as he is. He has not left behind 'wife and child': the Maiden indeed seems partly to fulfil the role of both, and she is still more dear to him than God is, so that he would rather disobey God's prohibition against crossing the river than endure separation from her, even though it is clear that she is herself enjoying the perfect bliss of communion with the Lamb. And he has certainly not set aside 'the wantoun questyons of the wilde goostly wittys', for it is these that cause him to be so often disputing with the Maiden about God's ordering of heaven and earth, even though she has perfect knowledge of these things.

And yet, as I have said, this unfitness of the Dreamer for the role of mystic, which is, as it were, thrust upon him, makes him all the fitter to be the central figure of the poem. Were it not for his continuing and touchingly human love for the Maiden, the poem would not move us as it does; were it not for his continuing intervention with question and argument, it would not even engage our attention as a doctrinal work. Through the Dreamer, because he is as imperfect as we are, we are drawn into the poem, engaged in its issues, and brought

---

[1] *The Scale of Perfection*, p. 307.
[2] *The Cloud of Unknowing and the Book of Privy Counselling*, ed. Phyllis Hodgson, EETS OS 218, 2nd edn. (London, 1958), p. 152.

to a fuller understanding, both intellectual and emotional, of the difference between the human order and the divine order. The same paradox is to be found in *Piers Plowman*. There, too, the Dreamer is much given to protest and disputation, and is frequently warned that he will make no progress in understanding until he learns patience; but if he were patient from the beginning there could be no poem of *Piers Plowman*, but only an uninterrupted sermon. Langland's Dreamer is called Wille, which was no doubt Langland's own name; but he also seems to stand for the human will in general. It is the persistence of a similarly obstinate will in *Pearl*, despite Christ's teaching—

> Thagh kynde of Kryst me comfort kenned,
> My wreched wylle in wo ay wraghte (55–6)

—that gives the poem its liveliness and power to move. This crucial characterization of the Dreamer as a being far more complex than the neutral onlooker who is the 'I' of, say, the Apocalypse of St John is found in the work of other fourteenth-century poets than Langland, as a recent study of the latter has pointed out:

If we now examine the characterization of this Dreamer, the 'I' of *Piers Plowman*, we shall find a 'self-portrait' which is...not unlike those in Langland's contemporaries. With whatever differences of emphasis, the common tradition is one of humorous self-depreciation, ranging from mild self-mockery to rueful admission of stupidity...What is common to Chaucer, Gower and Langland is the presentation of an 'I' who exhibits both eagerness to learn and a residual stubbornness, so that in the long run the central truth of the poem must be asserted at the expense of the Dreamer.[1]

In this respect, then, *Pearl* belongs to a tradition that is secular as well as religious; and at this point it will be best for us to turn to the secular branch of the visionary tradition, to see what light that throws on *Pearl*.

Dream-poems

So complex is the interweaving of secular and religious motifs in medieval literature and thought, that he would be a bold man who would assert that any of the prevalent literary genres had its origin solely on one side or the other of the border between them. But it seems reasonably likely that secular dream-poetry of the kind Chaucer wrote in *The Book of the Duchess* or the Prologue to *The Legend of*

[1] John Lawlor, *Piers Plowman: An Essay in Criticism* (London, 1962), pp. 285–6.

Good Women originated as a deliberate secularization of the tradition of religious visions. That certainly seems to be the case, at any rate, with the *Roman de la Rose,* a seminal work which influenced, directly or indirectly, all subsequent secular dream-poems. One important motif to which it helped to give wide currency was that of entering in a dream into a paradisal garden of love, inhabited by the God of Love himself and by a company of courtly young people (who in the *Roman* are mostly personifications). Among the beauties of the garden is a rose which is the symbol of the lady beloved by the Dreamer. There seems good reason to suppose that *Pearl* is influenced by this tradition, and indeed that it makes explicit use of the tradition of secular dream-poetry, and was intended to be understood in the light of it. However, the dream-landscape of *Pearl* has recently been studied by Miss P. M. Kean, and she throws doubt on this view of the poem. She shows, with detailed illustration, how much the dream-landscape owes to traditional descriptions of the Earthly Paradise, found in such works as the *Alexander* romances, *Mandeville's Travels,* the *Liber Scalae,* and St Bonaventura's *Arbor Vitae.* And she concludes that there is very little connection between *Pearl* and the tradition established by the *Roman de la Rose:* 'All the details which go to make up the description of the blissful country in *Pearl* are, thus, associated with descriptions of the surroundings of the Earthly Paradise, rather than with the Garden of Love.'[1] Miss Kean's investigations have thrown valuable light on *Pearl,* but, in my view, her 'rather than' makes a distinction between the two traditions much more rigid than was made in the Middle Ages. To begin with, there can be no doubt that the Garden of Love in the *Roman de la Rose* is a version (even if only a parodic version) of the Earthly Paradise. The Dreamer tells us that:

> whan I was inne, iwys,
> Myn herte was ful glad of this,
> For wel wende I ful sikerly
> Have ben in paradys erthly.
> So fair it was that, trusteth wel,
> It semede a place espirituel.
> For certys, as at my devys,
> Ther is no place in paradys
> So good inne for to dwelle or be
> As in that gardyn, thoughte me. (*Romaunt of the Rose,* 645–54)

[1] Kean, p. 113.

He tells us that the birds in the garden:

> songe her song as faire and wel
> As angels don espirituel, (671–2)

and he subsequently compares both the company of people who dance in the garden and the God of Love himself to angels (742, 916–17). So Guillaume de Lorris saw the dream-landscape in the first part of the *Roman*. It is true that his continuator, Jean de Meun, later made it clear that this Garden of Love was only a parody of the true paradise, and that the fountain at its centre was not truly the river of life, but one that made the living drunk and killed them. It is also true that, in the light of this continuation, one might even find hints in the earlier part that all is not so innocent as it seems in the Garden of Love, for its identification as paradise is based on a false assumption about merely human love:

> A! Lord, they lyved lustyly!
> A gret fool were he, sikirly,
> That nolde, his thankes, such lyf lede!
> For this dar I seyn, oute of drede,
> That whoso myghte so wel fare,
> For better lyf durst hym not care;
> For ther nys so good paradys
> As to have a love at his devys. (1319–26)

Yet in *Purity*, as we have seen, just this assumption is attributed to God himself, when he asserts that 'Wel nyghe pure paradys moght preve no better' (704) than true love between a man and a woman.[1] In any case, it would be quite wrong to assume that between the (ultimately) false paradise of the *Roman* and the true paradise of religious writings there existed on the imaginative level a dichotomy so complete as to make any mutual influence impossible. On the contrary, medieval literature is full of minglings of the secular and the religious, and of cases where what began or could be justified as mere parody carries with it much of the genuine feeling of what is parodied. I believe this to be the case with *Pearl*.

Miss Kean argues that in medieval art and literature there is a clear distinction between the motif of the enclosed garden (such as is described in the *Roman de la Rose*) and that of the open landscape in which the Dreamer of *Pearl* finds himself in his dream.[2] In fact,

---

[1] See above, pp. 72–3. [2] Kean, p. 94.

however, the Pearl Maiden herself refers to her new setting as 'this gardyn gracios gaye' (260), so it would appear that she does not observe this distinction. It is only a few lines after this that the Maiden uses the image of the rose to refer to her former, earthly self, which she contrasts with the pearl she has now become:

> For that thou lestez watz bot a rose
> That flowred and fayled as kynde hyt gef.
> Now thurgh kynde of the kyste that hyt con close
> To a perle of prys hit is put in pref. (269–72)

There can be no doubt, surely, that at this point the poet has in mind the *Roman de la Rose* and its tradition of secular love allegory in dream form. Nor does he forget it later, when the Dreamer addresses the Maiden as 'so ryche a reken rose' (906). Of course the poet is not merely reproducing the secular tradition, but is using it as the basis for a transformation—from rose to pearl, from God of Love to Lamb of God. The 'gardyn gracios gaye' of *Pearl* contains not the gay company of courtly personifications found in the *Roman* but only the Maiden, separated from her fellows and from the Lamb, who are in the heavenly city. But the dream-landscape is also haunted by ghosts of those personifications, faint reminders of the rose garden, such as Desire, Confusion, and Fear:

> To calle hyr lyste con me enchace,
> Bot baysment gef myn hert a brunt. (173–4)

> More then me lyste my drede aros. (181)

It was precisely to express such states of inner conflict that the personifications were used in medieval allegories of love. More substantially, there can be no doubt that secular love of the kind treated in such allegories is an important element in the powerful current of feeling that flows between the Dreamer and the Maiden. At the very beginning, the narrator uses the characteristic phrase *luf-daungere* (frustration in love) to define his attitude towards the lost pearl: 'I dewyne, fordolked of luf-daungere' (11). Daunger in the *Roman de la Rose* is one of the Dreamer's greatest enemies, the beloved lady's 'standoffishness' as C. S. Lewis put it.[1] In *Pearl* this term, with its potent associations, is transferred firstly to the death of the lost 'pearl', which causes the narrator the feelings of frustration and

[1] *The Allegory of Love* (Oxford, 1936), p. 124.

misery usually aroused by the lady's *daunger*, and then, even more appropriately, to the separation and change of attitude in her brought about by the transfiguration she, but not he, has undergone:

His frustration is akin to that of the courtly lover in that, though he may look again on his love, he may not join her as he wishes by crossing the stream which divides them:

> Now haf I fonte that I forlete,
> Schal I efte forgo hit er ever I fyne?
> Why schal I hit bothe mysse and mete?
> My precios perle dotz me gret pyne. (327-30)

And, like the courtly lover who fails to recognize the power which separates him from his love, he accuses her of heartless indifference to his suffering.[1]

Miss Kean admits that the phrase *luf-daungere* 'would carry some overtones from' works such as the *Roman de la Rose,* but finds its parallel rather in a Scriptural source, the Song of Songs: 'vulneraverunt me...quia amore langueo' (v. 7-8) ('They...wounded me... that I languish with love ').[2] What we must do, surely, is to keep both parallels in mind, because *Pearl* keeps up connections both with the secular allegories of love and with the religious texts that lie behind them. In this particular case, the religious text was itself originally a secular love-poem, which was then allegorized and understood in the Middle Ages as a religious love-poem. The tradition—to make the point once more—is so complex as to be beyond disentangling; and we ought to recognize that its rich confusion may have been a strength rather than a weakness to a medieval poet. Another example may be found in the words with which the Maiden says that the Lamb summoned her to him:

> Cum hyder to me, my lemman swete,
> For mote ne spot is non in the. (763-4)

This is based on the words addressed by Christ to his Bride in the Song of Songs according to its traditional exegesis:

> Tota pulchra es, amica mea, et macula non est in te.
> Veni de Libano, sponsa mea, veni de Libano, veni. (iv. 7-8)

> (Thou art all fair, O my love, and there is not a spot in thee.
> Come from Libanus, my spouse, come from Libanus, come.)

[1] W. R. J. Barron, 'Luf-Daungere', in *Medieval Miscellany Presented to Eugène Vinaver* (Manchester, 1965), 1-18; pp. 13-14.
[2] Kean, pp. 16-17.

But the words used by the medieval poet also carry associations of the most secular kind, suggesting the love-song of the time that Chaucer's Pardoner was in the habit of singing: 'Com hider, love, to me'.[1] There is nothing blasphemous about this suggestion: popular love-songs were often put to religious purposes, and inevitably carried with them some of their original feelings.

The same kind of ambiguity may even be felt about the nature of the vision itself. We have seen that *Pearl* has links with a tradition in which sleep and dreaming are metaphors relating to devotional experience of a genuinely religious kind. But, in its links with the allegory of love tradition, it is also connected with an idea of the dream as a fiction, constructed by the sleeping mind from its own contents, and fully explicable in terms of a naturalistic psychology. Chaucer's dream-poems regularly make use of such a conception of the dream. In the Prologue to *The Legend of Good Women* the narrator before going to sleep has been looking at daisies and admiring them; therefore in his dream he sees a daisy transfigured into a beautiful lady. Love too was in his mind, and he had heard the birds singing of it; therefore in his dream he meets the God of Love, and is ordered to compile stories of his saints. In *The Book of the Duchess* he had also been thinking of his own frustrated love, and had read the story of Ceyx and Alcyone to send himself to sleep; therefore he dreams of a knight who has lost his wife, as Alcyone lost her husband, by death, and who (like the Dreamer of *Pearl*) suffers thereby a frustration paralleling on a higher level the Dreamer's own. Similar psychological trails are laid to account for the dreams in *The Parlement of Foules* and *The House of Fame*. *Pearl* fits readily into this pattern. The narrator had been pondering on the loss of his pearl; what could be more natural than a wish-fulfilling dream in which he found her alive again, and yet the sense of loss and alienation of his waking life was also carried into the dream? This happens at harvest-time; John of Salisbury notes that dreams are particularly frequent in autumn.[2] In its ending, too, the dream in *Pearl* follows the same pattern as the Chaucerian dream-poems, in that the Dreamer is woken up by some event apparently in the dream itself. In *The Book of the Duchess* it is the striking of a bell in his dream that rouses him; in *The Parlement of Foules* the clamour of dream-birds; in *Pearl* his

---

[1] *Canterbury Tales* I [A], 672. The suggestion was made by Gollancz, ed. *Pearl*, 2nd edn. (London, 1921), p. 154.

[2] See *Policraticus*, ed. C. C. J. Webb (Oxford, 1909), I, 90.

own dreamed-of effort to cross the dream-river. Nor can it be supposed that the many allusions in *Pearl* to the authentic and authoritative visionary experiences in Scripture automatically exclude it from this category, for similar references may be found in Chaucer. In *The House of Fame*, for example, the narrator alludes to just that paradisal experience of St Paul touched on in *Pearl:*

> Thoo gan I wexen in a were,
> And seyde, 'Y wot wel y am here;
> But wher in body or in gost
> I not, ywys; but God, thou wost!' (979–82)

And this Chaucerian narrator goes on, in much the same way as the narrator of *Pearl*, to mention other authorities who have described the heavenly world; but his authorities are not Scriptural (they are Martianus Capella and Alanus de Insulis), and his line of argument is not 'Their visions authenticate mine' but 'My vision authenticates theirs':

> And than thoughte y on Marcian,
> And eke on Anteclaudian,
> That sooth was her descripsion
> Of alle the hevenes region,
> As fer as that y sey the preve;
> Therefore y kan hem now beleve. (985–90)

My purpose is not to argue that there is no difference between *Pearl* and such secular dream-poems, but rather that *Pearl* was able to draw, and did draw, on a wide range of traditions, because those traditions were themselves closely intertwined. It is a poem that makes a new and individual use of materials and conventions with which there is reason to suppose that its audience would have been familiar.

Lastly, in this consideration of *Pearl*'s place in the tradition that derives from the *Roman de la Rose*, we must return to the question of the characterization of the Dreamer. 'Characterization' here is not so much something uniquely given, as an elaboration of function, and it is for this reason that there is a recognizable similarity between the Dreamers of poems so different as *Piers Plowman, The House of Fame*, and *Pearl*. What all such Dreamers have in common is that, by dreaming, they are thrust involuntarily into an unfamiliar world which is in no way under their control. (This feature no doubt derives from the real experience of dreaming.) In *The Book of the Duchess* for example, the dream-Chaucer finds himself inexplicably impelled to follow a little dog into an extraordinarily regular forest, where he finds a man dressed in black, who is evidently a complete stranger to him. In *The House of Fame*, when he is standing in bewilderment in an almost surrealistically conceived desert, he is suddenly seized by an enormous golden eagle, who carries him off into the sky, and insists of informing him about medieval physics. There could be no more dramatic indication of the Dreamer's helplessness, and he expresses a baffled reluctance which seems to parody Dante's 'Io non Enea, io non Paolo sono':

> 'O God!' thoughte I, 'that madest kynde,
> Shal I noon other weyes dye?
> Wher Joves wol me stellyfye,
> Or what thing may this sygnifye?
> I neyther am Ennok, ne Elye,
> Ne Romulus, ne Ganymede,
> That was ybore up, as men rede,
> To hevene with daun Jupiter,
> And mad the goddys botiller.' (584–92)

In *The Parlement of Foules*, again, as the Dreamer stands indecisively before the gates of a walled park, his heavenly guide, Scipio Africanus, seizes him bodily and 'shof in at the gates wide' (154). The world in which the Chaucerian Dreamer thus finds himself at the mercy of events tends to be paradisal, or pseudo-paradisal, or at least in some way 'higher' than the everyday world; and the Dreamer himself is thrown into relief by it as being 'lower'—ill at ease, clumsy, 'all too human'. It is a world, normally, in which something is to be learned of love—love in its highest and most spiritual secular sense—yet the Dreamer seems scarcely capable of taking it in. In *The House of Fame*, though he is granted a sight of Fame and her suppliants, he is no wiser, and tells someone who asks why he is there that 'these be no suche tydynges/As I mene of' (1894–5). In *The Book of the Duchess*, he persistently questions the man in black about the loss of his lady, but as persistently fails to grasp what we already know, that he has lost her through death. In this poem, particularly, the disparity between the Dreamer and the world of his dream is seen in social terms. The man in black is a great nobleman, and both his love and his grief have an aristocratic perfection; the Dreamer, a somewhat bourgeois figure, stands so far outside this perfection that, though awed by it, he fails even to recognize his inability to understand it.

Professor Lawlor is, I believe, right in asserting that in this poem 'all proceeds from the conception of the Dreamer as the bookish servant of love, his unshaken doctrinaire position, and its final inadequacy to experience where the experience is of perfection itself'.[1] Here indeed is a close parallel to *Pearl*; nor need we be surprised, since both are courtly poems about the impact of death upon love, and combine elegy with instruction. The Dreamer of *Pearl* is also, in his way, a doctrinaire, whose experience is inadequate not in respect to human love but to divine love. He is always ready to quote authority against his informant—

> Me thynk thy tale unresounable.
> Goddez ryght is redy and evermore rert,
> Other Holy Wryt is bot a fable.
> In Sauter is sayd a verce overte,
> That spekez a poynt determynable. (590–4)

—and to impose his own preconceptions on her, and this very readiness makes him less open to the astonishing experience imposed on him by his vision. It is as if he is bound to cling to his earthly notions as a protection against the overpowering brilliance of the heavenly world; and his obstinate earthliness is felt often as a social deficiency, an inability to grasp the hierarchy and manners of the heavenly court, in which all are kings and queens.

So far I have been speaking of the characterization of the Dreamer as if he were as complete and fixed a character as those he meets in his dream—the Maiden in *Pearl* or the eagle in *The House of Fame*. This is, I believe, less misleading than to think of him as being a direct expression of the poet, and thus of the poem as being literal autobiography. There is no reason whatever to suppose that Chaucer or the *Gawain*-poet really had, even in dreams, the visionary experiences described in their poems. On the other hand, the situation is not quite so simple as I have been implying. For there can be no doubt that Chaucer's dreamers are in some sense based on himself: the Dreamer of *The House of Fame* is called Geoffrey and works as a customs official; the Dreamer of the Prologue to *The Legend of Good Women*, simpleton though he is, has written Chaucer's poems; and if the Dreamer of *The Book of the Duchess* seems socially inferior to the man in black, this only reflects the actual social inferiority of

[1] John Lawlor, 'The Pattern of Consolation in *The Book of the Duchess*', *Spec*, XXXI (1956), 626–48; p. 643.

Chaucer the winemerchant's son to his grand patron, the Duke of
Lancaster. The same is generally true of fourteenth-century dream-
poems. A recent study of the authorship of *Piers Plowman* argues that
it was 'an established practice, a convention, for fourteenth-century
authors of dream-vision poems to sign their work by naming the
dreamer-narrator after themselves', and continues:

A concomitant of the signing of poetry in this period was the involvement
of the author in the action of his poem. The Lover in the *Roman de la Rose*
was little more than a personified abstraction; fourteenth-century imita-
tions of that model often have a more particularized narrator who is,
furthermore, made in the image of the poet. This is particularly notable
in the case of Machaut who may have established the practice... The poets
who claimed authorship by this means made no difficulty over assigning to
the personages named after themselves experiences necessarily fictitious
because impossible in the actual world. They created the ambiguous
situation where encouragement to identify poet and narrator is given by
their possession of the same name and checked by the character of what
is narrated; that they did this suggests that the ambiguity had a purpose.[1]

Professor Kane declines to speculate about this purpose. I would
suggest that one part of it at least was to engage the audience more
fully in the drama of the poem without forcing them to adopt throughout a single point of view. The role of the fourteenth-century
Dreamer is not fixed but fluctuating; he is a 'character' not constantly
but only intermittently. In *The Book of the Duchess*, to take a simple
example, when the Dreamer as narrator repeats to us the song he
overheard the man in black singing, a song in which he disclosed
that his lady was dead, we are not faced in reality with any problem as
to why the Dreamer later appears not to know this simple fact. There
is no need to try to decide whether he is so stupid as to have forgotten
it, or so tactful as to pretend not to have overheard it, because at the
moment of the song itself we are not conscious of him as a character,
an overhearer, but simply as a neutral narrator. It is only at other
points in the poem, when Chaucer the poet supplies Chaucer the
dreamer with distinctive reactions and modes of speech, that we are
conscious of a difference between the two. We are not to expect any
overall consistency which will enable us to say either that the poet is
completely identified with the Dreamer or that he is completely detached from him; and as a result we ourselves can be more fully

[1] George Kane, *Piers Plowman: the Evidence for Authorship* (London, 1965), pp. 53,
54–5, 57.

engaged in the encounter between the Dreamer and the man in black, taking now the former's point of view and now the latter's. It is obvious that there is a similar kind of ambiguity in *Pearl*: we have already seen that the 'I' of the poem presents a mixture of two different kinds of experience—that of one who is freshly undergoing the astonishing vision and that of one who has already undergone it and learned from it. It is part of this ambiguity that the poem should both begin and end in the present tense, the initial, unconsoled sense of loss being felt as immediately as the final reconciliation. The poem indeed forms a kind of circle, in which we could pass from the end to the beginning without a break, and past and present coexist in simultaneity. Yet the simultaneity is not that of arrested motion, as on Keats's Grecian urn:

> Fair youth beneath the trees, thou canst not leave
> Thy song, nor ever can those trees be bare;
> Bold lover, never, never canst thou kiss,
> Though winning near the goal—yet, do not grieve;
> She cannot fade, though thou hast not thy bliss,
> For ever wilt thou love, and she be fair!

It is rather the simultaneity with which we see the spokes of a turning wheel; for the Dreamer and his experience are treated not statically but dynamically, and in order to grasp the meaning of the poem we must follow it through in detail, experiencing it as a temporal, sequential process, out of which meaning grows little by little. That must be a task for later sections of this chapter.

The problem of interpretation

We can now return to the question, 'What is *Pearl* about?' The scholars who have discussed it supply us with a wide variety of answers. When the poem first began to be studied, in the late nineteenth century, it was generally assumed that it was an autobiographical elegy. The pearl itself was taken to stand for a dead girl, who is seen after her death in her true form as a pure maiden. She had died in infancy, which is why the Dreamer exclaims to her, 'Thou lyfed not two yer in oure thede' (483), and she was the poet's own daughter, which is why the Dreamer says of her 'Ho watz me nerre then aunte or nece' (233). Such an interpretation of course draws no distinction between the poet and the 'I' of the poem; and indeed in some cases scholars felt justified in using the poem as an aid to reconstructing a hypothetical biography of the poet.[1] Few would now hold to the strict form of the autobiographical theory, though an extraordinary variant of it has more recently been advanced, according to which the dead girl was not a child but an adult who came from a foreign country, and had only recently been baptized, and who was not the poet's daughter but his beloved.[2] Literary criticism in general has in this century moved out of the naïve autobiographical phase which attempted to use even Shakespeare's plays as documents from which to reconstruct his life. In the case of a medieval poet whose very name is unknown to us, we can have no means of telling whether or not his works do reflect his life in any direct way; and, as we have just seen, even a poet who writes as 'I' may assign fictitious experiences to himself in a dream-poem. Moreover, even if we could be sure that the *Gawain*-poet did at one stage of his life mourn the loss of a daughter or mistress, this would not necessarily advance our appreciation of his work, for the crucial question would still remain of how, and how effectively, he turned this experience into literature.

A more promising line of approach might seem to be one which achieved some popularity in reaction against the autobiographical interpretation, and which is still very influential today. This is the view that the poem is an allegory, in which the pearl and Pearl Maiden do not represent a person who has died,[3] but a quality or abstraction which the narrator has in some other sense lost. Interpretations of this kind have been offered in great variety. I make no attempt to give a comprehensive survey, but mention a few by way of illustration. W. H. Schofield has argued that the pearl is a symbol of 'Clean Maidenhood', though he admits that it is a 'Protean' symbol. R. M. Garrett sees it as a symbol of the Eucharist. Sister Mary Madeleva believes that the pearl is 'spiritual sweetness' and that the 'dream-child...is the personification of [the poet's] own soul in the state of such potential perfection and happiness as is congruous to it

[1] See, for example, Sir Israel Gollancz in his edition of *Pearl* (London, 1891) and in the *Cambridge History of English Literature* (Cambridge, 1907), I, 320–34; the autobiographical view was also held by G. G. Coulton, 'In Defence of *Pearl*', *MLR*, II (1906–7), 39–43.

[2] Mother Angela Carson, 'Aspects of Elegy in the Middle English *Pearl*', *Studies in Philology*, LXII (1965), 17–27.

[3] Or at least not a person related to the narrator; J. B. Fletcher held that the pearl symbolized the Blessed Virgin ('The Allegory of the Pearl', *JEGP*, XX (1921), 1–21).

at this time of his life'. More recently, Sister Mary Vincent Hillmann has offered a view somewhat similar to this, though differing in detail. For her, the narrator of the poem is not metaphorically but literally a jeweller who has lost an actual pearl, while the Pearl Maiden is not his lost pearl but his own soul in the mystical union with God it might achieve (though at times too she is the 'symbol of any justi-fied soul'). Another variant of this equation of the pearl with the soul is suggested by M. P. Hamilton, who sees the pearl as standing both for the regenerate soul and for eternal life and beatitude. D. W. Robertson has found in the poem a four-level allegory, according to which the pearl means literally the actual gem, allegorically innocent souls, tropologically the soul that attains innocence, and anagogically the life of innocence in the Celestial City. M. R. Stern, adopting a similar approach, has gone one better, and argues that 'the Pearl Poet quite consciously intended to make his poem one huge typological metaphor of orthodox Christian behavior'; though admittedly he finds that as a consequence of this 'the 101st stanza of resolution and reconciliation is gratuitous and facile'.[1]

To meet each of these allegorical interpretations on its own ground would be an impossibly lengthy task, and I do not propose to attempt it. On the other hand, to discuss only the principles underlying the allegorical interpretation of the poem would inevitably involve entering a complex theoretical controversy about exegesis in general; for some at least of those who would allegorize *Pearl* would evidently do so because they believe virtually all of medieval literature to be allegorical.[2] We can however make certain points without entering

---

[1] See W. H. Schofield, 'The Nature and Fabric of *The Pearl*', *PMLA*, XIX (1904), 154–215 (with a rethinking of the problem in 'Symbolism, Allegory, and Autobiography in *The Pearl*', *PMLA*, XXIV [1909], 585–675); R. M. Garrett, *The Pearl: An Interpretation* (Seattle, 1918); M. Madeleva, *Pearl: A Study in Spiritual Dryness* (New York, 1925), esp. p. 132; M. V. Hillmann, ed. *The Pearl* (Notre Dame, 1967), esp. pp. xix–xxi and 89; M. P. Hamilton, 'The Meaning of the Middle English Pearl'; D. W. Robertson, 'The Pearl as a Symbol', *Modern Language Notes*, LXV (1950), 155–61; M. R. Stern, 'An Approach to *The Pearl*', *JEGP*, LIV (1955), 684–92, esp. pp. 689 and 691 n. 29. There is a useful analysis of the earlier work on the poem by R.Wellek, 'The *Pearl*: An Interpretation of the Middle English Poem', *Studies in English* (Charles University, Prague), IV (1933), 5–33 (reprinted with revisions in *Sir Gawain and Pearl: Critical Essays*, ed. R. J. Blanch [Bloomington, 1966], pp. 3–36).

[2] See, for example, D. W. Robertson, 'Historical Criticism', *English Institute Essays* 1950 (New York, 1951), pp. 3–31, p. 14: 'Medieval Christian poetry, and by Christian poetry I mean all serious poetry written by Christian authors, even that usually called "secular", is always allegorical when the message of charity or some corollary of it is

the trenches on the exegetical front. One of these is that we have so far found little tendency towards allegory in the *Gawain*-poet's work. On the contrary, in his two Old Testament poems, we have seen him aiming consistently to elaborate the literal sense of his sources; and, on the whole, where he has made use of allegorical interpretation (as in the parable of the wedding feast in *Purity*) he has expounded his own exegesis with great clarity, rather than leaving it to be worked out by his audience. Only in the equation of Jonah with Christ did he rely on hints demanding some effort of interpretation from his audience; there he was employing a piece of typology so traditional as to be part of the literal sense of the New Testament, and in any case the equation was only a very minor part of the meaning of the poem. Similarly, as we have noted, when he makes use of a Scriptural parable in *Pearl* itself, the Maiden first elaborates its literal sense, and then supplies her own directions for its allegorical interpretation:

> Bot now thou motez, me for to mate,
> That I my peny haf wrang tan here;
> Thou sayz that I that come to late
> Am not worthy so gret fere...
>
> Bot innoghe of grace hatz innocent.
> As sone as thay arn borne, by lyne
> In the water of babtem thay dyssente:
> Then arne thay boroght into the vyne.
> Anon the day, wyth derk endente,
> The niyght of deth dotz to enclyne:
> That wroght never wrang er thenne thay wente,
> The gentyle Lorde thenne payez hys hyne. (613–32)

The Maiden is one of the last-hired workmen; coming into the vineyard equals baptism; nightfall equals death. From these clues, we are able to deduce without any hesitation who is the lord of the vineyard and what is the payment of the workers. The intended meaning of the crucial elements in the parable is expounded as it would

---

not evident on the surface'. For some discussion of the theoretical issues, see M. W. Bloomfield, 'Symbolism in Medieval Literature', *MP*, LVI (1958–9), 73–81; and the essays by E. T. Donaldson, R. E. Kaske, and Charles Donahue in *Critical Approaches to Medieval Literature*, ed. Dorothy Bethurum (New York, 1960), pp. 1–82; also now Ian Bishop, *Pearl in its Setting* (Oxford, 1968), pp. 49–98.

have been by a medieval preacher in a sermon: that is to say, in a work which *uses* allegorical exegesis but for that very reason does not require allegorical exegesis. Again, the poet's treatment of the Old and New Jerusalems strongly suggests that he is not relying on his audience to draw out allegorical meanings from his poem. The distinction between the two Jerusalems is elementary enough, but the Maiden is nevertheless allowed to explain it at some length:

> Of motes two to carpe clene
> (And Jerusalem hyght bothe nawtheles),
> That nys to yow no more to mene
> Bot 'ceté of God' other 'syght of pes'. (949–52)

As we have seen, the Maiden is here doing what the writers of medieval devotional works do: expounding allegory, not writing in it. It is true, of course, that she is doing so for the sake of a Dreamer characterized as mundane and even rather simple in his intelligence; but the poet would hardly expect his audience to endure the exposition if they were allegorizers as practised as some modern medievalists. On these grounds it seems to me fair to say that the probability is against other parts of the poem having allegories concealed in them.

A second argument which points in the same direction is this. I have remarked that the allegorical approach to *Pearl* arose partly in reaction against the autobiographical approach; and it is still often the case that allegorical interpreters present their view of the poem as a critique of a more literal interpretation of the Dreamer's paternal relationship to the Maiden. A weapon they were quick to seize on is the absence from the poem of any reference to the Maiden's mother. If the Maiden is literally the Dreamer's daughter, then she must have had a mother; why then should the narrator refer to her exclusively as '*my* privy perle' (24)? It was not beyond the ingenuity of the autobiographical interpreters to devise an answer to this, and so we find Gollancz discreetly hinting that she was a 'love-child', *privy* because illegitimate.[1] It is easy to see the fallacy underlying both question and answer: they are based on the assumption that the poem simply transcribes a real-life situation. If we decline to make this assumption, we are not necessarily forced back into the view that it is an allegory; we can adopt the simpler solution of seeing it as a fiction. If this is so, then the *Gawain*-poet is no more obliged to explain what happened to the Maiden's mother than Shakespeare is

---

[1] *Cambridge History of English Literature*, I, 331.

obliged to tell us 'Where was Hamlet at the time of his father's death?' There is no reason why such questions should have answers at all, unless to answer them is to the poet's purpose. We cannot therefore argue that because the Pearl Maiden has no mother she must be an allegory of the Dreamer's soul or of purity. More recently different and more plausible reasons have been given for rejecting the father-daughter theory in favour of an allegorical interpretation. Sister Mary Vincent Hillmann, for example, comments as follows on the surprise the Dreamer expresses on first finding his pearl in the paradisal world of his dream:

> I segh hyr in so strange a place,
> Such a burre myght make myn herte blunt. (175–6)

These lines definitely undermine the theory that *The Pearl* is a lament for a dead child. For, though the dreamer, knowing that his pearl had been lost in the ground, might indeed receive a shock at seeing it (as he fancies the maiden to be) in 'so strange a place' as *Paradyse* (137), he could not reasonably, as a Christian, be surprised at seeing his little dead daughter there.[1]

An obvious objection to this comment is that there is no cause to suppose that the Dreamer will always think and feel 'reasonably, as a Christian'. On the contrary, we have been told that when he was in the garden that was exactly what he was failing to do: he persisted in mourning for his pearl despite the persuasions of 'resoun' (52) and 'kynde of Kryst' (55). It seems to be part of his character or function in the poem to fail in precisely this way. Moreover, like other allegorical interpreters of the poem, Sister Hillmann stumbles over the indications in the text itself that the pearl was a person, and that her relationship with the Dreamer was a personal one. She is able to make sense of a sort of the Dreamer's remark that the pearl 'lyfed not two yer in oure thede' (483) by explaining that 'she (it) had been imported into a Christian country (England) from the *Oryent* only two years before its (her) disappearance'. But of his earlier explanation that the pearl 'watz me nerre then aunte or nece' (233) she can only say that it is inexplicable: *nerre* must refer to the Maiden's physical position on the brink of the stream, while *aunte or nece* is 'used in all probability as a rhyme-tag...for no

---

[1] Hillmann, ed. *The Pearl*, note on lines 175–6, p. 83. As Sister Hillmann acknowledges, the same point had been made by Sister Madeleva (*Pearl: A Study in Spiritual Dryness*, p. 131).

apparent reason'.[1] It is true that the statement 'Ho watz me nerre then aunte or nece' is difficult to interpret (and, as we shall see, it may be designedly so), the difficulty being chiefly to decide whether it implies 'Within the range of family relationships, her relationship to me was closer than that of aunt or niece' or 'Her relationship to me was closer than any mere family relationship'. But it has recently been shown, with great ingenuity, that an apparently disconnected line towards the end of the poem helps to make the former interpretation far more likely. In the final stanza, the narrator shows his acceptance of his loss by formally committing his pearl into the hands of God:

> And sythen to God I hit bytaghte
> In Krystez dere blessyng and myn. (1207–8)

Professor Davis has shown from a study of medieval English letters that the formula 'God's (or Christ's) blessing and mine' is frequently used as a salutation or valediction, and always from parent to child.[2] This puts it almost beyond question that, so far as the relationship between Dreamer and Maiden can be pinned down at all, it is intended to be that of father and daughter. Hence we must be intended to understand that the lost pearl was a child who died before the age of two.[3] This is why the Dreamer asserts that:

> Thou lyfed not two yer in oure thede;
> Thou cowthez never God nauther plese ne pray,
> Ne never nawther Pater ne Crede (483–5)

and why he needs to be reassured about the salvation of the innocent.

[1] Hillmann, ed. *The Pearl*, notes on lines 484 and 233, pp. 91, 84.

[2] Norman Davis, 'A Note on *Pearl*', *RES*, n.s. XVII (1966), 403–5; further evidence to the same effect may be adduced from the medieval religious drama. For example, in the Chester *Deluge* Noah agrees that his sons should bring his wife into the ark: 'yea, sonnes, in Christs blessinge and myne' (*Chester Plays*, vol. I, ed. H. Deimling, EETS ES LXII [London, 1892], p. 57, line 222). The York Noah uses the same formula to his sons: 'And wende we hense in haste,/In goddis blissyng and myne' (*York Mystery Plays*, ed. Lucy Toulmin Smith [London, 1885], p. 55, lines 321–2). So does the York Abraham, addressing Isaac: 'Farewele, in goddis dere blissyng/And myn, for ever and ay' (*Ibid.* p. 65, lines 295–6). In the last case, the situation of a father giving up his child to God and to death is very similar to that in *Pearl*.

[3] Ian Bishop (*Pearl in its Setting*, pp. 111–12) notes that this age may have been chosen for a child who is treated as an example of innocence because the Holy Innocents were 'two years old and under' (Matthew ii.16) at the time of their deaths.

We can make coherent sense of the poem if we assume this as the framework of its fiction, so that there is no need for us to take it as an allegory on the ground of its lack of literal coherence. A more positive argument against allegorical interpretation, whether it takes the pearl to stand for an abstract quality or for the Dreamer's own soul, is that it neglects the passion and conviction with which the poem treats the Dreamer's relationship with the Maiden as a *personal* relationship. I consider the detailed development of this relationship below; here, though, I can anticipate the detailed analysis by the assertion, which any reader can check against his own experience of *Pearl,* that it is pervaded with personal feeling.[1] There is evidence enough for this in its phrasing: the erotic terminology we have noted, and such intimacies as 'my blysfol beste' (279), 'my swete' (325), 'my dere endorde' (368), and, even after the Dreamer has grasped the truth about the Maiden's high status, the touchingly human 'my lyttel quene' (1147) (is this how a man refers to purity, or to his own soul?). But there is equally persuasive evidence in the very texture of the poem, in the tremulous passion of its rhythms, as the Dreamer's love for the Maiden and his incredulous delight in finding her again first flow out and then are painfully broken by the recognition of how she is changed and exalted. It is precisely this painfully intense combination of desire and denial that justifies the elaborate external form of *Pearl.* The *Gawain*-poet might, like the authors of *Winner and Waster* or *The Parliament of the Three Ages* or *Death and Life,* have expressed his dream-vision in the same un-rhymed alliterative lines that he uses in his other poems; but the peculiarly personal content of *Pearl* demanded a form which would convey a perpetual tension between human passion and divine order. This is found in the tension between the difficult and constricting pattern of the stanzas fixed in their groups and the irregular rhythms of the feelings they contain and are modified by. In particular, for all the outward impulses of longing, the stanzas with their repeated last lines bring us back and back to the same difficult truths. But in insisting on the passionate qualities of the poem, I am not of course going back to the autobiographical theory. As one critic wrote over forty years ago: 'The mourning and the loss are in the poem and cannot be explained merely by being ignored. They can be explained not by interpreting the maiden as the symbol of purity but by in-

---

[1] Miss Kean argues to this effect cogently and in detail (Kean, pp. 114 ff.).

terpreting the loss of the maiden and the grief of the poet as a literary fiction.'[1]

On these grounds, then, it seems improbable that *Pearl* is an allegory in the sense of containing some systematic concealed meaning. It may be added that the very variety of interpretations proposed by allegorizers of the poem also detracts from their plausibility. Even if we dismiss as obviously mistaken the suggestions that the pearl stands for the Eucharist and for the Blessed Virgin, we are still left with a choice of 'clean maidenhood', 'spiritual sweetness', 'eternal life', or the various multilayered interpretations, not to mention others that we have not discussed; and each allegorizer tends to claim that his is the only true meaning of the poem, and all others are obviously mistaken. All the same, we are left with a difficult poem, and one whose central object, the pearl, has an undeniable complexity of meaning. Here, indeed, the very profusion of proposed allegorical interpretations may be helpful in reminding us how rich in meaning the pearl is, so long as we are willing to see the richness as suggestive rather than rigidly systematic. It seems likely enough, indeed, that for an educated fourteenth-century reader or listener the idea or word 'pearl' would in itself have been felt to be pregnant with symbolic potentiality, even if the poem *Pearl* had never been written. No doubt W. H. Schofield was right to state that 'a learned man of the fourteenth century was so used to interpretations of the pearl that the word could hardly be mentioned without a great many rising to his memory instantly'.[2] Likely enough this was true of the thing as well as the word and the idea, so that a fourteenth-century courtier, seeing a pearl on a ring or at a lady's breast, might have exclaimed, like Yeats on seeing a swan, 'Another emblem there!' And it would be foolish to claim that the poem *Pearl* has nothing to do with the pearl symbolism of its time; for the particular kind of success the poet has achieved by his 'poetic method at once condensed and allusive'[3] would scarcely have been possible if he had not shared with his audience a common pre-existing symbolism. But this must not lead us to suppose that there is no difference between the pearl symbol as it existed in the common educated consciousness of the fourteenth century and the pearl symbol as it exists in *Pearl*. If this were so, then in order to discover the meaning of the latter we should need

[1] W. K. Greene, 'The *Pearl*—a New Interpretation', *PMLA*, XL (1925), 814–27; p. 823.
[2] 'Symbolism, Allegory, and Autobiography in *The Pearl*', p. 639.
[3] W. R. J. Barron, 'Luf Daungere', p. 15.

only to look up lapidaries, Scriptural commentaries, and so forth, for evidence about the former. This indeed has been the tendency of modern interpretation of the poem, even among those who do not believe it to be a systematic allegory. Miss Kean, for example, besides using Scripture to interpret the jeweller image, and the Fathers to interpret the flower and garden images, delves into alchemical writings (even though she admits that 'there is little evidence that they influenced poets in the fourteenth century'[1]) to interpret the pearl image. To approach *Pearl* in this oblique way is surely to show little confidence in it as a poem, for it is to assume that the essential creative work had already been done in non-literary writings, and that all the poet had to do was to transcribe it. In fact however, if the tautology may be permitted, the poet of *Pearl* was a poet. He *used* the symbols provided for him by his age, and if we wish to understand his poem as a work of art we must begin not by superimposing on it some system of allegorical significances drawn from external sources, but by reading the poem as sensitively and intelligently as possible to discover what symbolism is created by its actual words. In saying this, I have no wish to profess or encourage historical ignorance, for I know well that it is only by historical studies that we can understand what the words mean. But there comes a point at which, if we really believe *Pearl* to be a great work of literature, we must be prepared to trust the poem rather than its background. To suppose otherwise, indeed, would be to confuse the poem with its background, and to find nothing distinctive in it. Within the religious verse of the Middle Ages there are many short pieces (the great majority, for example, of the surviving religious lyrics), and many longer works too, which are parasitic upon the symbolic consciousness of their age. They depended upon that consciousness for whatever power they possessed in their own time, they gave nothing in return, and the consequence is that they belong solely to their own age: they have no permanent value as literature. To try to understand the appeal of such works, we have to reconstruct artificially the world of symbolism that lay behind them in the life of their own time (and this is something eminently worth doing). But there are also certain longer poems which are successful as poems, which reconstruct current symbols within themselves, and in doing so give them a lasting and unique validity. *Pearl* is an outstanding example of this second kind of poem (others are *Piers Plowman*

[1] Kean, p. 140.

and, on a different scale of magnitude, *The Divine Comedy*). The way in which these poems work is to reconstruct symbols by incorporating them in an extended dramatic narrative in which a man like ourselves is involved in one or more human encounters. The result is that we do not have to try to apprehend the significance of their central symbols and images instantaneously, but can feel it being built up, piece by piece, over a period of time. In the fourteenth century the pearl could symbolize any of a very wide range of things; if a coherence is established within this variety, it is established by the poem itself, not by its sources and analogues.[1] In some ways it may be that we can better take *Pearl* as a guide to medieval symbolism than medieval symbolism as a guide to *Pearl*.

My purpose in what follows, then, is to read the poem with care: by no means an original aim, but more novel than it ought to be. It will be found, I believe, that Schofield was right in saying that 'The author's plan is to let the symbolism of his poem disclose itself slowly'.[2] The pearl image is not static but dynamic. It will be recalled that we found the same to be true of the central concept of *clannesse* in the poem *Purity*. We saw how, in the course of his poem, the *Gawain*-poet redefined that concept so completely as in effect to re-create it, and how he did so by setting it in a variety of contexts taken from real situations, so that the idea developed in meaning as the poem extended itself in time. In *Pearl* the poet treats his central image, and perhaps other images such as that of the jeweller, in the same way, but now the development in meaning is co-ordinated with and expressed through a single developing human drama—the encounter between the Dreamer and the Pearl Maiden. The result is a poem more economical and more powerfully moving than *Purity*. The whole force and poignancy of *Pearl* derives from its basic structure as an encounter involving human relationship; and it is through the synthesis of symbol with this human drama that the poet conveys his meaning, and not, I believe, through any concealed layers of allegory.

Symbol and drama

The pearl symbol is first mentioned as the first word of the poem's first line—'Perle, pleasaunte to prynces paye'—and the similarity

---

[1] This point is forcefully made by A. R. Heiserman, 'The Plot of *Pearl*', *PMLA*, LXXX (1965), 164–71.
[2] 'Symbolism, Allegory, and Autobiography in *The Pearl*', p. 588.

between this line and the closing lines of the poem has not escaped notice. At the end, the reference is to the Prince of heaven, to whom the pearl now belongs; the narrator wishes that we too may be 'precious perlez unto his pay'. I have suggested that the poem has a circular effect, its head biting its own tail; but this does not mean that its tail is the same as its head. None the less, even so moderate an interpreter of the poem as Gordon has followed the earlier commentators cited by Schofield and has claimed that the prince of the first line means 'literally a prince of this world and symbolically Christ'.[1] It is true of course that the parallel between the opening and closing lines is deliberate, and that on a second and subsequent readings of the poem the first line may recall the last, so that we shall have from the very beginning a sense of the nature of the development in meaning which is to take place. But this is not to say that the first line will mean the last, even symbolically. To agree that it does mean the last is surely to deny the nature of the poem as an object which, for its reader, is extended in time, and is therefore capable of discursive or dramatic development. And in this case we may miss the point of the first section of the poem. It begins with an exclamation in praise of 'the pearl' (i.e. pearls in general), and already a development in meaning begins as 'the pearl' slides unobtrusively across into another sense (i.e. one particular pearl):

> Perle, plesaunte to prynces paye
> To clanly clos in golde so clere!
> Oute of oryent, I hardyly saye,
> Ne proved I never her precios pere. (1–4)

Those lines, taken by themselves, might belong to a verse lapidary, and refer to the pearl as a literal precious stone, valued by literal earthly princes. This sense remains throughout the opening section: we can always understand that the narrator is referring to a jewel, and to the loss of a jewel. But there are also suggestions in this opening section that he is using the language of a lapidary in order to refer to something else: a girl or woman. They begin with the reference to the pearl as *her*. This indication that the pearl is feminine might be simply a matter of grammatical gender, *perle* deriving from a word which is feminine in French.[2] But the next two lines intensify the

[1] Schofield, *ibid.* pp. 589 ff.; Gordon, ed. *Pearl*, note on lines 1–4, p. 45.
[2] Cf. M. W. Bloomfield, 'A Grammatical Approach to Personification Allegory', *MP*, LX (1962–3), 161–71: 'One might say that languages with grammatical gender, unlike [modern] English, have automatically built-in personification of some sort' (p. 162).

suggestion of femininity in such a way as to hint at sex rather than gender:

> So rounde, so reken in uche araye,
> So smal, so smothe, her sydez were. (5-6)

Here *araye* could mean either the setting of a stone or the dress of a person, and *sydez* could mean either the surface of a pearl or the flanks of a woman. Other suggestions that the pearl is an image used of a person come from what the narrator goes on to tell us of his feelings about its loss, particularly when the loss is first mentioned:

> Allas! I leste hyr in on erbere;
> Thurgh gresse to grounde hit fro me yot.
> I dewyne, fordolked of luf-daungere,
> Of that pryvy perle wythouten spot. (9-12)

In later stanzas in the opening section he speaks of the grievous affliction of his heart, the burning and swelling of his breast, of clasping his hands in misery, of the fierce obstinacy of his grief. These are feelings that would be highly extravagant, Shylock-like indeed, if directed towards a jewel, but which are normal as part of the conventional language of love-suffering in medieval poetry. We noted earlier that *luf-daungere* suggests *fine amour*. It remains a case of suggestion, however: the implications of the phrasing are not pinned down by any explicit statement. We are faced with suggestiveness of a kind that belongs to poetry rather than to theology, and what it suggests is that the relationship between the narrator and the lost pearl is in some sense a human love-relationship, and that the loss involved is the death of a beloved girl or woman. She is 'clad in clot' (22) rather than in 'golde so clere', the earth is accused of marring her beauty, and she is now rotting. Yet at the same time as these hints of a human relationship broken by death are given, the original indications that the pearl is simply a pearl are by no means dropped. The refrain line throughout this section is some variant of 'that precios perle wythouten spotte', and the pearl is also referred to as a 'myry juele' (23) which 'trendeled doun' on to a 'huyle' (41), and as 'such rychez' (26).

Now we may, if we choose, refer to this deliberate intermingling of human suggestions and jewel suggestions as 'allegory', though the word is usually employed to indicate some more precise system of equivalences. But if we do call it allegory we need to recognize that it is the narrator who is being an allegorist, not necessarily the poet. This narrator is imposing on waking reality some vague equivalent to the kind of allegorical structure that the Lover in the *Roman de la Rose* finds ready-made in the world of his dream. The narrator, we gather, has lost by her death someone dear to him, and he thinks it appropriate to speak of the death of a person in terms of the loss of a precious stone: that is to say, that he sees it as the total and irrevocable loss of a valuable object, towards which the proper response is one of passionate and hopeless mourning. His attitude in this opening section is somewhat reminiscent of that of the man in black in *The Book of the Duchess*, a poem from which all hint of an otherworldly consolation is carefully excluded, even to the extent of omitting the consolatory metamorphosis from the story of Ceyx and Alcyone. In *Pearl*, even more than in Chaucer's dream-poem, this dramatic grief is made attractive, framed as it is in a scene which delights the senses with strange music and with the brightness and fragrance of flowers and herbs. But our response to the narrator's grief should not be one simply of surrender. The garden in which it is set forms a traditional pleasance or *locus amoenus*,[1] but the season in which the narrator enters it is not the traditional one of spring or Maytime but August, harvest-time, 'Quen corne is corven wyth crokez kene' (40). This unusual season may have had symbolic associations of one sort or another, as indeed may the flowers and herbs,[2] but it also has a compelling poetic effect. This effect is in harmony with the landscape's noticeable lack of one constant feature of the traditional *locus amoenus*, namely the stream or river. The

[1] For this literary convention, see E. R. Curtius, *European Literature and the Latin Middle Ages*, trans. W. R. Trask (New York, 1953), pp. 183–202.

[2] C. A. Luttrell, '*Pearl*: Symbolism in a Garden Setting', *Neophilologus*, XLIX (1965), 160–76, points out that the 'harvest-time and August opening' is by no means unique: there is an example in Nicole de Margival's *Panthere d'Amors*. It remains unusual, however. For suggestions as to the possible symbolic associations of the season, see Gollancz, ed. *Pearl*, pp. 118–19 (Lammas); C. G. Osgood, ed. *Pearl* (Boston, Mass., 1906), p. xvi (Assumption of the Virgin); Schofield, 'Symbolism, Allegory, and Autobiography in *The Pearl*', p. 616, n. 2 (St John's Great Reaper); Kean, pp. 48–52 (cycle of seasons connected with Passion and Resurrection, and with sin and regeneration). Miss Kean also considers the possible symbolism of flowers at some length (p. 59–70). As is usual with scholarly discussions of medieval symbolism, the scholars disagree so thoroughly among themselves that they can scarcely be said to clarify the poem for us, or even to convince us that there was any generally accepted system of symbols in the poet's own time, on which he was drawing. August could perhaps 'mean' almost as as many different things in the fourteenth century as it can today; and we are left with the poem.

landscape provides, we may say, an 'objective correlative' to the emotions of the narrator. About both there is a hint of the over-ripe, the unrefreshed, the drowsy, and perhaps of the merely passive: the corn awaiting the sickle, the narrator surrendering to his over-powering emotion. He does not see things with May-morning clarity; though he feels deeply the value of the lost pearl, by relying merely on feeling he underestimates its preciousness, seeing it not, as at the end of the poem, as precious to the Prince of heaven, but as precious only to earthly princes. As the opening lines hint, and as is made explicit later in the poem, the narrator is defined as a 'jeweller', aware only of material values.

That we are intended to adopt a critical attitude towards the narrator, even while feeling fully the pathos of his situation, is suggested by the way in which he refers to the flowers growing on the spot where his pearl was lost (that is, in human terms, the grave of the beloved):

> Blomez blayke and blwe and rede
> Ther schynez ful schyr agayn the sunne.
> Flor and fryte may not be fede
> Ther hit doun drof in moldez dunne;
> For uch gresse mot grow of graynez dede;
> No whete were ellez to wonez wonne. (27–32)

The last two lines embody an allusion to a familiar Scriptural text, John xii. 24–5:

Amen, amen dico vobis, nisi granum frumenti cadens in terram mortuum fuerit,
Ipsum solum manet; si autem mortuum fuerit, multum fructum affert.

(Amen, amen, I say to you, unless the grain of wheat falling into the ground die,
Itself remaineth alone. But if it die, it bringeth forth much fruit.)

But it is clear that the narrator has misunderstood this text: he has taken the fruit which grows from the dead grain to be material, like the flowers on the grave. If he recalled the next words in John, he would have understood that it was the spiritual fruit of eternal life:

Qui amat animam suam, perdet eam; et qui odit animam suam in hoc mundo, in vitam aeternam custodit eam. (John xii. 25)

(He that loveth his life shall lose it; and he that hateth his life in this world keepeth it unto life eternal.)

The narrator, then, has been mistaken to talk about the dead person as something which can be lost as completely as a jewel. Once a pearl is lost in the earth, it is lost for ever, but a person is an immortal soul as well as a corruptible body, and, by physical death, can gain eternal life. The narrator's grief, however touching and understandable, is mistaken, because it leaves out of account the immortality of the dead person's soul. His pearl may be lost to him for the time being, but it is not absolutely lost. His mistakenness comes close to being explicitly acknowledged in the final stanza of the opening section, where the earliest openly Christian reference occurs:

> A devely dele in my hert denned,
> Thagh resoun sette myselven saght.
> I playned my perle that ther watz spenned
> Wyth fyrce skyllez that faste faght;
> Thagh kynde of Kryst me comfort kenned,
> My wreched wylle in wo ay wraghte. (51–6)

It is not clear to what extent this perception represents the narrator's awareness at the time, or the awareness he achieved later as a result of the experience recorded in the poem. It does not need to be clear (we have noted that such ambiguity is part of the poem's technique), for its work has been done once it points towards a conflict between the narrator's violent and persuasive emotions and some as yet undefined rational and Christian attitude. The conflict is not immediately developed, for at this point the narrator is overcome by sleep, and becomes the Dreamer.

His body remains *in hoc mundo*, in the garden, but his spirit is transported to the new landscape of 'life eternal'. It is, as we have seen, another 'gardyn gracios gaye' (260), another version of the traditional *locus amoenus*, but this time a different version, shining with brilliant light and hard with metal and precious stones. This other world is conceived with the *Gawain*-poet's usual concreteness, but the concreteness is not used in quite the same way as when he re-creates Old Testament scenes in *Purity* or *Patience*. There the purpose of the concreteness is to naturalize and familiarize: it is a matter of introducing table-cloths and oaktrees into the deserts of Palestine. Coming from *Purity*, we might expect in *Pearl* to find the other world full of angels having picnics under the oaktrees, but in fact what the poet does is to evoke an exotic and genuinely otherworldly landscape, but still to re-create it in full solidity, with no hint of any vagueness or uncertainty. The more homely aspects of the Old Testament poems here become part of the Dreamer's naïveté, not part of the reality he naïvely regards. In this other world, the crystal cliffs, the blue-trunked trees with silver leaves, the gravel made of pearls, make up a kind of science-fiction landscape: it is planetary or lunar in its strangeness, and has a technicolour harshness in its brilliance. We have seen how the poet uses metallic similes to sharpen the sensory effect. He also employs one or two ingeniously precise similes of the 'as mote in at a munster dore' type for the same purpose. For example:

> In the founce ther stonden stonez stepe,
> As glente thurgh glas that glowed and glyght,
> As stremande sternez, quen strothe-men slepe,
> Staren in welkyn in wynter nyght. (113–16)

In the first of these similes describing the stones at the bottom of the rivers, the suggestion is perhaps of stained glass with the sun shining through it. The second simile, while seeming to be developed into an independent scene almost for its own sake, in fact heightens the original sensory effect with its strongly evocative details of the winter night and of men sleeping while the stars burn. Sound and rhythm, as always, have their part to play in calling up the scene, as in the two lines preceding those just quoted, where s's and r's create a whispering effect, while repeated present participles suggest the irregular, halting progress of the swirling water as it turns back on itself:

> Swangeande swete the water con swepe,
> With a rownande rourde raykande aryght. (111–12)

Or one might mention the pebbly feel of

> The gravayl that on grounde con grynde
> Wern precious perlez of oryente. (81–2)

That last line contains the first mention of pearls in the poem's second section, and the context of the landscape of which it forms part draws out two further aspects of the meaning latent in the pearl symbol: its brilliance and its hard permanence. Light, the effusion of God, is the favourite medieval image of beauty, and here the more human beauty which the pearl had at first in the narrator's memory —'So smal, so smothe her sydez were'—has begun, through emphasis on new aspects of the same symbol, to merge into a heavenly beauty. The pearl is now part of a landscape dazzling, overpowering in its brightness:

> For urthely herte myght not suffyse
> To the tenthe dole of tho gladnez glade. (135–6)

And the preciousness which was susceptible of death has in the same way begun to turn into a more permanent but harder preciousness. Thus, although the pearl symbol has for the moment reverted to its original sense of a precious stone, it has done so only to develop in new directions. We shall find that none of its separate senses is abandoned in the course of the poem, but any of them may momentarily come to the surface for the sake of a further development of associations.

This is the only mention of pearls in the second or third sections of the poem, but in the third section the Maiden appears for the first time. She is not at once identified with the lost pearl; by making use of the slow perception of his Dreamer, the poet is able to unfold his symbol gradually. At first what the Dreamer sees in her is the hard brilliance of the pearl, and an almost unbearable purity of whiteness. She is sitting on the other side of the river that cuts through the dream landscape, at the foot of a glittering crystal cliff, a courteous and gracious lady, dressed in a gleaming white mantle, who shines 'As glysnande golde that man con schere' (165): another characteristically precise simile—not just like gold, but like freshly cut gold. Not even in the feverish jargon of washing-powder advertisements does modern English have enough words meaning shining, glittering, radiant, and so on, to translate all the poet's different ways of expressing the effusion of light. Within all this overpowering glitter, the Dreamer comes only slowly to recognize the Maiden; and he says so with a naïve simplicity that will be characteristic of his attitude towards her in this encounter. He remarks only, 'I knew hyr wel, I hade sen hyr ere' (164), and again:

> On lenghe I loked to hyr there;
> The lenger, I knew hyr more and more. (167–8)

At last, this figure, at first still as a statue, begins to move. First she raises her head, so that the Dreamer can see 'Hyr vysayge whyt as playn yvore' (178), then she rises to her feet, and walks down to the river bank. This slow process of encounter and recognition is one of great emotional turmoil for the Dreamer. His heart is stunned (*blunt*,

176) and full of astonished confusion (*ful stray atount,* 179), and he is afraid that having seen her he may lose her again. It is through this moving and convincing crisis of human feeling that the meaning of the symbol is developed for us, rather than through the existence from the beginning of parallel allegorical layers.

At this point it is still not perfectly clear who it is that the Dreamer recognizes when he recognizes the Maiden, but it becomes clear in the course of the next section of the poem, section IV, in which her appearance and dress are described in great detail. Here pearls are mentioned again and again, as part of a 'fashion plate' description of her dress. The normal medieval descriptive method, of accumulation rather than selection, is used, but more effectively here than in the description of the temple vessels in *Purity*, because it is directed to a single end, the intensification of pearl qualities. (It has often been pointed out that there was a special enthusiasm for pearls in four-teenth-century courtly society, so that at the same time the Maiden is shown to be a great and fashionable lady.)[1] She is wearing a white linen mantle, open at the sides, and trimmed with pearls, with hanging sleeves also decorated with pearls. Her kirtle is to match, and again is covered with pearls. She wears a crown of pearls, and her complexion is as pearl-like as the pearls with which she is adorned:

> Her depe colour yet wonted non
> Of precios perle in porfyl pyghte. (215–16)

The culmination of this description is reached with a single flawless pearl at her breast:

> Bot a wonder perle wythouten wemme
> Inmyddez hyr breste watz sette so sure;
> A mannez dome moght dryghly demme
> Er mynde moght malte in hit mesure.
> I hope no tong moght endure
> No saverly saghe say of that syght,
> So watz hit clene and cler and pure,
> That precios perle ther hit watz pyght. (221–8)

To attempt to distinguish the symbolic significance of this one pearl from that of the Pearl Maiden herself would be to misunderstand, indeed to resist, the poet's methods. Certainly this pearl seems to have special associations with purity or virginity, in such phrases as

---

[1] See Gordon, ed. *Pearl*, p. xxxiv and note on line 228.

wythouten wemme, but these only recall and develop an idea which had been present from the first section of the poem, with its use of *wythouten spot* as the refrain phrase. The *order* in which the poem's symbolism is unfolded is significant, but it is a single symbol, with a single though complex meaning, which is being evolved, and any attempt at minute allegorical distinctions will only obscure the poem's central achievement. Even more mistaken is Sister Hillmann's attempt to distinguish the Pearl Maiden from the lost pearl. It is true that the Maiden 'does not identify herself with the material pearl'[1] explicitly, but the continuity of the symbol is beyond question. When the Dreamer first sees the Maiden move there are striking verbal reminiscences of the lost pearl of the poem's opening stanza:

> That gracios gay wythouten galle,
> So smothe, so smal, so seme slyght,
> Rysez up in hir araye ryalle,
> A precios pyece in perlez pyght. (189–92)

'So smothe, so smal' recalls 'So smal, so smothe her sydez were' (6), while 'hir araye ryalle' is in keeping with the royal associations of 'Perle, plesaunte to prynces paye' (1). The Maiden curtsies to the Dreamer, takes off her crown to him, and greets him; and his first words to her, though their form is interrogative, work through their repetitions to complete the identification of the Maiden with the lost jewel:

> 'O perle,' quod I, 'in perlez pyght,
> Art thou my perle that I haf playned,
> Regretted by myn one on nyghte?' (241–3)

There can surely be no doubt, if only we respond to the poem, that this Pearl Maiden *is* (though no doubt in some complex sense of the word 'is') his lost pearl. I have already argued that the lost pearl is to be seen as a person, and that, if we wish to reconstruct a specific human situation, she is most plausibly seen as the Dreamer's daughter dead in infancy. This is a convenient point to pause and ask why the poet did not make it easier for us to reconstruct this situation. Why did he mystify us with talk about aunts and nieces, and why did he allow the Dreamer to use the language of *fine amour* as well as that of fatherly love in referring to the pearl? We have been seeing how the poem works not by making clear-cut identifications and distinctions

---

[1] Hillmann, ed. *The Pearl*, p. xx.

of the kind that belong to theology, but by vague mergings and emergings of an essentially poetic kind. We may now be prepared to see that the same could be true of the (fictional) situation 'behind' the poem. If the poet left the relationship between the Dreamer and the Maiden vague, perhaps he did so because he wanted it to be vague. It is true, of course, that he gained certain advantages by the hints of a father-daughter relationship. It has been pointed out, for example, that 'there seems to be a special significance in the situation where the doctrinal lesson given by the celestial maiden comes from one of no earthly wisdom to her proper teacher and instructor in the natural order'.[1] Because the Dreamer at once recognizes the Maiden as one who in her earthly existence was 'So smothe, so smal, so seme slyght' (190), he is unable for a long time to grasp that the statement

> A mannez dom moght dryghly demme
> Er mynde moght malte in hit mesure (223–4)

is true of her doctrine as well as of the pearl at her breast. But the poet could gain further advantages by leaving the father-daughter relationship as a matter of hints only, and adding to it hints of other relationships, such as that of lover and beloved. One such advantage would be that of widening the poem's appeal for a courtly audience, who would be used to poems about *fine amour*, but less ready to respond to a poem about fatherly love. A more important advantage was that it enabled the poet to write a poem not about one particular relationship, but about human relationship in general: about earthly relationship, and its meaning in the context of death and of the other world beyond death. It was for this reason, no doubt, that he reserved the clinching phrase 'In Krystez dere blessyng and myn' (1208) for the final stanza: he did not wish to pin the poem down to a single specific relationship until the last possible moment. My argument has been that the *Gawain*-poet's central subject is the impact of the more than human upon the human, and the reassessment of human values that must follow from this. This is, I believe, the central subject of *Pearl* too, and before returning to the text of the poem I shall examine this idea further.

The situation in which the Dreamer finds himself in the heavenly world of *Pearl* reminds me of an incident in the life of Jesus recorded by St Matthew. The Sadducees, 'who say there is no resurrection' (Matthew xxii. 23), put to Jesus a problem about a woman who was

---

[1] Gordon, ed. *Pearl*, p. xiii.

married seven times in succession, to seven men who were all brothers—an imaginary situation, no doubt, intended to trap Jesus, rather than a difficulty that was always cropping up in real life. She outlived them all, and then eventually died herself, and the Sadducees wanted to know whose wife she would be in the resurrection. Jesus answered, 'in the resurrection they shall neither marry nor be married, but shall be as the angels of God in heaven' (xxii. 30). One meaning of this answer is to indicate that in the heavenly world the terminology of earthly relationship simply ceases to apply. One way of seeing *Pearl* is as an imaginative extension of this statement and of other New Testament statements like it (for example, in some of the parables of the kingdom) about the nature of the heavenly world. In our world, people exist above all through human relationships. Man is a social animal, and his very personality is largely formed by a succession of relationships: a series of marriages, as it were, including that with his parents and that with his children, and centring usually in marriage itself. Take away this network of human relationships, and the individual withers. Nevertheless, in the kingdom of heaven as postulated by the Christian revelation, this familiar network is dissolved away, and yet the individual soul survives. In *Pearl*, this is the state of which the Dreamer has a visionary foretaste: human relationship itself is dissolved away, and in the case of the Maiden, who, through having died, truly belongs to this other world, it has been replaced by relationship of a different and utterly strange kind. We shall be examining that in detail shortly, but for the moment let us consider simply how the Maiden explains to the Dreamer that in the heavenly world she is a bride of the Lamb and Queen of Heaven. He protests that this position can belong to the Blessed Virgin alone, but she explains further that *all* the 144,000 virgins in the heavenly city are also brides of the Lamb and Queens of Heaven. Now in human terms this is meaningless nonsense: we are obviously not to imagine something like the Wife of Bath's 'octogamye' multiplied many times over. But it is evidently only by inventing such nonsense that human language can be used to hint at the transcendent system of relationships, centring in God, that exists in the heavenly world. All that is clear to the Dreamer is that he is excluded from this new order: he has lost his pearl on earth, through her death, and even by visiting the other world in a vision he cannot regain her, because he has no part in this new system of relationships, and cannot even understand it except in terms of the old. Hence the pain his vision causes him; and he seems to feel an even sharper anguish at being confronted with the Maiden inexplicably at home in an incomprehensible other world than he did at the simple fact of her death in this world. It is in this sense, then, that *Pearl* can be said to be about relationship itself. To say 'Ho watz me nerre then aunte or nece', without specifying further, implies *all* close human relationships, in such a way as to enable the individual reader or listener to fill out the vagueness with his own experiences of human relationship. At the same time, to talk of aunts and nieces when confronted with a transfigured heavenly being betrays an inability to see reality in any other terms than those of the family relationships with which we are most familiar. The effect of this inability on the Dreamer's part is one of mingled pathos and comedy.

In the heavenly world of his dream, the Dreamer is certainly a figure at once pathetic and comic. At first, on seeing the Maiden, he is simply stunned:

> Wyth yyen open and mouth ful clos,
> I stod as hende as hawk in halle. (183–4)

Then he discloses expectations that not only contradict his earlier attitude in the garden but are quite out of keeping with the heavenly order of things. In the garden, he had mourned his pearl as though she were irrevocably lost. In the dream, recognizing that she still exists, he expresses new assumptions, though still of a kind familiar to us. We find them innocently and pathetically expressed nowadays in the obituary and memorial columns of newpapers. In the heavenly world, we shall achieve a reunion with the dear departed 'on the other shore'; the threads of earthly relationship will be picked up just where they were dropped, nothing essential will be altered, but all the difficulties and tensions involved in earthly relationships will miraculously be dissolved away. These are the dreams with which modern Christians often console themselves, despite all that the Gospels have to say about the essential strangeness and incomprehensibility of the heavenly order. And they are the Dreamer's expectations too. His first words to the Maiden (to return to the text where we left it) express his surprise at finding her alive after all, when previously, for all his theoretical Christianity, he had assumed that she was dead. He is almost reproachful towards her. He has been suffering the agonies of a rejected lover, yet now he finds her very pleasantly accommodated after all:

O perle', quod I, 'in perlez pyght,
Art thou my perle that I haf playned,
Regretted by myn one on nyghte?
Much longeyng haf I for the layned,
Sythen into gresse thou me aglyghte.
Pensyf, payred, I am forpayned,
And thou in a lyf of lykyng lyghte,
In Paradys erde, of stryf unstrayned.
What wyrde hatz hyder my juel vayned,
And don me in thys del and gret daunger?' (241–50)

Along with the genuineness of this suffering, which arouses our
compassion, the last question, coming from a Christian, is almost
ridiculously inept. What else could he have expected to find?
The Maiden answers him without giving the reassurance he is
groping for. She is grave, exact, and severe: 'Sir, ye haf your tale
mysetente' (257). She goes on to explain, in a passage we have already examined, that all that he lost was in fact a rose, subject to the
natural process of decay; but the rose has now proved to be 'a
perle of prys' (272). The Dreamer begs her pardon for his misunderstanding, only to flounder confidently into the further error of the
'on the other shore' theory:

'Iwyse,' quod I, 'my blysfol beste,
My grete dystresse thou al todrawez.
To be excused I make requeste;
I trawed my perle don out of dawez.
Now haf I fonde hyt, I schal ma feste,
And wony wyth hyt in schyr wod-schawez,
And love my Lorde and al his lawez
That hatz me broght thys blys ner.
Now were I at yow byyonde thise wawez,
I were a joyful jueler.' (279–88)

This facile hope of a happy-ever-after reunion is met with an
even more stinging rebuke from the Maiden, and a devastatingly
complete analysis of his error, divided into three parts. She begins
with a question and an exclamation which decisively withdraw her
from the realm of humanity—you human beings!—'Wy borde ye
men? So madde ye be!' (290). In the cruelty of this one might sense
the callousness of a small child, not seeing how much words can hurt;
yet at the same time it can be seen as deliberate and necessary harsh-

ness, for the Dreamer has no hope of gaining further understanding unless he can be shocked out of his fool's paradise. She continues:

> Thre wordez hatz thou spoken at ene:
> Unavysed, for sothe, wern alle thre.
> Thou ne woste in worlde quat on dotz mene;
> Thy worde byfore thy wytte con fle.
> Thou says thou trawez me in this dene,
> Bycawse thou may wyth yyen me se;
> Another thou says, in thys countré
> Thyself schal won wyth me ryght here;
> The thrydde, to passe thys water fre—
> That may no joyfol jueler. (291–300)

She then corrects each of his false statements separately. In the case of the first, it is important not to misunderstand her correction. She is not saying that he is mistaken in trusting the evidence of his eyes that she is 'in this dene' of paradise, but that he is mistaken in believing her to be there *only* because he can see her with his eyes.[1] She really is there (there is no hint of her being in the dream landscape only potentially), but he should have known that she would be without seeing her, because, as a Christian, he knew of God's promise of immortality for the soul. Her answer helps to define the failing that the Dreamer has in common with most Christians: the failure to take with full seriousness, to realize to himself, religious truths that he knows perfectly well in theory:

> I halde that jueler lyttel to prayse
> That levez wel that he segh wyth yye,
> And much to blame and uncortayse
> That levez oure Lorde wolde make a lyye,
> That lelly hyghte your lyf to rayse,
> Thagh fortune dyd your flesch to dyye.
> Ye setten hys wordez ful westernays
> That levez nothynk bot ye hit syye.

---

[1] Miss Kean appears to take it that 'in this dene' means 'on earth', and that the Dreamer 'had believed that she was on earth' (Kean, p. 128). But if this were so, why should the Maiden not explain that she is not on earth, rather than (as she does) that she is where she is not because he can see her, but because that was God's promise? Miss Kean asserts that 'As the Maiden points out, she is not, in fact, in the country in which he thinks she is' (p. 129), but without giving any line-reference. There is no equivalent in *Pearl* to the statement of Beatrice in the *Paradiso* which Miss Kean quotes as a parallel: "Tu non se' in terra, sì come tu credi".

And that is a poynt o sorquydryye,
That uche god mon may evel byseme,
To leve no tale be true to tryye
Bot that hys one skyl may deme. (301–12)

The Dreamer's second error, in supposing that he can now dwell
with the Maiden 'in this bayly' (315), she corrects by pointing out
that he must first ask permission, and that this may not be granted.
His third error, in proposing to cross the river-barrier which separates
them, she corrects by reminding him that Adam's sin makes it neces-
say that he should die before he can do so.

Discourse and drama

At this point, a complete change has begun to come over the course
of the poem. Previously, the burden of meaning had been carried by
the pearl symbol itself; but, by his evident failure to understand the
Maiden's complex and highly poetic image of the transformation of
the rose into the pearl, the Dreamer has shown that he is unable to
make any further progress through the development of symbolism.
He is hopelessly literal-minded, as dreamers in fourteenth-century
poems tend to be. We may recall, for example, how in *The Book of
the Duchess* the man in black tries to explain the nature of his loss
to the Dreamer by using chess imagery: he was playing at chess with
Fortune and lost his queen. The Chaucerian Dreamer is utterly
bewildered by this:

> ther is no man alyve her
> Wolde for a fers make this woo! (740–1)

And so the man in black has to turn to more literal language, and
tell his life-story. In *The Book of the Duchess*, however, chess imagery
is only peripheral; in *Pearl* pearl imagery is absolutely central, and it
is therefore all the more striking that from this point on it is simply
dropped. For more than four hundred lines the pearl symbol undergoes no further development, and simpler, more explicit forms of
exposition take its place. The Maiden's division of the Dreamer's
error into three parts occurs at the end of section v. In section vi
the word *perle* occurs only twice, as a name:

> My precios perle dotz me gret pyne; (330)

> When I am partlez of perle myne. (335)

In section VII it again occurs only twice, in the form of references to what has already occurred when the poem begins:

> Fro thou watz wroken fro uch a wothe,
> I wyste never quere my perle watz gon; (375–6)

> Thow wost wel when thy perle con schede,
> I watz ful yong and tender of age. (411–12)

In sections VIII, IX, X, XI and XII the word *perle* does not occur at all. Throughout this large central part of the poem the human drama of the encounter between Dreamer and Maiden continues to unfold itself, but it is accompanied not by any symbolic development but by the development of argument and explicit doctrine.

This has begun with the Maiden's threefold analysis of the Dreamer's error. In answer to her correction, the Dreamer persists in seeing the situation in terms of his own misery; for him (and this is eminently natural) the crucial fact about her careful statement is not that it is true but that it hurts him. It throws him into a despair like that in which Jonah wishes that God would slay him, though in the Dreamer's case the misery is more genuine and less histrionic:

> Now rech I never for to declyne,
> Ne how fer of folde that man me fleme.
> When I am partlez of perle myne,
> Bot durande doel what may men deme? (333–6)

Once more the Maiden rebukes him with what seems like cruelty— a cruelty that may again suggest a child in its apparent inability even to understand his suffering. The rebuke is now more clearly directed not at his opinions and expectations, but at the attitude of mind that underlies them:

> 'Thow demez noght bot doel-dystresse,'
> Thenne sayde that wyght. 'Why dotz thou so?
> For dyne of doel of lurez lesse,
> Ofte mony mon forgos the mo.
> The oghte better thyselven blesse,
> And love ay God, in wele and wo,
> For anger gaynez the not a cresse.
> Who nedez schal thole, be not so thro.
> For thogh thou daunce as any do,
> Braundysch and bray thy brathez breme,
> When thou no fyrre may, to ne fro,
> Thou moste abyde that he schal deme.' (337–48)

The picture the Maiden paints of him here is a cruel caricature, using an undignified animal image like the image of the hawk he had earlier applied to himself, and suggesting a thwarted child stamping and shouting in anger. It relates him very clearly to the anti-hero of *Patience*, the impatient man who foolishly resists the power of God, refusing to acknowledge that he lives in a world over which God has absolute control, and in which ultimately man has no choice but to do God's will. The conclusion 'Thou moste abyde that he schal deme' is hard but just, and a full response to the poem will take account of both its hardness and its justice. Our own thoughts and feelings should be engaged on both sides of the encounter; we shall recognize the absurdity of the Dreamer's position, and yet—because it is based on a completely natural human response, and because the Dreamer is 'I', not 'he'—we shall also share in his suffering.

The Dreamer now begins to undergo a development that was beyond the scope of Jonah, and still more of any of the examples of *fylthe* in *Purity*. He learns from the Maiden's insistence on the need to recognize facts, and especially the fact of God's omnipotence. He apologizes to God—'Ne worthe no wraththe unto my Lorde' (362) —and shows a new humility towards the Maiden:

> Rebuke me never wyth wordez felle,
> Thagh I forloyne, my dere endorde. (367–8)

He begins to recognize that there is a distance between them, but he persists in seeing that distance in earthly terms. Sometimes this produces an acute pathos, as when he begs her:

> God forbede we be now wrothe,
> We meten so selden by stok other ston. (379–80)

Here the tag 'by stok other ston' has an effect similar to that of the other tag 'aunte or nece': by its very nature as a cliché belonging to earthly meetings and separations it makes us feel the Dreamer's loneliness in the strange world of his dream. Such tags seem to be used for this purpose almost systematically. In the next stanza the Dreamer begs the Maiden to tell him 'What lyf ye lede erly and late' (392), and there again 'erly and late' touches one by its reminder of the familiar earthly world in the midst of the timeless heavenly world to which it is so strikingly inapplicable. Having grasped that there is now an unbridgeable distance between himself and the Maiden, the Dreamer can only see that distance as it might be in this world: as a social distance. She has somehow gone up in the world, and joined an aristocracy before the courtly grandeur of which he feels as abashed as the Chaucerian dreamer faced with the man in black or the God of Love. The distance between them is one of manners:

> Thagh cortaysly ye carp con,
> I am bot mol and manerez mysse. (381–2)

Yet he can at least take vicarious pleasure in her advancement:

> For I am ful fayn that your astate
> Is worthen to worschyp and wele, iwysse. (393–4)

And he is naturally curious about her new way of life.

At this point a digression may be necessary if I am to make my view of the poem clear. The *Gawain*-poet really is presenting the transcendent heavenly order in terms of material royalty, luxury and grandeur; it really is the case that for him an earthly kingdom is a valid 'image...of the Kingdom (significant word) of Heaven'.[1] And in this he is following a powerful tradition in medieval religious writing, found in English from the time of such twelfth-century texts as the *Ancrene Riwle*, where God is figured as a powerful and knightly king, full of *deboneirté*, who woos a lady besieged in her castle; or as *The Wooing of Our Lord*, where Christ is represented as wooing the human soul, and possessing in himself all the qualities that would be most desirable in an aristocratic husband—wealth, *largesce*, power, beauty. (The images of wooing and marriage, deriving from the Song of Songs, also reappear in *Pearl*.) And of course in the medieval visual arts God is regularly represented as a king, and heaven as an earthly court. If the heavenly order is to be represented in earthly images at all (and earthly images are all we know), what images could an aristocratic society better choose than those of earthly royalty? But intelligent people in the fourteenth century knew as well as we do that these images were only images, not realities; and so we find the author of *The Cloud of Unknowing* referring scathingly to those naïvely devout men who 'wil make a God as hem lyst, and clothen Hym ful richely in clothes, and set Hym in a trone, fer more curiously than ever was He depeynted in this erthe. Thees men wil maken aungelles in bodely licnes, and set hem aboute ich one with diverse minstralsie, fer more corious than ever was any seen or herde in this

---

[1] D. S. Brewer, 'Courtesy and the *Gawain*-Poet', p. 59.

liif.'[1] What the *Gawain*-poet has done in *Pearl* is to find a way of simultaneously using such material images for the divine and making us aware of their inadequacy. He does this by means of his naïve Dreamer, who can see the grandeur into which his pearl entered on the other side of death only in grossly material terms, as a higher social status. It would not be a great exaggeration to think of him as something of a snob; he has at least a keen sense of social status, a tendency to see reality in terms of social differences (one of his first thoughts on seeing the Maiden in her new state was that her face was 'sade *for doc other erle*' [211]), and a powerful curiosity about how the great live in their heavenly world. This must not be taken to imply that the *Gawain*-poet is as scornful as the *Cloud*-author of the use of royal and courtly images for heaven, or that he totally dissociates himself from the Dreamer's view of them. On the contrary, they are an essential part of his poem, and he clearly takes a real and unashamed delight in describing the grandeur and glitter of the heavenly world and the heavenly city. For him, as not perhaps for us, such images remained natural and viable. But it is significant that he represents God himself not as a great king or lord, but (following the Apocalypse) as the Lamb, a far more mysterious and unearthly image, in which magnificence is strangely mingled with suffering.

To return to the text: the Maiden expresses her approval of the Dreamer's new humility:

> 'Now blysse, burne, mot the bytyde,'
> Then sayde that lufsoum of lyth and lere,
> 'And welcum here to walk and byde,
> For now thy speche is to me dere.
> Maysterful mod and hyghe pryde,
> I hete the, arn heterly hated here.' (397–402)

His emotional readjustment makes possible further intellectual progress, and she at once explains, simply and openly, the terms of her new life. She is married to the Lamb of God, he has crowned her as his queen forever, and as such she is 'sesed in alle hys herytage' (417). Inevitably, the Dreamer takes this explanation with complete literalness, and understands it in earthly terms. Taken in this way, it is indeed startling, and his first reaction is a shocked remark, halfway between question and exclamation: '"Blysful," quod I,

---

[1] Ed. Phyllis Hodgson, p. 105.

"may thys be trwe?"' (421). He quickly pulls himself up, afraid of
having offended her, only to repeat the question:

> Dysplesez not if I speke errour.
> Art thou the quene of hevenez blwe,
> That al thys world schal do honour? (422–4)

He imagines that she must be claiming to have supplanted the Blessed
Virgin herself, for the kingdom of heaven, like earthly kingdoms, can
surely have only one queen at a time. She carefully explains that this
is not so:

> The court of the kyndom of God alyve
> Hatz a property in hytself beyng:
> Alle that may therinne aryve
> Of alle the reme is quen other kyng,
> And never other yet schal depryve,
> But uchon fayn of otherez hafyng. (445–50)

This straightforward explanation makes as clear as possible the
difficulty of using the language of everyday affairs, rather than that of
poetic symbolism, about the divine. The Maiden's words are as
exact as possible, *depryve* belonging (like *herytage* earlier) to the
technical language of law, and *property* either to the same technical
language or to that of scholastic philosophy,[1] yet taken together they
make up a statement which in earthly terms is nonsensical. The
Dreamer makes the best effort he can to accommodate himself to
what he says:

> 'Cortaysé,' quod I, 'I leve,
> And charyté grete, be yow among.' (469–70)

But he still cannot swallow it entirely, and, with indignation breaking
through his caution, he continues:

> Bot—my speche that yow ne greve—
> Thyself in heven over hygh thou heve,
> To make the quen that watz so yonge! (471–4)[2]

It is her youth that sticks in his throat. If only she were a little older,
she might somehow deserve this extraordinary promotion; as it is,

---

[1] On legal terminology in *Pearl*, see Kean, pp. 185 ff.
[2] There is a discrepancy in the line-numbering here, because Gordon and other editors
assume that a line has accidentally been omitted from the manuscript between *greve*
and *Thyself.*

he cannot bring himself either to believe or to approve anything so
out of keeping with his ideas of justice:

> That cortaysé is to fre of dede,
> Yyf hyt be soth that thou conez saye.
> Thou lyfed not two yer in oure thede;
> Thou cowthez never God nauther plese ne pray,
> Ne never nawther Pater ne Crede;
> And quen mad on the fyrst day!
> I may not traw, so God me spede,
> That God wolde wrythe so wrange away.
> Of countes, damysel, par ma fay,
> Wer fayr in heven to hald asstate,
> Other ellez a lady of lasse aray;
> Bot a quene! Hit is to dere a date. (481–92)

It is delightful that he should think of the court of heaven in such
thoroughly earthly terms as to feel that it would be tolerable for her
to be a countess in it, but not a queen; and this is perfectly in keeping
with the sense of social distinctions he showed on first seeing her,
when he thought her face 'sade for doc other erle' (211). A countess
is the wife of an earl. And the speech is amusing not only in its
naïve assumptions, but in the vigorous colloquialism of their expression. His indignation reaches its height when he has to mention the
offensive word 'queen': we notice the almost angrily emphatic mono-
syllables of 'And quen mad on the fyrst day!' and the outraged
squeak in the last line of the stanza: 'Bot a quene! Hit is to dere a
date.' He would rather accuse God of extravagance than accept
that. As everywhere in his work, the *Gawain*-poet shows a brilliant
gift for mimicking tones of voice; to do this within the intricate metrical form of *Pearl* demands a virtuosity unusual even for him.

It is in answer to this indignant incredulity of the Dreamer's that
the Maiden repeats and expounds the parable of the vineyard, which
we examined earlier. That part of the poem (lines 493–588) is purely
discursive, not even dramatic, and I need say no more about it here.
Not till after the Maiden has finished re-telling the parable does the
Dreamer once more intervene, with his insistence on judging things
for himself—an insistence for which we may feel grateful, even
while recognizing its unwisdom, since he voices doubts we may share.
He has made some progress; though his tone of voice has its usual
resolute earthliness, he is now measuring the Maiden's statements not
merely against common sense but against Biblical authority:

> Then more I meled and sayde apert,
> 'Me thynk thy tale unresounable.
> Goddez ryght is redy and evermore rert,
> Other Holy Wryt is bot a fable.
> In Sauter is sayde a verce overte.' (589–93)

Perhaps his characteristic 'Me thynk' may remind us of the repeated 'uus thynk' (552–3) of the disgruntled workmen in the parable; he has much in common with them. The Maiden recognizes his mood of scholastic disputatiousness—'Bot now thou motez, me for to mate' (613)—and once more answers in purely discursive terms, with an exposition of the roles of grace and justice in determining the fate of human souls, in which she first reverts to the parable to expound it allegorically, and then produces appropriate Scriptural texts to confirm her argument. We examined her treatment of these at an earlier stage. She concludes by referring to the Crucifixion as a deed more powerful than any abstract argument:

> Forthy to corte quen thou schal com
> Ther alle oure causez schal be tryed,
> Alegge the ryght, thou may be innome,
> By thys ilke spech I have asspyed;
> Bot he on rode that blody dyed,
> Delfully thurgh hondez thryght,
> Gyve the to passe, when thou arte tryed,
> By innocens and not by ryghte. (701–8)

After so much discourse, this plain reference to the Crucifixion as an irreducible human event has an extraordinary emotive power. It leads the Maiden back to speak of the Ministry of Christ, again in simple and human terms: her place in heaven is to be justified ultimately not by bandying texts and arguments but by Christ's saying,

> Do way, let chylder unto me tyght,
> To suche is hevenryche arayed. (718–19)

Symbolism resumed

On the question of the salvation of the innocent there is no more to be said; but now that this question has been settled, the poem can at last revert to its former course and former method of developing symbolism. Christ's words about 'the kingdom of heaven' lead

159

naturally into another parable of the kingdom, this time one of the shortest, that of the pearl of great price:

Iterum simile est regnum caelorum homini negotiatori quaerenti bonas margaritas;

Inventa autem una pretiosa margarita, abiit, et vendidit omnia quae habuit, et emit eam. (Matthew xiii. 45–6)

(Again the kingdom of heaven is like to a merchant seeking good pearls.

Who, when he had found one pearl of great price, went his way and sold all that he had and bought it.)

The mention of pearls makes possible the resumption of pearl symbolism, after the long discursive central section:

> Ther is the blys that con not blynne
> That the jueler soghte thurgh perré pres,
> And solde alle hys goud, bothe wolen and lynne,
> To bye hym a perle watz mascellez. (729–32)

The fact that we have here a planned resumption of the symbolism, rather than one dependent on chance associations, is demonstrated by the way in which the symbol is taken up again in section XIII at precisely the point at which it was abandoned in section v. The point at which the Dreamer's understanding failed was the image of the transformation of the rose into the pearl, and at that point, for the first time, the pearl was called a 'perle of prys' (272). Now, over 450 lines later, comes the parable of the pearl of great price. Moreover, in the refrain-lines of section v, the Dreamer was being referred to as a jeweller, with implications perhaps of materialism. The Maiden, for example, seemed to be using the language of trade, of profit and loss, for his benefit in a very pointed way:

> And thou hatz called thy wyrde a thef,
> That oght of noght hatz mad the cler. (273–4)[1]

Now the image of the jeweller is redeemed by that of the merchant of the parable. Both the pearl and the jeweller remain viable as symbols, because they can include heavenly as well as earthly meanings. Recognition of this should perhaps modify the light in which one sees the human drama of the encounter between Dreamer and Maiden. I have been emphasizing mainly the gap between the two,

[1] I think this a more plausible interpretation of the lines than A. L. Kellogg's suggestion (*Traditio*, XII [1956], 406–7) that they allude to the doctrine of *creatio ex nihilo*, for this would not explain *thef* or *cler* (cf. 'a clear profit').

with its consequences of the Dreamer's misunderstanding and the Maiden's apparent cruelty towards him. But symbols provide the means of bridging the gap between earthly and heavenly understanding, as the Scriptural parables of the kingdom bear witness. There is difference between the heavenly and earthly worlds, but there is also continuity, a continuity figured, for example, in the fact that the 'gardyn gracios gaye' of the dream is only another version of the 'erber grene' in which the narrator fell asleep. The earthly rose does not disappear, to be replaced by the heavenly pearl; it is 'put in pref' to (proves to be) a pearl. This complex relationship between the earthly and the heavenly is easily misunderstood. It is misunderstood by the Dreamer, who persistently sees only continuity between them; it is misunderstood by those modern scholars who see only difference.[1] But the poem itself, with the delicacy and subtlety of poetic symbolism, opens the way to a truer understanding.

The Maiden proceeds immediately with a stanza in exposition of the parable of the pearl which seems designed to sum up the pearl symbolism as so far developed, and to take it further through the association with the kingdom of heaven:

> This makellez perle, that boght is dere,
> The joueler gef fore alle hys god,
> Is lyke the reme of hevenesse clere:
> So sayde the Fader of folde and flode;
> For hit is wemlez, clene, and clere,
> And endelez rounde, and blythe of mode,
> And commune to alle that ryghtwys were.
> Lo, even inmyddez my breste hit stode.
> My Lorde the Lombe, that schede hys blode,
> He pyght hit there in token of pes.
> I rede the forsake the worlde wode
> And porchace thy perle maskelles. (733–44)

Here some of the associations previously accumulated by the symbol are gathered together. 'Wemlez, clene, and clere' reminds one of previous phrases such as 'wythouten wemme' and 'wythouten spot',

---

[1] For example, Sister Hillmann, ed. *The Pearl*; W. S. Johnson, 'The Imagery and Diction of *The Pearl*', *ELH*, xx (1953), 161–80: 'The result is an emphasis upon a ubiquitous sense of contrast between the nature of heaven and the nature of earth, the revelation of which seems, for our present reading, to be the poem's main purpose' (p. 163); and S. de Voren Hoffman, 'The *Pearl*: Notes for an Interpretation', *MP*, LVIII (1960–1), 73–80: 'in the poem we find together several meanings of the pearl figure and…they are kept distinct' (p. 76).

and attention is now focused on the single pearl at the Maiden's breast, as it were the symbol of the symbol. This is available to the Dreamer as well as to the Maiden; but there would surely be no point in trying to distinguish separate layers of meaning in the pearl, and to differentiate between the pearl as the Maiden and the pearl as the kingdom of heaven, which is not her private possession but is 'commune to alle that ryghtwys were'. These figurative senses are inextricably entangled, and any attempt to schematize them is only too likely to result in an impoverished perception of the richness of the symbolic whole. The poetry works not by distinction but by fusion. The mingling of the various senses is recognized by the Dreamer in the very phrasing of his answer, in which 'he sums up the complex symbolism of the passage'[1] we have been discussing:

> 'O maskelez perle in perlez pure,
> That berez,' quod I, 'the perle of prys.' (745–6)

The Dreamer goes on to ask who created her beauty, but before she can answer that question he asks another, which betrays once more his preoccupation with status: 'quat kyn offys' (755) does she hold in heaven? She answers that she is the bride of the Lamb of God, and repeats the invitation of the Song of Songs which he addressed to her:

> Cum hyder to me, my lemman swete,
> For mote ne spot is non in the. (763–4)

The Dreamer then asks who this Lamb of God is; and in doing so he shows in its most materialistic form his preoccupation with social advancement. He imagines her progress as one of ruthless social climbing, elbowing aside all possible rivals, and culminating in an unparalleled triumph over them:

> Quat kyn thyng may be that Lambe
> That the wolde wedde unto hys vyf?
> Over alle other so hygh thou clambe
> To lede wyth hym so ladyly lyf.
> So mony a comly on-uunder cambe
> For Kryst han lyved in much stryf;
> And thou con alle tho dere out dryf
> And fro that maryag al other depres,
> Al only thyself so stout and styf,
> A makelez may and maskellez. (771–80)

[1] Dorothy Everett, *Essays on Middle English Literature*, p. 93.

The Dreamer is now prepared to accept that the Maiden really has achieved the highest rank, but he has clearly not understood her earlier explanation of the universal kingship and queenship of the blessed. The tone of his remarks is roughly that of a bourgeois father's astonished admiration at his daughter's unexpected marriage with the royal family's most eligible bachelor. And this tone is supported by the strikingly secular implications of some of the terms he applies to her. 'Comly on-uunder cambe' is a formula belonging to a formulaic system regularly applied to ladies in romances and love-poems; two other examples are 'lufsum under lyne', applied to the lady in *Sir Gawain and the Green Knight* (1814), and 'geynest under gore' from the Harley lyric *Alysoun*.[1] 'Stout and styf' is another alliterative formula, belonging to medieval romance, but implying the heroic resolution of the warrior rather than the modesty appropriate to a lady.[2] We can reasonably deduce that such phrases would have seemed glaringly inappropriate to the Maiden's true nature, and it is possible that for a courtly fourteenth-century audience they would have called up the vulgar world of popular romance (such as Chaucer parodies in *Sir Thopas*). Certainly they reveal the Dreamer's absurd failure to grasp the truth about the Maiden's position.

Patiently, she explains once more that she is *maskelles* but not *makeles*; indeed, she is only one of the Lamb's 144,000 brides. She goes on to attempt an answer to the question 'Quat kyn thyng may be that Lambe?' She does so by quoting the main Scriptural sources for the doctrine of the Lamb of God. The first of these is in Isaiah liii, the passage concerning the 'man of sorrows' on whom the sins of the world were laid, and who 'shall be led as a sheep to the slaughter and shall be dumb as a lamb before his shearer, and he shall not open his mouth' (Isaiah liii. 7). She relates this in turn to the second source, John the Baptist's welcoming of Christ as the fulfilment of the prophecy in Isaiah: 'The next day, John saw Jesus coming to him; and he saith: Behold the Lamb of God. Behold him who taketh away the sin of the world' (John i. 29). Finally she links these two texts to the Apocalypse, in which the other St John saw the Lamb standing in the midst of the throne of God (Apocalypse v. 6). Thus the poet brings together the three chief Scriptural occurrences of the Lamb: the foreshadowing in Isaiah, the historical event in St John's Gospel, and the heavenly fulfilment in the Apocalypse. The typological

---

[1] *English Lyrics of the Thirteenth Century*, ed. Carleton Brown (Oxford, 1932), p. 140.
[2] See the detailed discussion of *styf* in Borroff, pp. 79–81.

pattern is complete, explicitly completed by the poet, rather than left hidden as an allegory.

The Maiden repeats her earlier explanation that, by being married to the Lamb, she is not keeping out anyone else: every day, she says, the Lamb brings in a new supply of brides, and yet they never quarrel with each other. On the contrary, their attitude is 'the more the merrier'; this is the very phrase she uses: 'The mo the myryer, so God me blesse' (850). The down-to-earth colloquialism is no doubt intentionally comic, and it throws a comic light back upon the Dreamer, whose materialism makes it necessary. The Maiden proceeds to quote the Apocalypse to him at some length, to prove that what she says is true, but we need not examine the passage here. Now at last it seems that the Dreamer has grasped that she is only one among many royal brides, but this leads him to think of another question, in which his materialism shows itself once more. He prefaces it with an elaborate complimentary address, very different from his blunt contradictions earlier in the poem. He has understood and accepted the distance between them, and has found a *cortays* rhetoric appropriate to her grandeur and his lowliness:

> 'Never the les let be my thonc,'
> Quod I, 'My perle, thagh I appose;
> I schulde not tempte thy wyt so wlonc,
> To Krystez chambre that art ichose.
> I am bot mokke and mul among,
> And thou so ryche a reken rose,
> And bydez here by thys blysful bonc
> Ther lyvez lyste may never lose.
> Now, hynde, that sympelnesse conez enclose,
> I wolde the aske a thynge expresse,
> And thagh I be bustwys as a blose,
> Let my bone vayl neverthelese.
>
> 'Neverthelese cler I yow bycalle,
> If ye con se hyt be to done;
> As thou art gloryous wythouten galle,
> Wythnay thou never my ruful bone.' (901–16)

In this open acknowledgment of his own inferiority the Dreamer achieves a real dignity, but at last he brings out his naïve question. If she is only one of a great company of brides, wherever do they live?

Haf ye no wonez in castel-walle,
Ne maner ther ye may mete and won? (917–18)

In giving the Dreamer these thoughts of a castle or mansion as possible dwelling-places, the poet is of course following the technique
explained earlier: he is making use of the traditional images for
heavenly things used in his time, but at the same time, by letting the
Dreamer employ them with exaggerated and comic naïveté, he is
indicating that they cannot really be taken literally. The Maiden
has spoken of Jerusalem, but the Dreamer knows that that is in
Judaea, so the brides cannot dwell there, yet their sheer numbers must
demand a great city for them to live in:

> Thys motelez meyny thou conez of mele,
> Of thousandez thryght so gret a route,
> A gret ceté, for ye arn fele,
> Yow byhod have, wythouten doute.
> So cumly a pakke of joly juele,
> Wer evel don schulde lyy theroute! (925–30)

One would not be wrong, I think, to detect in those last two lines a
delightfully breezy colloquialism, which at the same time conveys the
Dreamer's innocently kindly masculine concern at the thought of a
crowd of helpless girls sleeping rough.

The Maiden reassures him with her explanation of the existence
of two Jerusalems, one earthly and the other heavenly. In answer to
his request to see the heavenly city where she dwells, she tells him
that 'thurgh gret favor' (968) of the Lamb he may see it from outside,
though not from within. There follows the detailed description,
closely based on the Apocalypse. This again is a passage we have
considered already, with its jewel imagery and brilliant light, and
the Dreamer's assurance that his experience would not have been
possible 'in the body'. Just as during the earlier long passage based
on Scripture (the parable of the vineyard, lines 497 ff.), symbol and
drama are here in abeyance. There they gave way to narrative and
exposition; here to description. Miss Kean is right, I think, in judging
that there is a certain lack of pressure in the poetry of this part of
Pearl: 'Necessary as an effective set piece is to the plan of the poem, it
does not, in fact, seem to engage the poet's concentrated attention;
and he seems to depend on his reader's reaction to the general effect,
and to recognition of a familiar context, rather than on his usual

technical skill'.[1] We found a similar failing (so it appears to a modern reader) in the description of the temple vessels in *Purity*: a mere collection of details, in which poetry attempts to do the work of painting, and necessarily fails to embody the required significance. Such failures are so common in medieval literature that we can perhaps do no better than to record that we have encountered something that appealed to medieval taste but does not appeal to ours. For medieval poets and their audiences, exhaustive descriptions and lists seem to have had an attraction so great that they often demanded nothing more. A parallel example from a fourteenth-century dream-poem is the list of fourteen varieties of trees in *The Parlement of Foules*; one from elsewhere in the *Gawain*-poet's work is the lengthy explanation in *Sir Gawain and the Green Knight* of the various symbolic significances of the pentangle. In none of these cases would we be prepared to call the passage poetry; it is rather an inset into the poem of a different kind of material, highly relevant to its significance but not continuous with it in literary substance. This descriptive passage, however, becomes once more enlivened with drama from the point at which the Dreamer reminds us of his own presence as a witness, so overcome as to be certain that he could not have been 'in the body', and amusingly undignified in his stunned state: 'I stod as stylle as dased quayle' (1085). What follows certainly is poetry. Heralded by the haunting simile of moonrise in daylight comes the procession of virgin-brides, in which the development of the pearl symbolism is taken a stage further, for they are all arrayed like his own pearl:

> Depaynt in perlez and wedez qwyte;
> In uchonez breste watz bounden boun
> The blysful perle wyth gret delyt. (1102–4)

The Dreamer can now see for himself that they are not jostling for position, as an earthly procession might, and he innocently notes this surprising fact: 'Thagh thay wern fele, no pres in plyt' (1114). At their head is the Lamb himself. In describing the Lamb, the poet does not, as we might expect, allow the Dreamer's naïve vision to make him familiar or homely. On the contrary, he brings out the full exoticism of the Apocalypse, the almost nightmare quality of St John's apprehension of the nature of God. The Lamb, 'Wyth hornez seven of red golde cler' (1111) and pearly-white coat, surrounded by

[1] Kean, p. 215.

prostrate elders and incense-scattering angels, suggests for the moment the god of a totemistic cult stranger and crueller than Christianity as we usually think of it. Only for the moment, however. This is no cruel beast-god, but one with 'lokez symple, hymself so gent' (1134), and he has in his side the bleeding wound of the crucified Christ. The wound is described with the simplest of alliterative formulas, 'wyde and weete' (1135)[1]—it is an ordinary wound, gaping and messy—and it arouses in the Dreamer a touchingly simple compassion and incredulity that anyone could have been so cruel as to cause it. It is as if he were feeling the reality of Christ's sufferings for the first time:

> Bot a wounde ful wyde and weete con wyse
> Anende hys herte, thurgh hyde torente.
> Of hys quyte syde his blod outsprent.
> Alas, thoght I, who did that spyt?
> Ani breste for bale aght haf forbrent
> Er he therto hade had delyt. (1135–40)[2]

The mixture of feelings aroused by this description of the Lamb and his procession has, I find, an extraordinarily disturbing power: squalor in majesty, pain in triumph. Already disturbed by this, the Dreamer is still more agitated by the sight of his 'lyttel quene' (1147) among the virgin-brides. All that he has learned about the necessary distance between them is overwhelmed by 'luf-longyng' (1152), and he makes his ill-fated attempt to cross the stream.

This attempt, as the Dreamer ought to have recognized before making it, is displeasing to God—'Hit watz not at my Pryncez paye' (1164)—and in consequence 'That braththe out of my drem me

---

[1] Cf. *The Destruction of Troy*, ed. Panton and Donaldson, 'wyde woundes and wete' (1329); *York Mystery Plays*, ed. Lucy Toulmin Smith, 'woundes wete' (p. 406, line 200 and p. 411, line 283) (these are Christ's wounds).

[2] Miss Kean (p. 210) notes the 'prosaic terms' in which the wound is described, and compares the Dreamer's reaction, which she sees as 'lack of comprehension', with that of the Chaucerian Dreamer in *The Book of the Duchess* to the news that the man in black's lady is dead. She remarks; 'What is appropriate to a courtly poem addressed to a patron, seems oddly at variance with a moment which, we feel, would normally call for a much higher emotional tension.' It is true that 'the glimpse of the New Jerusalem and its triumphant host cannot be a personal triumph for the Dreamer' (p. 211), but I think Miss Kean underrates the emotional charge that can be carried by simple language. To see and feel for the first time the reality of Christ's suffering, and to see that suffering as borne at the very heart of triumph, is to achieve illumination (admittedly not of an advanced kind), not misunderstanding.

brayde' (1170). He is suddenly returned to the waking world, to the garden and pearl of the poem's opening:

> Then wakned I in that erber wlonk;
> My hede upon that hylle watz layde
> Ther as my perle to grounde strayd. (1171–3)

He has shown the sin of Jonah, impatience, and he ruefully reflects that if he had submitted to the will of God he might have seen more of his secrets:

> To that Pryncez paye hade I ay bente,
> And yerned no more then watz me gyven,
> And halden me ther in trwe entent,
> As the perle me prayed that watz so thryven,
> As helde, drawen to Goddez present,
> To mo of his mysterys I hade ben dryven. (1189–94)

The moral he draws is entirely in keeping with *Patience*:

> Lorde, mad hit arn that agayn the stryven,
> Other proferen the oght agayn thy paye. (1199–1200)

But the situation is more complex than at the end of *Patience*. The 'hero' of *Patience* is 'he', and there is no sign that Jonah has learned anything from his experience: the moral is for us. But the 'hero' of *Pearl* is 'I', and the Dreamer has learned something himself, as well as providing an *exemplum* for us. The dream-experience has not been wasted on him, for the moral he draws from it also applies to the rebellious feelings he had been displaying at the beginning of the poem towards the loss of his pearl. Now, assured by his vision that she is not really lost, but is one of the circle of the blessed, he is able to win through to acceptance of her death and even, through seeing how happy her state now is, to rejoicing at it:

> If hit be veray and soth sermoun
> That thou so stykez in garlande gay,
> So wel is me in thys doel-doungoun
> That thou art to that Prynsez paye. (1185–8)

The Dreamer has been changed by his dream, yet we feel the change to be precarious—as precarious, say, as the change brought about at the end of *The Tempest*. It will always be possible to return from the end of the poem to its beginning, and to start the wheel revolving once more. But for the moment a genuine change of attitude has occurred, and it is not implausibly extreme. The Dreamer still finds the world a 'doel-doungoun', but he can now recognize his own impatience, and is ready to commit his pearl voluntarily into the hands of God:

> And sythen to God I hit bytaghte,
> In Krystez dere blessyng and myn. (1207–8)

One question remains to be considered: does the poem tell us anything about the nature of the further *mysterys* that the Dreamer might have seen if he had not been impatient and tried to cross the river? It is of the essence of *Pearl* that, through the Dreamer's imperfection, the visionary experience should remain incomplete, and indeed, if the poem is to remain a poem, it has to break off short of any closer approach to the ineffable. But the necessary sense of incompleteness, by which the Dreamer is made miserable at the end—

> Me payed ful ille to be outfleme
> So sodenly of that fayre regioun,
> Fro alle tho syghtez so quyke and queme.
> A longeyng hevy me strok in swone... (1177–80)

—could be conveyed to us all the more fully if we had some hint of what further illumination he had lost. I believe that the poem does offer such a hint, and that the clue to it is found once more in the development of the pearl symbolism. A final and incomplete stage in this development has been taking place during the long passage based on the Apocalypse. The qualities of the pearl have been gradually extended, as we have seen, to include the other world of the dream, the kingdom of heaven and the new Jerusalem, which had

> uch yate of a margyrye,
> A parfyt perle that never fatez. (1037–8)

But in particular there are suggestions that the Lamb of God too can be seen as an aspect of the poem's central symbol (or rather that the pearl can be seen as a reflection of the Lamb). In answering the Dreamer's question 'Quat kyn thyng may be that Lambe?' (771), the Maiden has referred to Christ as 'My Lombe, my Lorde, my dere juelle' (795). *Juelle* is a term which has previously been applied to the Maiden herself—

> That juel thenne in gemmez gente (253)

> A juel to me then watz thys geste,
> And juelez wern hyr gentyl sawez (277–8)

169

—and it is later applied once more to the Lamb, whose followers 'Al songe to love that gay juelle' (1124). Other key qualities of the pearl are also found in him. He is white and spotless:

> Thys Jerusalem Lombe hade never pechche
> Of other huee bot quyt jolyf
> That mot ne masklle moght on streche,
> For wolle quyte so ronk and ryf; (841–4)

> The Lompe ther wythouten spottez blake. (945)

Finally, when the Dreamer actually sees the Lamb for the first time he sees this whiteness as explicitly pearl-like; 'As praysed perlez his wedez wasse' (1112). We seem to have here the briefest glimpse of a potential culmination of the visionary experience, by which the Lamb and the pearl would be identified, and the Dreamer would see in the precious stone the ground of its own preciousness; or, to put it differently, would recognize in the human soul the image of God. Such a perception would belong to mystical experience, however, and, as I have argued earlier, though the *Gawain*-poet probably knew the devotional writings of his time, he neither was nor supposed himself to be a mystic. Still less is his Dreamer a mystic; but I think it likely that, in the potential identification of Lamb and pearl (similar to, but higher than, the achieved identification of pearl and rose), the poet hinted at a culmination from which the Dreamer was excluded.

5

Sir Gawain and the Green Knight

The story

Sir Gawain and the Green Knight, the *Gawain*-poet's best known
and most admired work, differs from his other three poems in being
more essentially a narrative than they are. It is not an *exemplum* set
in a homily, or a vision with explicit and detailed doctrine at its heart,
but a story. Like *Patience* and *Pearl*, it has its tail in its mouth; but
what it emerges from and returns to is not a moral truth but the
process of legendary British history, that larger tale of alternating
'blysse and blunder' (18) in which it is only an incident. This essentially narrative quality of the poem gives it a self-sufficiency, and
independence of moral schemata, whose consequences we shall have
to examine later. For the moment, let us consider the story which is
the poem's principle of structure or, in Aristotelian terms, its 'soul'.
This story is made up of a number of traditional elements—the
Beheading Game, the Temptation, the Exchange of Winnings—
which can be traced back over several centuries, but it is generally
agreed that these elements are not found linked together in any
possible source for the poem.[1] It may be, of course, that the poet was
using a lost source in which they were linked, and that we should take
literally his claim to be repeating the story 'as I in toun herde' (31)
or 'As hit is breved in the best boke of romaunce' (2521). Perhaps
some such source may one day be brought to light out of the tangled
forest of medieval French romance. But it is perfectly possible that
it was the poet himself who first brought the plot-elements together.
As we shall see later, the skill with which he employs his narrative
structure to convey his meaning makes this more likely. At any rate,
in reading his poem, we are not in a position, as we were with

---

[1] Source studies have exercised a peculiar, and perhaps unjustifiably great, fascination
over students of *Gawain*. For accounts of analogues and possible sources, see L. H.
Loomis, in *Arthurian Literature in the Middle Ages*, ed. R. S. Loomis (Oxford, 1959),
pp. 530–7; Norman Davis, ed. *Sir Gawain and the Green Knight*, pp. xv–xxi; and
above, p. 15, n. 3.

Purity, Patience and *Pearl*, to compare it line by line with an immediate source. It stands by itself, and it is generally agreed to stand as an excellent story, admirably told: the finest of all the romances in Middle English. The poem offers no problems of structure, and its division into four 'fitts', indicated by large decorated initials in the manuscript, seems satisfactory and has usually been retained by editors.[1] No reader could possibly have any difficulty in following the beautifully articulated plot; and when the plot is complete, so is the poem.

But though *Sir Gawain and the Green Knight* is essentially a story, it is not purely a story. Reading it for the first time, we are eager to know 'what happens next', but we also delight to read it again and again, long after the mere sequence of events is well known enough to surprise us no more. In part this lasting fascination of the poem is due to the satisfaction its plot gives as an aesthetic structure, in which the three main plot-elements are ingeniously linked together, and certain patternings recur throughout. Many of these are threes of one kind or another: three days' hunting, three meetings of the Lady and Gawain in Gawain's bedroom, three axe-blows at the Green Chapel, and many other minor groups of three.[2] Other patternings involve the recurrence of certain colours: green, predominantly, but also the gold with which it is often intertwined, and the red of blood.[3] Others again involve the repetition of events such as the two Christmas feasts, the two halves of the Beheading Game, the kisses Gawain receives from the Lady and passes on to her husband, and so on. Such effects, involving repetition and variation, are regularly found in oral literature, or literature with an oral basis, such as *chansons de geste* and ballads, and we whose training is with written literature may need reminding not to underestimate their power. But *Sir Gawain and the Green Knight,* though it belongs to a tradition with its roots in oral poetry, is far from being a ballad or *chanson de geste.* These are what we might call 'pure' narratives: works which are narratives and nothing else, in which the burden of interpreta-

[1] But cf. above, p. 43, n. 2.

[2] J. A. Burrow (p. 96, n. 29) notes that 'All threes in the poem are connected with Hautdesert', and lists a number of other threes.

[3] See J. F. Eagan, 'The Import of Color Symbolism in *Sir Gawain and the Green Knight*', *St Louis University Studies*, series A, Humanities I, 2 (1949), 11–86; William Goldhurst, 'The Green and the Gold: the Major Theme of *Gawain and the Green Knight*', *College English*, XX (1958), 61–5; and Burrow, pp. 14–16 and 39–40.

tion, of finding meaning and coherence in the events narrated, is thrown entirely upon the audience. *Sir Gawain and the Green Knight* is a romance, and it possesses those characteristics which Professor Vinaver has seen as fundamental to the genre:

romance was primarily a *literary* genre in the strict and perhaps somewhat narrow sense of the term: it was the product of trained minds, not of an uncritical and ingenuous imagination. To such minds an event in a work of narrative art could not be expressed merely by a plastically significant gesture or scene: it called for description and elaboration, it had to be related to its context and given its proper place in a sequence of co-ordinated occurrences. It was not enough for it to be impressive: it had to be made fully intelligible.[1]

Sir Gawain and the Green Knight offers its own detailed commentary on the story it tells, a commentary which both elaborates and inter-prets, in such a way as to make the story at once more specific and more general in its significance. This fact seems often to have been disregarded by those who have offered their own interpretation of the poem in terms of the primitive origins, real or supposed, of its plot-elements. Such interpreters will see in Gawain, 'the traditional Gawain who...was the hero, the agent who brought back the spring, restored the frozen life processes, revived the god—or (in later versions) cured the king', and will see in his pentangle 'an ancient life-symbol',[2] before they have exhausted or fully come to terms with the commentary included in the poem on the hero and his token. Gawain is a thoroughly self-conscious and articulate hero. His articulateness indeed is an essential part of his traditional virtue of courtesy, and his self-consciousness is used at crucial points in the poem to throw a clear light upon his feelings and motives. Thus when the Lady of the castle first comes creeping into his bedroom and he pretends to be asleep, we are left in no doubt as to what is going on in his mind:

> The lede lay lurked a ful longe quyle,
> Compast in his concience to quat that cace myght
> Meve other amount—to mervayle hym thoght,
> Bot yet he sayde in hymself, 'More semly hit were

[1] Eugène Vinaver, 'From Epic to Romance', *Bulletin of the John Rylands Library*, XLVI (1963–4), 476–503; p. 488.
[2] John Speirs, *Medieval English Poetry: the Non-Chaucerian Tradition* (London, 1957), pp. 220, 230.

To aspye wyth my spelle in space quat ho wolde.'
Then he wakenede, and wroth, and to hir warde torned,
And unlouked his yye-lyddez, and let as hym wondered,
And sayned hym, as by his sawe the saver to worthe. (1195–1202)

That *concience* (self-awareness) of Gawain's is an essential part of
the poem, and it has nothing to do with his supposed origin as a
sun-god. In the passage just quoted, several different techniques—
what Gawain says to himself, how he would have appeared, or wished
to appear, to the Lady, what the omniscient narrator knows of his
consciousness—are run expertly together to give a complete picture
of his inner and outer behaviour. The narrator has no hesitation in
telling us from his omniscience what feelings and principles Gawain
is motivated by, when this is necessary for our understanding of the
action's significance. For instance, at the evening meal in the castle
after the second day's hunting, we are not left merely as observers of
the behaviour of the Lady and Gawain, but are taken into Gawain's
consciousness and given a most detailed and subtle account of the
eddying conflict in his feelings:

And ever oure luflych knyght the lady bisyde.
Such semblaunt to that segge semly ho made
Wyth stille stollen countenaunce, that stalworth to plese,
That al forwondered watz the wyye, and wroth with hymselven,
Bot he nolde not for his nurture nurne hir ayaynez,
Bot dalt with hir al in daynté, how-se-ever the dede turned
    towrast. (1657–63)

That *nurture* which prevents Gawain from repelling the Lady's
forwardness, though it is characteristic of him, is not a quality peculiar to himself. It is good breeding: a quality widely understood in
medieval courtly society, and one that we too can feel our way into
with only a little trouble (the trouble largely of reading this very
poem). Thus the significance of the scene is extended; it takes on a
relevance to its audience's own lives, and in entering into Gawain's
situation they are reassessing their own values. Here we have a conflict involving both values and impulses ('wroth with hymselven'
suggesting that it is not a simple case of one against the other). At
other points, values are in conflict among themselves in Gawain's
mind, so that the whole system of Christian courtliness to which he
is committed—a commitment which the poem's audience no doubt
shared—is put under strain. This is so on the next day, when the

Lady renews her assault, and Gawain's *cortaysye*, chastity and loyalty are set at odds among themselves:

> For that prynces of pris depresed hym so thikke,
> Nurned hym so neghe the thred, that nede hym bihoved
> Other lach ther hir luf, other lodly refuse.
> He cared for his cortaysye, lest crathayn he were,
> And more for his meschef yif he schulde make synne,
> And be traytor to that tolke that that telde aght. (1770-5)[1]

The pentangle, too, is used by the poet to articulate the involvement of the story in moral issues of general relevance. I shall have more to say later about its significance, but here it is worth at least remarking that it is not left as 'an ancient life-symbol', but is given a detailed symbolic interpretation which shows how Gawain goes forth on his quest as the representative of a delicate complex of civilized and religious values.[2] They may be summarized in the terms of the fifth and last of the pentangle's fives: *fraunchyse, felawschyp, clannes, cortaysye* and *pité*.

Gawain is not the only character whose motives and values are in this way made explicit. Whether or not the poet applies his omniscience to them, they are all splendidly articulate. Arthur, for example, plays only a minor part in the poem, but nothing could be clearer than the complicated sequence and synthesis of motives revealed in the economical little scene immediately after the Green Knight has galloped away from Camelot, carrying his head in his hand:

> Thagh Arther the hende kyng at hert hade wonder,
> He let no semblaunt be sene, bot sayde ful hyghe
> To the comlych quene wyth cortays speche,
> 'Dere dame, today demay yow never;
> Wel bycommes such craft upon Christmasse,
> Laykyng of enterludez, to laghe and to syng,
> Among thise kynde caroles of knyghtez and ladyez.
> Never the lece to my mete I may me wel dres,
> For I haf sen a selly, I may not forsake.'
> He glent upon Sir Gawen, and gaynly he sayde,
> 'Now sir, henge up thyn ax, that hatz innogh hewen'. (467-77)

---

[1] For more detailed comment on the meaning of this passage, see Burrow, p. 100; and below, pp. 204-6.

[2] It is fair to add that Mr Speirs admits that in *Sir Gawain and the Green Knight* 'the pentangle has acquired a Christian significance' (p. 230), but he thereafter disregards that significance as completely as if it were not there. For my further comments, see below, pp. 196-8.

Here the combination of narratorial penetration and the *Gawain*-poet's usual gift for imitating tones of voice catches and crystallizes a whole range of varied motives as they stream past. First there is Arthur's bewilderment, then the courage and sense of kingly responsibility that enable him to keep it to himself. He is *hende*, a man of *cortays speche* (that is why the *cortays* Gawain can fitly take his place as the representative of Camelot), and he therefore turns first not, as we might expect, to Gawain, the main participant in the extraordinary scene which has just been transacted, but to Guinevere. An event of disturbing abnormality has occurred, and Arthur's first concern is therefore to reassure the queen and the courtiers by pushing it into the realm of the normal. And so, with sang-froid and a quick wit, he immediately classes the scene they have witnessed among the usual courtly entertainments of the Christmas season, and recaptures the situation before the Green Knight's entry by admitting with rueful irony that now at last he cannot deny that he has seen the wonder he was waiting for. Now he can eat, and the feasting can be resumed, as if nothing untoward had happened. Only after this, having done what he can to re-establish an atmosphere of normality, does he turn to Gawain, and address him with an appropriate manly brevity. This brevity is one kind of *cortaysye*; the loquaciousness of Gawain, master of 'the teccheles termes of talkyng noble' (917), and especially admired by ladies, is another. Arthur is generally a man of few words—this is his longest speech in the poem—and he is evidently given to this masculine curtness especially when addressing someone like Gawain, who is at once his vassal and his kinsman. We remember the forceful advice he gave Gawain earlier—perhaps out of the corner of his mouth, certainly in confidence—when he was about to strike his blow at the Green Knight:

> 'Kepe the, cosyn,' quoth the kyng, 'that thou on kyrf sette,
> And if thou redez hym ryght, redly I trowe
> That thou schal byden the bur that he schal bede after.' (372–4)

His words now are similarly packed with meaning. Once more his aim is to absorb the abnormal into the normal, and so, with a reassuring joke which is at the same time a skilful compliment, he classes the all-too-real axe he is holding with the metaphorical one of the proverb 'Hang up thine axe', meaning 'Have done with this business'.[1] Gawain's axe, however, is to be 'hung up' as a trophy over the dais.

[1] See Davis, ed. *Sir Gawain and the Green Knight*, note on lines 476–7, p. 87.

Even now we have by no means exhausted the implications of these lines, for they have their part to play not only in making this scene as fully comprehensible as possible, but in enriching the meaning of the whole poem. Thus Guinevere's fear, which is implied by the promptness with which Arthur reassures her, will be useful two thousand lines later in rendering more plausible the Green Knight's explanation that Morgan la Fay sent him to Camelot

> For to haf greved Gaynour and gart hir to dyye
> With glopnyng of that ilke gome that gostlych speked
> With his hede in his honde bifore the hyghe table. (2460–2)

Again, Arthur's classification of the entry and beheading of the Green Knight with the *enterludez* appropriate to the Christmas season has a wider significance than might appear, for it seems likely that such pageants really could have formed part of the Christmas festivities in the court for which the poet wrote.[1] Arthur's words thereby help to reinforce the ambivalent suspension of the action between jest and earnest which is found throughout the poem. After all, the Green Knight announced that he had come to Camelot to seek 'a Crystemas gomen' (283).

We may surely say that in this little scene the *Gawain*-poet has succeeded in what Vinaver sees as the romance-writer's aim of making the event 'intelligible', and that he has done so with an economy that puts to shame the diffuseness of the kind of commentary that is necessary to bring out all its implications. And throughout the poem the *Gawain*-poet employs his exquisitely clarifying art to the same purpose: sometimes by the means we have been discussing, of revealing speech and explicit analysis of motive, at other times by other means that Vinaver mentions, such as description. Description is an essential part of the medieval *ars poetica*, and it is used with great skill in passages describing persons (such as the Green Knight at lines 137–220 and the old and young ladies at 943–69), seasons (the cycle of the year at 500–33), or places (the castle at 781–802, the Green Chapel and its surroundings at 2163–84).[2] But it cannot be said that the poem as a whole is rendered '*fully* intelligible' in this way. Not everything in it is equally clear. On the one hand, for example, we are never given any external description of Gawain's

---

[1] See Elizabeth Wright, '*Sir Gawain and the Green Knight*', *JEGP*, XXXIV (1935), 157–79, p. 158, followed by Speirs, *Medieval English Poetry*, p. 219. On the appearance of the somewhat similar 'wild man' figure in pageants, see Benson, pp. 79–80.

[2] See D. A. Pearsall, 'Rhetorical Descriptio in *Sir Gawain and the Green Knight*'.

appearance, comparable with that of the Green Knight just mentioned or that of the lord of the castle at lines 843–9. On the other hand—and this is a lack we feel much more sharply—the motives of the Green Knight in either of his roles are never laid bare in the way Gawain's are, and those of his accomplices are left in similar obscurity. We are occasionally given an insight into his wife's motives, of a delicacy comparable with that employed on Gawain or Arthur, with the outward appearance shown to conceal a complex inner experience. This occurs, for example, towards the end of her first visit to his bedroom, when she seems almost to give up hope of tempting him:

> And ay the lady let lyk as hym loved mych;
> The freke ferde with defence, and feted ful fayre.
> 'Thagh I were burde bryghtest,' the burde in mynde hade,
> 'The lasse luf in his lode'—for lur that he soght
>   boute hone. (1281–5)[1]

But such insights are rare in the case of the Lady, and altogether absent in the case of that puzzling character, the guide, who gives Gawain what appears to be a quite false account of the Green Knight, when they are on their way to the Green Chapel (2097–2109). And so far as the Green Knight himself is concerned, though he, like all the other characters, is thoroughly articulate in speech, there are only two points at which we are given even a hint of his inner thought and feelings. One is in his Sir Bertilak role, when Gawain arrives at his castle and discloses who he is, and Sir Bertilak gives a loud laugh, 'so lef hit hym thoght' (909). The other is in his Green Knight role, when Gawain, having received the slight cut in his neck at the Green Chapel, leaps up to defend himself, and the Green Knight sees his fearlessness and 'in hert hit hym lykez' (2335). Elsewhere, the Green Knight's inner life is left in complete darkness, and when, towards the end of the poem, Gawain attempts to pierce this and asks who he really is, he gets an answer concerning Morgan la Fay which has been widely felt to be nothing more than a sop to prevent him (and us) from asking more questions—'a bone for the rationalizing mind to play with, and to be kept quiet with'.[2] Moreover, the Green Knight

---

[1] It is not clear whether 'for lur that he soght/boute hone' is part of the Lady's thought or an explanation added by the poet. I believe the ambiguity to be intentional (as it could easily be in a poem written for reading aloud), and therefore revert to the punctuation of J. R. R. Tolkien and E. V. Gordon, ed. *Sir Gawain and the Green Knight*, corr. edn (Oxford, 1930), which brings it out better.

[2] Speirs, *Medieval English Poetry*, p. 218.

is provided with no equivalent to Gawain's pentangle—no explicit indication of the values to which he is committed.

One consequence of this failure of the poet to clarify the inner life or the ethical goals of the Green Knight in the way he does with Gawain and Arthur is that modern scholars and critics have felt the need to 'interpret' the Green Knight from outside, in much the same way that they have tried to interpret the central symbol of *Pearl*. It is on the face of it needless to interpret Sir Gawain in any other terms than those that are so abundantly supplied in the poem (though this has not stopped some modern readers from seeing him as a 'youthful hero whose task it is to bring back life' and who is tested 'to find out whether or not [he] is a fit agent to bring back the spring', or, more simply, as Everyman).[1] But there might seem to be more justification for finding an identity for the mysterious Green Knight, by relating him to symbolic systems outside the poem. The 'meanings' that have been found for the Green Knight have been almost as abundant and various as those that have been found for the pearl. Thus John Speirs has seen him as 'a recrudescence in poetry of the Green Man ...a descendant of the Vegetation or Nature god of almost universal and immemorial tradition...a reappearance in poetry of an old vegetation god.' L. D. Benson sees him as a combination of this Green Man with another figure in medieval iconology, the 'wild man' or 'wodwose', but he insists that the Green Man who appears in the poem as the Green Knight is not the pagan, folkloric figure Speirs describes but a courtly derivative, who had become fully acceptable to Christianity. By way of contrast with Speirs, who asserts that the Green Knight 'is life', and relates his greenness to vegetation, Heinrich Zimmer identifies him as death, and associates his greenness with that of corpses. A similarly total contrast may be found between B. S. Levy who sees him as the Devil and Hans Schnyder who identifies him as Christ.[2]

---

[1] For the former view, see Speirs, *Medieval English Poetry*, pp. 229, 236; for the latter, H. Schnyder, *Sir Gawain and the Green Knight* (Bern, 1961), and B. S. Levy, 'Gawain's Spiritual Journey: *Imitatio Christi* in *Sir Gawain and the Green Knight*', *Annuale Mediaevale*, VI (1965), 65–106.

[2] Speirs, *Medieval English Poetry*, pp. 219, 225, 226; Benson, pp. 56–95; Zimmer, *The King and the Corpse* (New York, 1956), 76–7 (a similar view is expressed by A. H. Krappe, 'Who *was* the Green Knight?', *Spec*, XIII [1938], 206–15); Levy, 'Gawain's Spiritual Journey' (and see also D. B. J. Randall, 'Was the Green Knight a Fiend?', *Studies in Philology*, LVII [1960], 479–91); Schnyder, *Sir Gawain and the Green Knight*, p. 41.

There have also been, as with the pearl symbol, attempts to 'explain' the Green Knight in biographical terms, by identifying him with some fourteenth-century nobleman, such as Amedeo VI of Savoy, known as the Green Count.[1] There can clearly be no reconciling of such divergent views, and, as with the symbolism of *Pearl*, the very variety of modern interpretations makes one inclined to doubt the validity of any claim to achieve a greater certainty of interpretation by studying external evidence than simply by reading the poem. As C. S. Lewis has written, with specific reference to the attempt to interpret the Green Knight in terms of pagan ritual, 'the surviving work of art is the only clue by which we can hope to penetrate the inwardness of the origins. It is either in art, or nowhere, that the dry bones are made to live again.'[2] It seems at any rate that there are dangers in beginning one's study of *Sir Gawain and the Green Knight* by asking 'Who is the Green Knight?' and expecting an answer to that question will somehow 'solve' the poem. It is true that many critics find him more interesting than any other character in the poem, 'more human, more alive', as one of them has written, 'than Arthur and even Gawain', but I believe, and have tried to show elsewhere,[3] that this may be partly due to the predilection of modern criticism for concreteness and muscularity in poetry, and to a consequent failure to respond to the power of the different kind of poetry associated with Gawain. Without wishing to deny the fascination of the Green Knight or his poetic vitality, I prefer to begin studying the poem not with him, but with the story in which he plays a part, and with the poet's way of telling it.

The linked plots

We have seen that *Sir Gawain and the Green Knight* is made up of a combination of three plot-elements: the Beheading Game, the Temptation, and the Exchange of Winnings. The poet has often been praised for the skill with which he links these elements together, but

---

[1] See J. R. Hulbert, '*Syr Gawayn and the Grene Knyȝt*', *MP*, XIII (1915–6), 689–730, pp. 716–28; and S. R. T. O. D'Ardenne, '"The Green Count" and *Sir Gawain and the Green Knight*', *RES*, n.s. X (1959), 113–26.

[2] C. S. Lewis, 'The Anthropological Approach', in *English and Medieval Studies Presented to J. R. R. Tolkien*, ed. Norman Davis and C. L. Wrenn (London, 1962), pp. 219–30; p. 223.

[3] D'Ardenne, '"The Green Count" and *Sir Gawain*', p. 120; Spearing, *Criticism and Medieval Poetry*, pp. 38–45.

he has not perhaps been sufficiently praised for the way in which he makes this linkage itself convey the meaning of his poem. It is not simply a case (as often with medieval romances) of a given narrative having a new meaning imposed on it by such devices as those Vinaver mentions as typical of romance, and which we have just been examining at work in the poem. It is rather that the story is so arranged that it *is* the poem's meaning; or, to put it differently, meaning is not only defined by style, analysis of motive, characterization, and so on, but is enacted by the shape of the narrative itself. If the plot of *Sir Gawain and the Green Knight* was found rather than invented, it was even better chosen for the poet's purpose than that of *Patience*. In consequence, the poem affords a degree of satisfaction arising from economy almost unparalleled in medieval romance. It will be remembered that the plot-elements are not linked consecutively, but inserted one into another. Thus the Temptation is inserted into the Beheading Game, and is completed between the blow Gawain gives and the blows he receives. In the same way, the three parts of the Temptation are each inserted inside one of the hunting scenes and thus the Exchange of Winnings is intertwined with the Temptation, not consecutive with it, and it too is inserted into the Beheading Game. We know of course that the Temptation and the Exchange of Winnings are linked, or at least we come to know by the end of the first day of Temptation; but it is very important that we do not know until almost the end of the poem that these two elements have any connection with the Beheading Game.

The action of the poem begins with the Beheading Game, but first we are given a picture of the court which the Green Knight is to disrupt. The Camelot of this poem is a young Camelot, a place of gaiety and elegance, where a 'fayre folk in her first age' (54) is ruled over by a 'childgered' king (86), who cannot bear to do any one thing for long, 'So bisied him his yonge blod and his brayn wylde' (89). It is a delightful place, an innocent version of the ideal aimed at by any of the great courts of Western Europe in the later Middle Ages. It combines the religious and the secular virtues, and when we first see it, it is celebrating the Christmas and New Year festival first with Mass and then with presents and kissing games. When the Green Knight abruptly enters this festivity, just as the first course of the feast has been served, his challenge sets up a test which is in itself sufficiently difficult and exciting to engross our interest. The Green Knight announces that he has been drawn to Arthur's court by its fame, and particularly by its 'kydde cortaysye' (263), to request a Christmas game. But the nature of this game is so horrific as to stun the courtiers into an even deeper silence than the Green Knight's extraordinary appearance, and he exults over their discomfiture and the injury done to their fame. But although the courtiers may be frightened, Arthur is not: he answers angrily, immediately takes up the challenge, and plays a few practice strokes with the unfamiliar axe, to get the feel of it. It is at this point that Gawain intervenes, and, in a speech of poised modesty, begs to be allowed to take Arthur's place. There has been a persistent feeling among recent critics that Arthur and his court show up rather badly in this initial encounter with the Green Knight; but this seems to me an exaggerated view. The courtiers perhaps are less heroic than they might be in their response to the Green Knight's entry, and in their silence there is a definite hint of fear:

> As al were slypped upon slepe so slaked hor lotez,
>   in hyghe—
> I deme hit not al for doute,
> Bot sum for cortaysye—
> Bot let hym that al schulde loute
> Cast unto that wyye.[1] (244–9)

But Arthur's response is surely impeccable, despite the various criticisms that have been made of it. Baughan asserts that he strikes great blows at the Green Knight himself, but finds that they are in vain; this, however, is based on a misunderstanding of the text. Benson argues that 'Arthur's failure is that when he does take up the challenge he does so in exactly the churlish manner that the Green Knight had demanded. His shame and anger lead him to forget his famous courtesy entirely'. But Arthur's initial greeting of the stranger is highly courteous, and he answers him angrily only after receiving from him a number of unprovoked insults. Moorman suggests that we are encouraged to compare Arthur's court with Sir Bertilak's, to the detriment of the former, because better hospitality is offered to Gawain on his arrival than had been offered to the Green Knight; but to say this is surely to forget that Gawain does

---

[1] Borroff points out (p. 119) that the narrator's defence of the court against the imputation of cowardice actually has the effect of suggesting that they were afraid. A similar narratorial 'smear' technique is commonly found in Chaucer, especially directed against Criseyde in *Troilus and Criseyde*.

not offer any insults to his hosts—quite the reverse—nor is he 'half etayn' and bright green.[1] In general, it is surely the case that Arthur performs very creditably in the face of a quite unfamiliar physical danger. Still more admirable is the performance of Gawain, once he has stepped forward to beg that he may be substituted for Arthur as the respondent. Gawain addresses his plea to be allowed to take on the challenge not only to the king but to his council and to the queen. Arthur is no Renaissance tyrant but a medieval prince, ruling by the counsel of his nobles; and the queen is presumably added out of Gawain's famous *cortaysye*, which especially demands deference to ladies. The nobles agree that Gawain should take up the 'game' (365) the intruder proposes. Thus, when Gawain, with a formal gesture of submission, receives the Green Knight's axe from the king, he is becoming both his personal substitute and, in the most open and official way, the representative of the whole court, who is to redeem their initial hesitance. He then proceeds to ask the Green Knight what his name is and how to get to his court, so that he can present himself in a year's time to receive the return blow. It is clear that he sees the challenge he has accepted as being essentially a test of physical skill, strength and courage, and that he is so far responding to it honourably. He has promised to accept a return blow from the Green Knight's axe, and, though it will presumably kill him if he does not succeed in killing the Green Knight with his first blow, he is taking pains to find out where he must go to keep the appointment. It is clear that the onlookers see the test in this light. I have already quoted Arthur's advice to Gawain, to make sure of his opponent with his own axe-stroke, and then he will not need to worry about any return blow. The Green Knight appears to take the same view, because he says that he will give Gawain the information he needs after receiving his axe-stroke,

> And if I spende no speche, thenne spedez thou the better,
> For thou may leng in thy londe and layt no fyrre. (410–11)

In fact, contrary to all expectation, the Green Knight *is* able to speak again even after Gawain's aim has been so good that he has com-

---

[1] D. E. Baughan, 'The Role of Morgan le Fay in *Sir Gawain and the Green Knight*', *ELH*, XVII (1950), 241–51, p. 246 (Baughan's error was pointed out by G. L. Engelhardt, 'The Predicament of Gawain', *Modern Language Quarterly*, XVI [1955], 218–25); Benson, p. 216; Charles Moorman, 'Myth and Mediaeval Literature: *Sir Gawain and the Green Knight*', *MS*, XVIII (1956), 158–72, p. 167.

pletely sliced his head off; and when he speaks, he once more emphasizes this straightforward physical test:

> To the grene chapel thou chose, I charge the, to fotte
> Such a dunt as thou hatz dalt—disserved thou habbez
> To be yederly yolden on Nw Yeres morn.
> The Knyght of the Grene Chapel men knowen me mony;
> Forthi me for to fynde if thou fraystez, faylez thou never.
> Therfore com, other recreaunt be calde the behoves. (451–6)

What is demanded of Gawain, it seems, is a response in the tradition of heroic behaviour to which we have seen alliterative poetry characteristically giving expression. The situation belongs to romance rather than to the epic ethos of Old English poetry as continued in the alliterative *Morte Arthure*: Gawain has taken up the challenge in the first place for the honour of Camelot, rather than, for example, to protect the weak from physical harm by the strong. But the action demanded of him in confronting the monstrous Green Knight is approximately the same as that demanded of Beowulf in facing his monsters, or of Arthur in facing the Giant of St Michael's Mount. The worst that can happen to him is death by beheading—an honourable form of execution at least. When the time eventually comes for him to set off, this is what the courtiers fear on his behalf:

> There watz much derve doel driven in the sale
> That so worthé as Wawan schulde wende on that ernde,
> To dryye a delful dynt, and dele no more
>   wyth bronde. (558–61)

Finally, at the very moment when the armed Gawain rides away on his quest, the poet, with a certain cynicism about human behaviour, lets us overhear the very courtiers who had earlier advised Arthur to allow Gawain to take up the challenge criticizing him for letting Gawain be 'britned to noght,/Hadet wyth an alvisch mon' (680–1).

In the light of all this, when Gawain is welcomed at the strange castle on Christmas Eve, neither he nor we have any reason to suppose that what happens there will have any connection with the Beheading Game. Throughout his stay there, he sees himself as enjoying a relatively pleasant interlude in the few days that are left to him before he is 'britned to noght' by the Green Knight. He cannot, of course, forget the terrifying goal of his quest, and this fact makes all the more impressive the display of the courtly virtues that he puts on for the sake of his host and hostess and their court. This is what they expect of him—'Now schal we semlych se sleghtez of thewez' (916)—and he does as much as any man could to be a pleasant guest. He eats, he drinks, he dances, he makes conversation, he plays games; but all the while there sits at his heart the knowledge that the real test still lies ahead of him. Here the poet uses his omniscience not only to render Gawain's behaviour 'intelligible' but to bring out most touchingly his genuine courage: not insensibility or forgetfulness, but a magnificent self-control. Gawain declines the lord's invitation to stay longer after Christmas because he knows where his duty lies: to reach the Green Chapel may mean death, but he would rather die than not reach it:

> Naf I now to busy bot bare thre dayez,
> And me als fayn to falle feye as fayly of myyn ernde. (1066–7)

After he has been informed that the Chapel is nearby, so that he can spend all three days at the castle, we are reminded on each of the three days of what lies ahead of him. I have quoted the first day's reminder, in the lines in which his hostess thinks to herself that even if she were the most beautiful of women, she would still be unable to gain Gawain's love, 'for lur that he soght/boute hone' (1284–5). On the second day Gawain begs to be allowed to leave for the Green Chapel at once, 'For hit watz negh at the terme that he to schulde' (1671), but his host assures him that it will be soon enough if he leaves at dawn on New Year's Day. And early on the next morning, that of the third day, we are told (so deep is the poet's penetration into his hero's experience) how even in his dreams the coming meeting was present to him:

> In dregh droupyng of dreme draveled that noble,
> As mon that watz in mornyng of mony thro thoghtes,
> How that destiné schulde that day dele hym his wyrde
> At the Grene Chapel, when he the gome metes,
> And bihoves his buffet abide withoute debate more. (1750–4)

From these dreams he is awakened by his hostess's morning visit; and throughout the three days the actual trials of the Temptation have been intertwined with these thoughts of the Beheading Game. It is, of course, the thought of this crucial test lying ahead of him that persuades him to accept and conceal the Lady's gift of the green girdle, even though he has previously said that he will receive no gift,

> er God hym grace sende
> To acheve to the chaunce that he hade chosen there. (1837–8)

When the Lady explains that the girdle will preserve his life,

> hit come to his hert
> Hit were a juel for the joparde that hym jugged were. (1855–6)

After this, ominously, we are told that he went to confession and was
absolved as completely as if 'domezday schulde haf ben dight on the
morn' (1884)—and again we think of the ordeal that lies ahead of him.
At the end of fitt III the poet reminds us of it once more, in a way
which is all the more sinisterly suggestive because this time he
declines to use his omniscience and in effect invites us to imagine
Gawain's thoughts for ourselves:

> Yif he ne slepe soundyly say ne dar I,
> For he hade muche on the morn to mynne, yif he wolde,
> in thoght.
> Let hym lyye there stille,
> He hatz nere that he soght;
> And ye wyl a whyle be stylle,
> I schal telle yow how thay wrogt. (1991–7)

With this minstrel-like intervention, the poet makes it clear that he is
deliberately winding up the tension, and pointing his audience's
expectations ahead to the completion of the Beheading Game.

In fitt IV the poet redoubles this effort to keep his audience on the
edge of their seats, waiting for the climax of the story. In the early
hours of the next morning, he does dare to tell us whether Gawain
slept soundly. He did not: snow fell, the wind blew it into great
drifts, and:

> The leude lystened ful wel that ley in his bedde;
> Thagh he lowkez his liddez, ful lyttel he slepes;
> Bi uch kok that crue he knwe wel the steven. (2006–8)

After he is dressed and armed, he engages in another brilliant display
of courtesy before leaving the castle, and then rides away in the company of the guide,

> That schulde teche hym to tourne to that tene place
> Ther the ruful race he schulde resayve. (2075–6)

The guide warns him, with detectable relish, of what a terrible monster the Green Knight is: he is bigger than any man on earth (so was
Beowulf's opponent, Grendel),[1] he kills everyone who passes by his

---

[1] Compare *Gawain*, 2100: 'And more he is then any mon upon myddelerde', with
Beowulf, ed. Klaeber, line 1353: 'Næfne he wæs mara þonne ænig man oðer.'

Chapel, and Gawain does not stand a chance against him. The guide then proposes that Gawain should ride away, and he will keep his secret, an episode which (though it has other purposes, to which I shall return) certainly has the effect of heightening the tension still further by introducing delay and indecision. When Gawain indignantly rejects the proposal, the guide gallops wildly away, shouting that he would not accompany Gawain a foot further for all the gold on earth. Gawain, left alone, arrives at the Chapel at last, and finds it as sinister as we could possibly expect—or, one feels inclined to add, hope, for the guide's relish in the horror of the situation is clearly shared by the poet, and transmitted to us. Once again we enter into Gawain's very mind, and share his fears, as he insists with almost hysterical emphasis that the Devil himself must be at hand, waiting to destroy him:

> 'Now iwysse,' quoth Wowayn, 'wysty is here;
> This oritore is ugly, with erbez overgrowen;
> Wel bisemez the wyye wruxled in grene
> Dele here his devocioun on the develez wyse.
> Now I fele hit is the fende, in my fyve wyttez,
> That hatz stoken me this steven, to strye me here.
> This is a chapel of meschaunce, that chekke hit bytyde!
> Hit is the corsedest kyrk that ever I com inne!' (2189–96)

Here, as is usual with the *Gawain*-poet's psychological realism, there is the most delicate touch of exaggeration, which gives the mimicry of Gawain's thoughts, however fundamentally sympathetic it may be, a definite comic edge. One is reminded of the moment in *Patience* when we entered Jonah's thought and learned directly, what the Bible did not explain, why he was fleeing from the Lord. In both cases, we observe a single fearful thought rapidly growing until its branching detail dominates the mind: in *Patience* that Jonah will be captured by the Ninevites, here that Gawain's adversary is really the Devil. The situation is terrifying, and Gawain has perhaps more right to his fear than Jonah has, for Gawain has received no direct command from God; indeed the courtiers at Camelot had suggested that the Green Knight's challenge had only been accepted 'for angardez pryde' (681). But we are not quite so terrified as Gawain is: the hint of exaggeration in his thought enables our sympathy to be accompanied by a certain detachment. We certainly share his expectation, however, that the goal of his adventure lies immediately ahead. It is at this point that he hears the terrible noise, 'As one upon a gryndelston hade grounden a sythe' (2202)—not just an axe this time. Gawain is startled—his sudden 'Bi Godde!' (2205) suggests something like a nervous leap—but then he summons up the last ounce of courage left to him after all that he has gone through, and calls out his challenge aloud:

> Who stightlez in this sted me steven to holde?
> For now is gode Gawayn goande ryght here.
> If any wyye oght wyl, wynne hider fast,
> Other now other never, his nedez to spede. (2213-16)

The movement of these lines seems to impose a quiver on one's voice as one reads them; and the implication of the emphasis on speed in the courageous shout is very clear. Now or never: if the challenger fails to answer on the instant, Gawain will feel he has done his duty and will be off like lightning. Significantly, the answer he gets, without a moment's pause, is one that mocks him for his apparent impatience:

> 'Abyde,' quoth on on the bonke aboven over his hede,
> 'And thou schal haf al in hast that I the hyght ones!' (2217-18)

We and Gawain are made to wait a moment longer still, both by the Green Knight's determination to finish grinding his blade and by the poet's own delaying tactics in supplying information, before we find with relief that the challenger is the Green Knight, exactly as before, not even the more hideous monster described by the guide:

> Yet he rusched on that rurde rapely a throwe,
> And wyth quettyng awharf, er he wolde lyght;
> And sythen he keverez bi a cragge, and comez of a hole,
> Whyrlande out of a wro wyth a felle weppen,
> A denez ax nwe dyght, the dynt with to yelde,
> With a borelych bytte bende by the halme,
> Fyled in a fylor, fowre fote large—
> Hit watz no lasse bi that lace that lemed ful bryght—[1]
> And the gome in the grene, gered as fyrst . . . (2219-27)

---

[1] Editors normally explain this line as referring to a *lace* or thong similar to that mentioned in line 217. But the Green Knight now has a new axe, the former one having been hung up as a trophy at Camelot, and, as Gollancz remarks, 'one hardly expects the present weapon to be in any way ornamental' (I. Gollancz, ed. *Sir Gawain and the Green Knight*, EETS OS 210 [London, 1940], note on line 2226, p. 127). Gollancz continues, 'The only lace that has been recently mentioned is the one worn

It will be noted that only after the fearsome weapon has been fully described does the poet disclose who it was that was carrying it. Now the tension is wound up once more as the two knights carry out the second part of the Beheading Game. The tenseness of this scene is so obvious as to need no detailed comment. First Gawain ducks as he sees the axe-blade descending on him 'as marre hym he wolde' (2262), and the Green Knight halts his stroke and pauses to taunt Gawain. We enter fully into Gawain's situation, seeing the descending axe-blade from the viewpoint of one underneath it.[1] Next the Green Knight deliberately feints at him, and Gawain irritably tells him to get on with it. Then at last the genuine blow is struck, and cuts Gawain only slightly. The tension that has been built up throughout the whole episode between Gawain's eagerness to get the Game finished and the slowness with which events have actually proceeded (a slowness enacted by the lingering detail in which they have been described) is at last released, and Gawain leaps up and away with an energy that expresses our relief as well as his. Up to this point, though Gawain's honour has sometimes seemed balanced on a knife-edge, it has always been possible that he would come successfully through the test of the Beheading Game. Now at last it seems that he has done so. He draws his sword and challenges his opponent to a fair fight if he wishes—only to find, to our astonishment and his, that the Green Knight is not preparing to strike a fourth blow. He is standing aside, resting on his axe, looking at Gawain; and, with an almost vertiginous shift of perspective, instead of seeing the Green Knight through Gawain's eyes, as we have done all through this last scene, for a brief moment we see Gawain through the Green Knight's. The effect is as disturbing as if an Italian Renaissance picture had somehow been turned inside out; though it must be remembered that such shifts of perspective were still possible within the freer spatial conventions of medieval art. What the Green Knight sees is:

---

by Gawain himself (2037-9)'—i.e. the green girdle—but he goes on to suggest a different solution. I am attracted, however, by the suggestion of S. Malarkey and J. B. Toelken, 'Gawain and the Green Girdle', *JEGP*, LXIII (1964), 14-20, that the line does refer to the green girdle, and means 'the gleaming girdle that Gawain wore had no effect in making that horrible four-foot blade seem any smaller' (p. 16). The slightly detached irony of the narrator's remark, thus interpreted, is perfectly in keeping with what I judge to be the tone of the scene.

[1] Noted by Borroff, pp. 126-7.

> How that doghty, dredles, dervely ther stondez
> Armed, ful awlez; in hert hit hym lykez. (2334–5)

That pleasure of the Green Knight's is not entirely flattering to
Gawain. He is pleased with him, from the same standpoint of superio-
rity that might enable one to be pleased with a small boy or a pet dog
that showed fighting spirit. His first words express an almost teasing
reproof:

> Bolde burne, on this bent be not so gryndel.
> No mon here unmanerly the mysboden habbez (2338–9)

and they strikingly echo God's words to Jonah at the end of *Patience*:

> Be noght so gryndel, godman, bot go forth thy wayes:
> Be preve and be pacient in payne and in joye. (524–5)

One might well ask, what else could Gawain do? For it soon appears
that he has been conspired against not just by the Green Knight but,
in a sense, by the plot of the poem and by the poet who contrived it.
He learns that the Green Knight was the lord of the castle; that he
knew of all Gawain's dealings with his wife, including his secret
acceptance of the girdle; and that the conclusion of the Beheading
Game functioned not as the supreme test Gawain had to face, but as
a symbolic representation of a test which had already taken place,
and which Gawain had already failed. The three axe-blows which
made up the second part of the Beheading Game were only symbols of
the three days of the Temptation, and in this sense the Beheading
Game was a game indeed: it was a way of enacting in play a quite
different form of challenge. What makes this dénouement all the more
galling is that it is delivered by the Green Knight as something absolutely matter of course, as if Gawain might have known about it all
along. This is particularly true of the disclosure that the Green
Knight and the lord of the castle were the same person in different
forms, a fact which is never formally disclosed at all, but simply
implied by the *we* of 'the forwarde that we fest in the fyrst nyght'
(2347). Gawain feels himself to have been made the butt of a cruel
and unfair joke, and he gives vent to violent anger and shame.

I have been tracing out this thread of plot in such detail, trying to
recapture the reactions of someone hearing the poem read for the
first time, in order to emphasize what seems to me a crucial point.
This is that the audience of the poem, along with Gawain himself,
have been led all the time to look forward to the conclusion of the

Beheading Game as the true climax of the poem, in the form of a test of Gawain's physical skill, strength and courage; but that, quite unexpectedly, they are then brought to understand that what had seemed the climax was only an anticlimax, that what had seemed an interlude was the main subject of the poem. The crucial test Gawain had to undergo was not the test at the Green Chapel but a test in the castle: a moral test, not a physical test, a test not outside but inside the bounds of courtly society. What the conclusion of the Beheading Game brought was not the expected climax, but only knowledge of what had happened already, and consequent self-knowledge. If we accept this, then a question immediately presents itself. It was very clear what was tested by the Beheading Game: it proved that Gawain was not a 'recreaunt' (456) or a 'knyght kowarde' (2131) but truly, if only just, 'gode Gawayn' (2214). But, if not the Beheading Game but the Temptation was the crucial experience Gawain had to undergo, what was tested by that? What qualities in Gawain were tested during his stay at the strange castle?

The testing of Gawain

At its simplest level, the test Gawain undergoes at the hands of the Lady is one of sexual temptation. Throughout her first and second visits to his bedroom, and through part of the third visit, she is attempting to seduce him, and persuade him to become her lover. This fact is worth mentioning, and worth substantiating, because it seems sometimes to be disregarded, in favour of more complex and elevated ethical issues. Such issues are certainly present, and I shall come back to them, but the Temptation would not work at all if it were not for its fundamental sexual content. A major danger to Gawain lies in the Lady's sexual attractiveness; he responds to this (otherwise it would be no danger to him), and I believe that we are made to respond to it too. The Lady, it is true, is a demure medieval beauty in her appearance, rather than the bolder type that has been fashionable in our own time—

> Wyth chynne and cheke ful swete,
> Bothe quit and red in blande,
> Ful lufly con ho lete
> Wyth lyppez smal laghande (1204–7)

—but, as the persistent hint of laughter on her lips suggests, she is none the less provocative for that. We are left in no doubt that Gawain finds her attractive from the moment he first sees her and thinks her 'wener then Wenore' (945). She makes the most of her physical charms, wearing a low décolletage:

> Kerchofes of that on, wyth mony cler perlez,
> Hir brest and hir bryght throte bare displayed,
> Schon schyrer then snawe that schedez on hillez. (954–6)

Such charms are all the more piquant as part of a contrast between the Lady and her aged chaperone, than whom she is so much 'More lykkerwys on to lyk' (968). Gawain at once 'lappez [her] a lyttel in armez' (973)—just politeness, no doubt, but the bodily contact is suggestive. Then at supper they sit next to each other and take great 'comfort of her compaynye' (1011), though the poet is careful to add, using the antithesis found throughout *Purity*, that their talk was 'clene' and 'closed fro fylthe' (1013). When the Lady begins to visit Gawain in his bedroom, her behaviour is of course highly provocative sexually. Quite apart from all she says, and from the laughter, at once mocking and enticing, that plays round her lips as she speaks— —'Al laghande the lady lanced tho bourdez' (1212)—she makes him fully aware of her physically, as she sits down on his bed, pretends to imprison him in it (making literal the prisoner-metaphor of love-poetry), and eventually, after rising,

> cachez hym in armez,
> Loutez luflych adoun and the leude kyssez. (1305–6)

There is a persistent contrast between the outward *clannesse* of their conversation and the actual suggestiveness of the lady's be-haviour, a contrast which offers a far more seductive temptation than greater openness and outspokenness could do. Highly suggestive, too, are her reminders that the bedroom door is firmly locked (she has locked it), that the two of them are quite alone, and that she, a poor weak woman, would be quite unable to resist Gawain if he should choose to impose his will on her:

> Me behovez of fyne force
> Your servaunt be, and schale.[1] (1239–40)

[1] Burrow (pp. 81–2) is surely right to stress the ambiguity of this offer of service. The two meanings, one respectable, the other not, that he finds in 'Ye ar welcum to my cors' (1237) are entirely in keeping with the contrast throughout these bedroom

On her second visit to his bedroom the Lady uses the same tactics again. She establishes physical contact between them from the beginning, at the same time giving her provocative laugh:

> Settez hir softly by his syde, and swythely ho laghez,
> And wyth a luflych loke ho layde hym thyse wordez. (1479–80)

Once more she reminds him of his masculine strength and her feminine weakness, which would make it impossible for her to resist any attempt he might make on her virtue; and this time she adds a strong hint that he would meet no resistance:

> 'Ma fay,' quoth the meré wyf, 'ye may not be werned,
> Ye are stif innoghe to constrayne wyth strenkthe, yif yow lykez,
> Yif any were so vilanous that yow devaye wolde.' (1495–7)

And once more she reminds him that they are alone together (as if he could forget it), and that her husband is safely out of the way:

> I com hider sengel, and sitte
> To lerne at yow sum game;
> Dos, techez me of your wytte,
> Whil my lorde is fro hame. (1531–4)

Her 'sum game' has a generous vagueness reminiscent of one of her remarks on her first visit, when she said that the true Gawain would by now have found a way of begging a kiss from her, 'Bi sum towch of summe tryfle at sum talez ende' (1301). Gawain's imagination (and ours) is to fill in the blanks in those *sum*'s. His evidently gets to work, for, as we have seen, when she sits next to him at supper that night, he is angry at her advances, and angry not with her but with himself, for responding to them:

> And ever oure luflych knyght the lady bisyde.
> Such semblaunt to that segge semly ho made
> Wyth stille stollen countenaunce, that stalworth to plese,
> That al forwondered watz the wyye, and wroth with hymselven.
> (1657–60)

Before paying her third visit to Gawain, the Lady makes a special effort to dress as seductively as possible. She rises early, and puts on

---

scenes between surface innocence and covert provocativeness. They are also in keeping with the earlier play on the literal and metaphorical meanings of the lover as his mistress's 'prisoner'.

> a mery mantyle, mete to the erthe,
> That watz furred ful fyne with fellez wel pured,
> No hwez goud on hir hede bot the hagher stones[1]
> Trased aboute hir tressour be twenty in clusteres;
> Hir thryven face and hir throte throwen al naked,
> Hir brest bare bifore, and bihinde eke. (1736–41)

Besides adding to the impression of luxury, the fur, next to the bare skin so generously displayed front and back, has an extraordinarily sexy effect. Gawain is lost in gloomy dreams when she enters, but is soon roused as she bends down over him, kissing him, with her usual laugh:

> The lady luflych com laghande swete,
> Felle over his fayre face, and fetly hym kyssed;
> He welcumez hir worthily with a wale chere.
> He sey hir so glorious and gayly atyred,
> So fautles of hir fetures and of so fyne hewes,
> Wight wallande joye warmed his hert. (1757–62)

Her care over her dress has not been wasted, and she wins from Gawain the most ardent response she has so far achieved. He is obviously in a highly inflammable state, and the poet at this point inserts one of his clarifying comments to indicate just how serious the danger is:

> Thay lanced wordes gode,
> Much wele then watz therinne;
> Gret perile bitwene hem stod,
> Nif Maré of hir knyght mynne. (1766–9)

There can surely be no doubt that here it is Gawain's chastity that is being tested. The reference to the Blessed Virgin is entirely apt, for there have been many signs of Gawain's special devotion to her. He had her image painted on the inner side of his shield, so that he could look at it when in battle (648–50). He prays to her at the most desperate point in his search for the Green Chapel, on Christmas Eve:

> The knyght wel that tyde
> To Mary made his mone,

---

[1] It is generally agreed that there is something wrong with this line as it stands and that emendation may be required. There is much to be said for Gollancz's suggestion of reading *hwe* ('head-covering') for *hwez* (Gollancz, ed. *Sir Gawain and the Green Knight*, p. 121); this would have the Lady, though married, dressing as if she were single.

That ho hym red to ryde
And wysse hym to sum wone. (736–9)

His dedication to her goes with a commitment to chastity on his own account. This is made explicit a few lines later in the account of the third day's visit. The Lady suggests that he must be rejecting her love because he has a mistress at home, 'a lemman, a lever, that yow lykez better' (1782). Such an excuse might ease his situation, but he quickly brushes it aside:

> The knyght sayde, 'Be sayn Jon,'
> And smethely con he smyle,
> 'In fayth I welde right non,
> Ne non wil welde the quile.' (1788–91)

His oath is carefully chosen, for St John was famous as a virgin.[1] Perhaps then we can accept Gollancz's summary of the poem as 'the story of a noble knight triumphing over the sore temptations that beset his vows of chastity'?[2] We should have to add, of course, that he does not entirely triumph over the temptations. He does not consent to become the Lady's lover, it is true, but it is only after he has been thoroughly 'softened up' by her sexual advances and the resulting turmoil in his own feelings that he falls into the trap of accepting the girdle that she says will save his life at the Chapel. Moreover, though on receiving the assurance that he is vowed to chastity she seems to abandon her attempts at sexual seduction, the offer of the gift also has its sexual side. He accepts it *because* it will save his life but *as* a love-token, a 'luf-lace'—so it is called by the poet at the moment of acceptance (1874), and again by Gawain when he understands how he has been trapped and is full of shame:

> And thus, quen pryde schal me pryk for prowes of armes,
> The loke to this luf-lace schal lethe my hert. (2437–8)

[1] Burrow points out that 'Oaths by St John sometimes seem to have this kind of significance', but he suggests that Gawain's claim to be dedicated to chastity is only 'a convenient polite fiction', and that he only wishes to be without a mistress 'for the time being', because he is on a quest (p. 101 and n. 35). There seems no reason, however, to suppose that Gawain's claim to celibacy is, within the poem, a fiction, for there is no hint anywhere else in *Sir Gawain and the Green Knight* that he has a mistress, and the Blessed Virgin seems to be his guardian. It seems more likely that he is being polite in his 'Ne non wil welde the quile', after the downright preceding line. It is as if a teetotaller were to soften down his 'Certainly not!' when offered a drink by adding '—not for the moment', to avoid making his abstinence conspicuous.

[2] *Cambridge History of English Literature*, I, 331.

When he puts it on on New Year's morning, it is referred to as 'his drurye' (2033). The Green Knight may assure him that he accepted the girdle neither for its fine craftsmanship nor through 'wooing'— 'Bot that watz for no wylyde werke, ne wowyng nauther' (2367)— and indeed it is true that Gawain did not accept it *only* through *wowyng*. But what Gawain blames himself for is:

> The faut and the fayntyse of the flesche crabbed,
> How tender hit is to entyse teches of fylthe. (2435-6)

We have seen from *Purity* that *fylthe* is the opposite of the *clannesse* that is especially associated with the Blessed Virgin.[1] In taking the girdle as a love-token, Gawain has committed *fylthe* not physically but symbolically; in wearing it openly as he sets out to face what he believes to be his supreme test, he is declaring himself the Lady's 'man', even though the inside of his shield still invisibly claims that he is Our Lady's 'man'.[2] It cannot be said, then, that the story is quite one of chastity triumphing over temptation, as Gollancz believed; but can we otherwise accept his formulation, and see the Temptation as a test simply of Gawain's chastity?

The situation is not so simple as Gollancz's summary indicates. Though Gawain certainly undergoes a dangerous sexual temptation at the hands of the Lady, it would be surprising if this were the sole significance of the Temptation, because before he sets out from Camelot we have already been warned that something more complex than chastity is the object of his commitment. On the inner side of his shield is the image of Mary; on the outer side is the pentangle. I have noted above how the poet, by expounding the symbolism of this sign, uses it to articulate the system of values as whose representative Gawain rides forth. We must now look more closely at the pentangle symbolism, as an indication of what there is in Gawain to be tested by his adventure. I remarked that the passage of exposition cannot strictly be regarded as poetry, but rather as an inset of doctrinal

---

[1] See especially *Purity*, 1069-84.

[2] It has often been assumed that, because he agrees to conceal the girdle from the Lady's husband, Gawain must be wearing it hidden underneath his armour when he sets out on New Year's morning. This is the view, for example, of Benson, who writes that 'he has left Bertilak's castle with the appearance of knighthood concealing the reality of the lace' (p. 227). But Gawain has said farewell to his host the night before, and so he is free to wear the girdle openly on top of his red coat-armour, as a sign of whose knight he is. This also enables him to fling it to the ground at line 2377, which he would certainly be unable to do if it were worn beneath his armour.

material into the poetic structure. This does not mean that for the poet it was of little importance, and that we can therefore disregard it. It offers important help towards an understanding of Gawain's adventure, and for the poet it was obviously of crucial importance for the 'intelligibility' of his story, for at this point alone is he willing to hold up the narrative:

> And quy the pentangel apendez to that prynce noble
> I am in tent yow to telle, thof tary hyt me schulde. (623–4)

Two main points receive emphasis in this description and allegorization. One is the 'five fives': the five sets of five qualities in Gawain himself that the pentangle symbolizes. They are all good qualities, naturally, and they are largely virtues with a religious basis. Gawain is without fault in his five senses, he does no wrong with his five fingers, his faith is in Christ's five wounds, he draws his fortitude from the five joys of the Blessed Virgin (it is in this connection that her image on the other side of the shield is mentioned), and finally comes a group of five more specific virtues: *fraunchyse* (generosity), *felaw-schyp* (love of his fellows), *clannes* (purity), *cortaysye* (courtesy) and *pité* (compassion or piety).[1] These are, as I have said, religiously based virtues, but this does not of course prevent many of them from being courtly virtues too. They are the virtues to which any great medieval court would be committed, at least in theory, and this part of the allegorization establishes Gawain as the personal representative of the qualities embodied in the courtly civilization whose reputation he defends. There is more emphasis on the religious aspect of these qualities in Gawain than in Camelot: in him the courtly aspirations are purified, taken a stage further in idealization, and hence, as we shall see, more dangerously stretched and exposed. The second point that receives emphasis in the pentangle passage, and very heavy and repeated emphasis, is the intertwining and interdependence of these separate virtues. Of the pentangle which is their emblem the poet says:

> uche lyne umbelappez and loukez in other,
> And ayquere hit is endelez; and Englych hit callen
> Overal, as I here, the endeles knot. (628–30)

And this emphasis on continuity is then applied to the virtues themselves, and is underlined very heavily:

---

[1] See below, p. 208 and n. 2.

Now alle these fyve sythez, for sothe, were fetled on this knyght,
And uchone halched in other, that non ende hade,
And fyched upon fyve poyntez, that fayld never,
Ne samned never in no syde, ne sundred nouther,
Withouten ende at any noke I oquere fynde,
Whereever the gomen bygan, or glod to an ende. (656–61)

The poet places more weight on the fact of 'endlessness' than on any of the separate virtues; here, in order to make sure that we grasp the point, he uses the rhetorical device of *expolitio*: 'dwelling on the same topic and yet seeming to say something ever new.'[1] It is evident that this passage is far from being merely decorative. The poet's main point about Gawain's virtues is their interdependence. They support each other everywhere, so long as the endless knot remains endless; but what this implies is that a failing at one point may bring about a failing at others too, because then the knot will no longer be endless. This has its bearing on what is going to happen to Gawain. It prepares us to see, in the test he has to undergo, not a single quality being tried, but a whole complex of virtues—those that go to make up the Christian and courtly civilization of Camelot—and it prepares us too for the possibility that, if he fails, his failure will not be in a single isolated quality, but in a number of linked qualities.[2]

We have seen that Gawain is tested in *clannesse* in the Temptation scenes, and that is one of the five specific virtues symbolized by the pentangle. Another is *cortaysye*, and this also has a special importance for the testing of Gawain. In order to understand this, we have to begin by looking outside the poem itself. As was remarked in chapter 1, Gawain had a reputation in Arthurian romance in general, quite apart from what a particular poet might make of him in a particular poem. His reputation was as the knight of courtesy, and of courtesy in a rather restricted sense of the word. He was a philanderer,

---

[1] *Rhetorica ad Herennium*, ed. and trans. Harry Caplan (London, 1954), p. 365. Geoffroi de Vinsauf's instructions for *expolitio* apply exactly to this passage: 'although the meaning is one, let it not come content with one set of apparel. Let it vary its robes and assume different raiment. Let it take up again in other words what has already been said; let it reiterate, in a number of clauses, a single thought. Let one and the same thing be concealed under multiple forms—be varied and yet the same' (*Poetria Nova of Geoffrey of Vinsauf*, trans. Margaret F. Nims [Toronto, 1967], p. 24).
[2] R. H. Green, 'Gawain's Shield and the Quest for Perfection', *ELH*, XXIX (1962), pp. 121–39, points out that Solomon, by whom the poet says the pentangle was established as a sign of *trawthe*, was 'a gravely flawed figure', and suggests the relevance of this to Gawain's subsequent failure (p. 130).

an expert in the art of love-talking and love-making. His usual role has been summed up as follows: 'Gawain is the casual, good-natured and well-mannered wooer of almost any available girl. If she acquiesces, good; if not, there is sure to be another pavilion or castle not far ahead. Rarely indeed do the authors pass a moral judgment on the hero's conduct.'[1] This was the part played by Gawain in French romances of the kind that are likely to have been familiar to the poet and perhaps to some of his audience, and that probably formed the sources of his poem. When the poet made Gawain the hero of his poem, and introduced him sitting next to queen Guinevere at the feast at Camelot, he would naturally lead his audience to expect the traditional performance from him. And within the world of the poem he clearly has his traditional reputation. When he arrives at the strange castle on Christmas Eve, and its inhabitants learn who their guest is, the poet lets us know (something presumably unknown to Gawain himself) how they whispered to each other their expectations of him:

> In menyng of manerez mere
> This burne now schal uus bryng;
> I hope that may hym here
> Schal lerne of luf-talkyng. (924–7)

And the Lady, as we shall shortly see further, expects or pretends to expect that she will learn from the *cortays* Gawain not only *luf-talkyng* but love-making:

> ye, that ar so cortays and coynt of your hetes,
> Oghe to a yonke thynk yern to schewe
> And teche sum tokenez of trweluf craftes. (1525–7)

Yet Gawain, we know, is committed not only to *cortaysye*, which lays him open to the Lady's advances, but also to *clannesse*, which must lead him to reject them. How is such a contradiction possible? One way out of the dilemma is to argue that the Temptation cannot be a test of Gawain's chastity, for if it is, 'the poet...has committed the major gaffe of selecting as exemplar of *clannes* the Arthurian figure least likely to qualify'.[2] Yet we have seen the evidence that

[1] B. J. Whiting, 'Gawain: His Reputation, His Courtesy and His Appearance in Chaucer's *Squire's Tale*', *MS*, IX (1947), 189–234; p. 203.
[2] Gordon M. Shedd, 'Knight in Tarnished Armour: the Meaning of *Sir Gawain and the Green Knight*', *MLR*, LXII (1967), 3–13; p. 5.

Gawain's chastity *is* tested by the Lady. Another and more subtle solution is to suggest that the poem clearly distinguishes between two kinds of *cortaysye*. One of these is the religious virtue so fully treated in *Pearl*, 'true' courtesy, as one might say; the other is the debased, 'false' courtesy of the promiscuous Lady, which she would try to impose upon Gawain. It would then be possible to argue that in the Temptation scenes we see the Lady attempting to 'manoeuvre Gawain into acting in accordance with *her conception* of what his identity involves' and that 'The existence of two views of Gawain, so to say, the lady's and the poet's, helps to increase the social tension in the scenes between them.'[1]

This is a more tenable view, but it still seems to me unsatisfactory, in the sharpness with which it distinguishes between true and false courtesy, and between two conceptions of Gawain's character. The most striking thing about true courtesy and false courtesy is that they are both called courtesy, or rather *courtoisie* or *cortaysye*. This is not a linguistic accident: we have to deal with a single, immensely rich complex of ideas and feelings, which is capable of specialization in any of a number of directions—towards heavenly grace, towards a politeness which shows itself in courteous speech and deference to ladies, towards elegant seduction and love-making. There are multiple links between these different aspects of the concept, which enable a medieval writer to pass rapidly and almost unnoticeably from one to another. Thus heavenly courtesy tends to be associated (as it is in *Pearl*) with devotion to the Blessed Virgin, often referred to in courtly literature in terms that are elsewhere applied to a human mistress; the whole imaginative feudalization of love-relationships characteristic of medieval courtly society reinforces this link. Again, the descent is easy from perfectly 'clene cortays carp' (1013) with a lady to love-making, particularly since the ordinary conversation of courtly society seems to have used the language of love between the sexes very freely. This is surely the root of Gawain's dilemma. He accepts and indeed is proud of his traditional reputation for *cortaysye,* with the skill in *luf-talkyng* that this implies; yet it is very difficult for him to reconcile this with his dedication to *clannesse,* precisely because there is no clear dividing line between a true and a false *cortaysye.* From the point of view of Christian morality—I mean as this was generally understood in the Middle Ages, rather than among modern Christian revisionists—this is the great weakness of a system

[1] Burrow, p. 80; Brewer, 'Courtesy and the *Gawain*-Poet', p. 84.

of values centring, as that of medieval courtly society did, in *cortaysye*, the virtue of courts. Such an ambiguity at the heart of a living system of values was the necessary condition for the construction of any system of *human* values on the basis of the ascetic morality into which Christianity had developed by the Middle Ages. It is found also in the even more central concept of love, the rich ambiguities of which are explored in works such as *Troilus and Criseyde*; though scarcely resolved, because in human terms no resolution is possible, all human love being condemned in the face of the love of God. There are occasional signs of the exploitation of the ambiguity of love in *Sir Gawain and the Green Knight*, as when the Lady reproaches Gawain for his coldness by saying:

> Blame ye disserve,
> Yif ye luf not that lyf that ye lye nexte. (1779–80)

Here it seems likely that she is deliberately confusing the love of 'Thou shalt love thy neighbour as thyself' with sexual love, 'thy neighbour' being 'that lyf that ye lye nexte'. But she does not press the point, and the central ambiguity of this poem lies in *cortaysye*. This is a weakness in the mutually dependent virtues of the pentangle. In one sense of *cortaysye*, it is perfectly compatible with *clannesse*, with which it is alliteratively paired in the same line: 'His clannes and his cortaysye croked were never' (653). Within the protection of Camelot, we may suppose that the problem of compatibility did not arise; but when Gawain is among strangers, though still in a courtly society, *cortaysye* is gradually pushed in a direction which wrenches the pentangle out of shape and eventually out of its 'endlessness'. It is not so much that, as Burrow puts it, when Gawain is at the castle, 'the members of the household reflect back at him his own values a little distorted, as it were a slightly lopsided pentangle',[1] but rather that the pentangle, and the balance of values it symbolizes, is itself unstable and therefore capable of distortion, and that Gawain's experience serves to bring out its instability. The equilibrium of Camelot, held with such apparent lack of effort, 'With rych revel oryght and rechles merthes' (40), is in fact highly precarious.

So much by way of generalization; now let us return to the Temptation scenes, and see in more detail how Gawain's *cortaysye*, as well as his *clannesse*, is involved in his testing by the Lady. It weakens his resistance to her temptation in several ways. One is that, inasmuch as

---

[1] Burrow, p. 63.

cortaysye involves unfailing deference to ladies and perfect politeness in conversation with them, it prevents him from taking the extreme measure of a pointblank refusal of the Lady's advances. The pleasure with which he responds to them shows that this would not be his natural reaction, but, were it not for his *cortaysye*, it might seem a way out of his intolerable situation. This is indicated at supper on the second day of the Temptation, when, as we have seen, he is bewildered and angry with himself at her advances and his inner response to them. He might feel tempted to give her a sharp rebuff, but, the poet says:

> he nolde not for his nurture nurne hir ayaynez,
> Bot dalt with hir al in daynté, how-se-ever the dede turned
> towrast. (1661–3)

More important is the public nature of his reputation for *cortaysye*. His reputation is the property of others besides himself, and he feels a strong obligation towards it which the Lady is not slow to exploit. Soon after she has first come to his bedroom she mentions his reputation as well known to her:

> For I wene wel, iwysse, Sir Wowen ye are,
> That al the worlde worchipez quere-so ye ride;
> Your honour, your hendelayk is hendely praysed
> With lordez, wyth ladyes, with alle that lyf bere. (1226–9)

From this point on, Gawain's reputation, and especially his reputation for *cortaysye* (or *hendelayk*) is almost the main topic of conversation between them. On this occasion, with great delicacy, he first denies that he is the Gawain she takes him to be, explaining not that she is mistaken about his true nature but that he cannot rise to the height she expects:

> 'In god fayth,' quoth Gawayn, 'gayn hit me thynkkez,
> Thagh I be not now he that ye of speken;
> To reche to such reverence as ye reherce here
> I am wyye unworthy, I wot wel myselven.' (1241–4)

Then he asserts that he has received exaggerated praise from others:

> the daynté that thay delen, for my disert nys even,
> Hit is the worchyp of yourself, that noght bot wel connez.
> (1266–7)

The Lady's insistence on bringing up again and again the subject of

Gawain's reputation puts him at a double disadvantage. It brings before him what is expected of him as the knight of *cortaysye*, and thus helps to sap his resolution; it also forces him to talk about himself and his fame to an extent that makes a proper modesty difficult to achieve. There is a delicate comedy in the very ingenuity with which he attempts to evade her allusions to his fame: every evasion seems to involve him in a more detailed discussion of the subject any modest man would wish to avoid. Moreover, the more his reputation is discussed, the clearer it becomes that it has a certain fascination for him as well as for her. It takes two to make a discussion, and once she has raised the subject, he seems unable to let it drop. His hidden concern for his name and fame emerges in his shocked response to a Parthian shot of the Lady's on the first day of the Temptation. She rises to go, says goodbye, gives her usual laugh, and then suddenly turns back with a seemingly innocent remark:

> Thenne ho gef hym god day, and wyth a glent laghed,
> And as ho stod, ho stonyed hym wyth ful stor wordez:
> 'Now he that spedez uche speche this disport yelde yow!
> Bot that ye be Gawan, hit gotz in mynde.' (1290–3)

His suspicions lulled by the expectation that she has already given up the contest for that day, Gawain betrays himself by the speed of his 'Why?'

> 'Querfore?' quoth the freke, and freschly he askez,
> Ferde lest he hade fayled in fourme of his castes. (1294–5)

The poet's explanatory comment makes it clear that it is his name for *cortaysye* that lies uppermost in his mind.

The Lady is obviously pleased with the speed with which he has risen to her bait, because her opening words on her next visit dangle the same bait before him again:

> Sir, yif ye be Wawen, wonder me thynkkez,
> Wyye that is so wel wrast alway to god,
> And connez not of compaynye the costez undertake,
> And if mon kennes yow hom to knowe, ye kest hom of your mynde.
> (1481–4)

Her complaint is that he has already forgotten the instruction she gave him the day before in how to beg for a kiss. Once more, Gawain rises immediately to the bait:

'What is that?' quoth the wyye, 'Iwysse I wot never;
If hit be soth that ye breve, the blame is myn awen.' (1487–8)

He neatly makes the kiss something requested of him rather than by
him, but the Lady then returns, at considerable length, to the subject of his reputation for *cortaysye*:

> so yong and so yepe as ye at this tyme,
> So cortayse, so knyghtyly, as ye ar knowen oute

> ye ar knyght comlokest kyd of your elde,
> Your worde and your worchip walkez ayquere

> ye, that ar so cortays and coynt of your hetes
> Why! ar ye lewed, that alle the los weldez? (1510–28)

This time Gawain does not deny possessing the reputation the Lady
attributes to him, but contents himself with the somewhat two-
edged assertion that she knows far more of *trwluf* than he does.

On her third visit, too, the question of Gawain's reputation comes
up, but this time, revealingly, it is brought up (if obliquely) by
Gawain himself, not by the Lady. She appears to accept his assertion
that he does not propose to have any mistress, but she asks for a
keepsake from him, if she cannot have his love. She suggests a glove,
but he excuses himself by saying that he has no collection of precious
objects with him, since he is travelling light; and no mere glove could
be worthy of her honour. But he also implies that no mere glove
would be worthy of *his* honour: a gift from Gawain ought to be something better than that:

> Hit is not your honour to haf at this tyme
> A glove for a garysoun of Gawaynez giftez. (1806–7)

It seems symptomatic that, like Shakespeare's Julius Caesar, he
should now be referring to himself in the third person.

Before this on the third day there has come a comment by the
poet which we have already seen as an example of how the poet
makes his story 'intelligible', and which, since it refers to Gawain's
concern to keep up his reputation for *cortaysye*, we must now examine
in more detail. It comes in explanation of the poet's remark that there
was great danger in the relationship between Gawain and the Lady,
'Nif Maré of hir knyght mynne'—

> For that prynces of pris depresed hym so thikke,
> Nurned hym so neghe the thred, that nede hym bihoved

Other lach ther hir luf, other lodly refuse.
He cared for his cortaysye, lest crathayn he were,
And more for his meschef yif he schulde make synne,
And be traytor to that tolke that that telde aght. (1770–5)

Here line 1772 outlines the dilemma in which Gawain finds himself, through his double commitment to *clannesse* and to *cortaysye*. The lady urges him so near the limit that he must either accept her love (thereby breaking the pentangle at the point of *clannesse*) or refuse it *lodly*, offensively (thereby breaking it at the point of *cortaysye*). So much seems undeniable; but there is some dispute about the meaning of the lines that follow, and it is important to try to settle the matter, since these lines give us a particularly clear insight into the poet's understanding of what was going on in the Temptation scenes. Gollancz's view was that 'lines 1773–5 show that Gawain's chief fear is that he may sin against God, and his duty of loyalty to his host takes the second place'.[1] It is evident from the context that by 'sinning against God' Gollancz meant breaking his chastity. Burrow, however, has sharply questioned this interpretation. In his view, line 1775 is to be taken not as adding a third consideration —that of loyalty to his host—to the considerations of accepting the Lady's love and offensively refusing her already mentioned, but as defining the nature of the sin in line 1774. Thus the dilemma is between discourtesy and disloyalty, and Burrow sees Gollancz's interpretation as involving 'two particularly mischievous errors: first, that the author was so preoccupied with chastity that he could use the word "sin", without further ado, to mean "sexual sin" or sin in the Sunday papers' sense; and second, that he did not regard treachery to the host as a sin, properly speaking, at all—or at least that he regarded it as "taking second place"'.[2] I believe, however, that in this case we must, with whatever reluctance, class the *Gawain*-poet with the Sunday newspapers. For one thing, as we have just seen, line 1772 establishes a dilemma between accepting love and refusing it offensively; and we should naturally expect lines 1773–5, whose function seems to be to expand and clarify line 1772, to repeat that dilemma, rather than to substitute for it a quite different dilemma between discourtesy and disloyalty. For another thing, the context of the whole passage surely makes it likely that the poet *is* using sin to mean sexual sin. Gawain has responded to the Lady's advances

[1] Ed. *Sir Gawain and the Green Knight*, p. xxi, n. 1.   [2] Burrow, p. 100.

more ardently than ever before, the poet has warned of the danger between them unless the Blessed Virgin should remember her knight —what could be more natural than that at this point he should tell us that Mary's knight was concerned above all with his chastity?

I do not wish to argue, however, that Gawain's fear of disloyalty to his host is of no importance. It does, I believe, 'take second place': it has not quite the importance Burrow attributes to it, for he sees the whole poem as turning on Gawain's fidelity to the agreements he undertakes, his *trawthe*. This view in its turn demands to be considered in our examination of the nature of the test Gawain undergoes, especially since Burrow's is probably the most sensitive full-scale analysis of *Sir Gawain and the Green Knight* that has yet been produced. His own summary account of the nature of Gawain's test is this:

In the course of the action of *Sir Gawain* the hero makes two contracts with his adversary, the beheading agreement and the exchange agreement, and the outcome of his adventure is made to depend on his fidelity to these contracts—what the poet calls his 'trawþe'. His trial is essentially one of 'truth' in this medieval sense; and we are expected to accept this truth-trial as a sufficient basis for the life-and-death moral judgment passed on him by the Green Knight in the last part of the poem.[1]

Trawthe, as Burrow defines it, is undoubtedly of considerable importance in the poem. Gawain promises to meet the Green Knight at the Green Chapel in a year's time, he promises to exchange his winnings with his host on the three days of the Temptation, and he promises the Lady, in contradiction of this last promise, to conceal from her husband the girdle she gives him to protect him when he goes to the Green Chapel. It is for keeping his promise to her (as *cortaysye* would demand), and thereby breaking his promise to her husband, that he receives the wound in his neck from the Green Knight. Burrow has brought this out admirably, and also the less clearly defined ties of loyalty that should bind Gawain to the host

---

[1] *Ibid.* pp. 23–4; see also pp. 42 ff. As a parallel example of the high importance that could be given to 'truth', in the sense of fidelity to contracts, in fourteenth-century literature, Burrow cites *The Franklin's Tale* and particularly the line, 'Trouthe is the hyeste thyng that man may kepe'. This remark is the Franklin's, however, not Chaucer's, and I have argued elsewhere that Chaucer does not fully identify himself with the Franklin, and that he surrounds the Franklin's conception of *trouthe* with some dubiety or ambiguity (see my edition of *The Franklin's Prologue and Tale* [Cambridge, 1966], esp. pp. 5–11 and 24–6).

with whom he has feasted. But to see the poem simply or even largely as a test of Gawain's *trawthe* is surely misleading. This would not be so if *trawthe* were taken to mean, in the most general sense, fidelity to a code of conduct; this must be what it means in the pentangle passage, when the poet tells us that:

> Hit is a syugne that Salamon set sumquyle
> In bytoknyng of trawthe, bi tytle that hit habbez,
> For hit is a figure that haldez fyve poyntez,
> And uche lyne umbelappez and loukez in other,
> And ayquere hit is endelez. (625–9)

Here the justification for using the pentangle as a symbol of *trawthe* has nothing to do with fidelity to contracts, but refers to the interlocking of Gawain's virtues. Similarly a little later, when the poet writes that:

> Forthy hit acordez to this knyght and to his cler armez,
> For ay faythful in fyve and sere fyve sythez
> Gawan watz for gode knawen, (631–3)

faythful surely means virtuous generally rather than in relation to the keeping of contracts (though that is certainly part of virtue). But to say that the poem is a trial of Gawain's *trawthe* in this general sense is to say no more than that it is a serious moral test. In the narrower sense of fidelity to contracts, it does not appear that the poem is centrally concerned with *trawthe*; it is rather that contractual agreements form the framework within which a far more complex testing of Gawain takes place. So far as the Beheading Game is concerned, we have seen that this is not the crucial test Gawain had to undergo; and in any case there is no real doubt that he will keep his agreement with the Green Knight. We have seen how, during his stay at the castle, he never forgets this agreement, and how anxious he is not to miss keeping it—so that, for example, he at first declines the lord's invitation to stay on once Christmas is over. And the scene with the guide is surely intended to make clear Gawain's faultlessness in this respect. He does not hesitate for a moment in rejecting the guide's proposal that he should simply ride away without meeting the Green Knight, while the guide for his part will keep the secret. Admittedly Gawain is now wearing the green girdle, which the Lady has promised will make him invulnerable, but his fears during the night have shown that his confidence in it is far from complete. Nevertheless, he sees at once what he must do:

'Grant merci,' quoth Gawayn, and gruchyng he sayde;
'Wel worth the, wyye, that woldez my gode,
And that lelly me layne I leve wel thou woldez.
Bot helde thou hit never so holde, and I here passed,
Founded for ferde for to fle, in fourme that thou tellez,
I were a knyght kowarde, I myght not be excused'. (2126-31)[1]

Where, as here, Gawain can see clearly what the ethical issues are, and he has to choose between the virtue of *trawthe* and the vice of cowardice, there can be no doubt what his choice will be. Even in private, and far away from the society to which his code of conduct belongs, his values are sufficiently internalized for him to be sustained by his conception of himself as a true knight. So far as the Temptation is concerned, Gawain's *trawthe* is one object of the moral test, but it is precisely because it is only one among several virtues tested that Gawain cannot make an equally clear choice of the right path.

Neither in Gawain's words or thoughts nor, more important, in what the poet says, is there any indication during the Temptation scenes that Gawain's *trawthe* to the exchange of winnings agreement is the crucial issue. The position it holds is exactly indicated in the lines we have examined giving us the poet's statement of what was in Gawain's mind on the third day: he was primarily concerned to find some way of not offending against either *cortaysye* or *clannesse*, and secondarily to avoid being a *traytour* to his host. In terms of the pentangle, he is concerned not to offend against *felawschyp*, by, for example, taking his friendly host's wife as his mistress. Moreover, when he does this not actually but symbolically by accepting and concealing the girdle, he also offends against *fraunchyse,* in which are included 'larges and lewté that longez to knyghtez', and the opposite of which is *covetyse* (all mentioned in Gawain's self-accusation in lines 2380-1). Thus four at least of the final group of five virtues symbolized by the pentangle are under test in the Temptation: and if *pité* might be taken to mean not compassion but piety (as it does in *Patience*, 31)[2] the fifth of the five would also be involved, for Gawain offends against piety in making himself the Lady's 'man'

---

[1] Benson (p. 229), writes that 'Gawain may be tempted by the guide's offer, for he answers "gruchyng," but he will have no part of it'. But in context surely what *gruchyng* refers to is Gawain's reluctance to wish the guide well for his offer. He is *cortays*, though unwillingly, even to someone who has suggested something dishonourable to him; there is no suggestion that the offer attracts him.

[2] See Gollancz, ed. *Sir Gawain and the Green Knight*, note on *pité*, p. 106.

instead of the Blessed Virgin's. I have no wish, however, to press this parallel in any detail;[1] my main point is the general one that the Temptation brings out the complexity and internal interdependence of Gawain's value-system as this is symbolized in the pentangle. His virtues are so closely interlocked that a test of any one of them cannot help being a test of others as well. Conversely, a failure in one cannot help being also a failure in others. It is this fact, no doubt, that helps to explain the variety of the accusations that Gawain makes against himself when all is made clear to him at the Green Chapel. He sees himself, at various times, as guilty of *cowarddyse* and *covetyse* (2374, 2379–80, 2508), *trecherye* and *untrawthe* (2383), foolish submission to the wiles of women (2414–28), *fylthe* (2436), and *unleuté* (2499). So complex is his situation in the Temptation scenes that in a single act he may indeed be guilty of all these vices and more.

The complexity of Gawain's situation helps to determine the tone of the Temptation scenes, which is predominantly one of delicate comedy. This comedy is sometimes directed against the Lady, on occasions when Gawain manages to slip in edged remarks about her behaviour, while still maintaining an outward *cortaysye*. Such, for example, is his apparent compliment that it is she, not he, who really knows about the *art* of love (1540–5), or his again apparently complimentary reminder that she has already chosen a better man than himself, in her husband, when she says that if she had to choose a *lorde* she would choose Gawain: '"Iwysse, worthy," quoth the wyye, "ye haf waled wel better"'' (1276). But, in the nature of the case, it is usually the Lady who makes the running in these scenes, and Gawain against whom the comedy is directed. He is forced into more and more elaborate 'sleghtez of thewez' (917), and particularly into feats of *cortays* speech, as she presses her attentions upon him, and he has to try to reconcile the many different demands his code of values makes of him in this difficult and embarrassing situation. This comedy directed against the hero we have come to see as characteristic of the *Gawain*-poet's work, particularly in the cases of the *Pearl* Dreamer and of Jonah. Lot, too (*Purity*, 861–4), was an

---

[1] Davis (ed. *Sir Gawain and the Green Knight*, note on lines 652–4, p. 95) denies that there is any significant parallel at all: 'Despite the importance given to this group of virtues by their climactic position, they do not seem to have been chosen by the poet with especially close regard to the adventure which follows, or to the particular qualities for which Gawain is later praised.' It would be surprising if the poet were as careless as this implies.

example of a hero forced into a comic role by his efforts to meet by polite speech the demands of an impossibly embarrassing situation. The poet is not by any means doing something completely new in allowing the hero of a chivalric romance to appear sometimes in a comic light.[1] Chretien de Troyes, the first great writer of chivalric romances, does this to the hero of his *Perceval* and also, in the view of some scholars, to Lancelot in his *Chevalier de la Charrette*. Later, a comic and even a burlesque approach is to be found in such romances as *Le Chevalier à l'Epée* and *La Mule sans Frein,* which have been suggested as possible sources for *Sir Gawain and the Green Knight*; indeed, a recent study of these works remarks that, 'In the French romances, Gauvain had taken a step or two towards becoming a medieval Don Quixote'.[2] But the realistic detail and the delicacy of the comedy are highly characteristic of the *Gawain*-poet. They have come to be widely appreciated and fully analysed among recent writers on the poem, and I shall therefore say little more about them here. It will be enough to examine a single exchange between Gawain and his temptress, in order to bring out some of its rich texture of comic implication—implication which depends, as so often in the *Gawain*-poet, on the exactness with which the written words define and control the tone of the speaking voice. The exchange is one we have already considered briefly. It occurs on the third day, when the Lady, appearing to accept that she has no hope of becoming Gawain's mistress, asks him for a keepsake instead:

> 'Now, dere, at this departyng do me this ese,
> Gif me sumquat of thy gifte, thi glove if hit were,
> That I may mynne on the, mon, my mournyng to lassen.'
>
> (1798–1800)

Her words have a confidence and smooth sweep that show her capable of remaining in command of any social situation, even this one of apparent defeat; and they put her request in such a way as to make denial almost impossible. There is the endearment with which she opens, the oblique assurance (quite misleading, as it turns out) that she is giving up the battle, and that this is a last request, and the attractive wistfulness of the last line. She is careful, while apparently

---

[1] On this matter Benson is somewhat misleading, writing for example (p. 209) that 'The poem's theme, like its subject, is completely traditional, though significantly modified by the touch of comedy that places it in a new and nonromantic perspective'. Non-romantic perspectives are themselves a traditional part of romance.

[2] D. D. R. Owen, 'Burlesque Tradition and *Sir Gawain and the Green Knight*', p. 145.

leaving Gawain freedom of choice, to slip in the suggestion that the gift might take the form of a glove—something so small that he could scarcely deny her it. What could be more innocuous? But Gawain, though he may be encouraged to relax by her reference to *departyng*, is still on the alert. He recognizes the symbolic significance of such a lover's gift, and he is determined to give her nothing, however small. For his excuse, he seizes on the very worthlessness of the gift she suggests; but first he embarks on an elaborately fulsome excuse and apology:

> 'Now iwysse,' quoth that wyye, 'I wolde I hade here
> The levest thing for thy luf that I in londe welde,
> For ye haf deserved, for sothe, sellyly ofte
> More rewarde bi resoun then I reche myght;
> Bot to dele yow for drurye that dawed bot neked,
> Hit is not your honour to haf at this tyme
> A glove for a garysoun of Gawaynez giftez.' (1801-7)

There is a delicious touch of exaggeration in this. Gawain is delighted with what he feels to be his own mastery of the situation, and he indulges himself a little, so that his praise of the Lady's efforts becomes positively patronizing. And precisely because she deserves so much, and he possesses so little, it would be insulting for him to give her anything at all. *Her* honour would be besmirched by any mere glove that he might give her; and, as I noted earlier, *his* honour is obviously in his mind too. Then another thought occurs to him, which enables him to embroider his argument still further. It is not merely that he possesses nothing worthy of her (or himself) as a memento of him, but that on his present mission he has left behind such precious objects as he does possess:

> And I am here an erande in erdez uncouthe,
> And have no men wyth no malez with menskful thingez. (1808-9)

The very absence of any of his treasures permits him safely to refer to them with tantalizing concreteness. He is beginning to feel rather pleased with himself, for getting out of an awkward situation with such skill. He airily relates his difficulty to the human situation in general—one must cut one's coat according to one's cloth—and expresses his regret with considerable self-satisfaction:

> That mislykez me, ladé, for luf at this tyme,
> Ich tolke mon do as he is tan, tas to non ille
> ne pine. (1810-12)

And then, with a last unexpected twist, of a kind often found in the bob-and-wheel of the *Gawain*-stanza, the tables are turned again. The Lady plays the card she has presumably held in reserve all the time, and that will win the match: if Gawain will not give her something, he must certainly receive a gift from her:

> 'Nay, hende of hyghe honours,'
> Quoth that lufsum under lyne,
> 'Thagh I hade noght of yourez,
> Yet schulde ye have of myne.' (1813–16)

It is noteworthy that this suggestion is deliberately kept back for the very last line (in the same way as, for example, the information that the Green Knight is green), and that the holding-back is done not only by the Lady but also by the poet, through his insertion of the formulaic 'Quoth that lufsum under lyne'. In reading such conversations sensitively the twentieth-century reader is bound to be at a disadvantage compared with the courtly reader or listener of the poet's own time. To an audience accustomed to practise and to hear *cortays* conversation in everyday life, the skill of both participants would have been more immediately apparent, and every nuance of tone would have made its point. We may often be mistaken in our judgments of such matters of detail, but there can surely be no mistaking the delicate comedy of the overall effect.

But the testing of Gawain is not simply comic. One way in which this is made clear is by the parallelism of the Temptation scenes with the hunting scenes. It might be suggested indeed that the Exchange of Winnings agreement functions chiefly as a means of justifying this parallelism and of focusing our attention on it, rather than as a test of *trawthe*. It must be said at once that the hunting scenes have more than one function in the poem. To a medieval audience they would certainly have had more interest for their own sake than they are likely to have for anyone who is likely to read the poem today. I have said something in chapter 1 about the importance of hunting as an aristocratic activity in the Middle Ages. Its technique was certainly as complex as that of courteous conversation, and one reason why both are displayed in *Sir Gawain and the Green Knight* is that courtly romance tends to be exemplary of courtly ways of life. Romances in the Middle Ages fulfilled the functions of modern 'gracious living' magazines as well as of novels. We may also imagine that the original audience of this poem was not entirely homogeneous in its interests, and that for some of the gentlemen the hunting scenes would have been a welcome relief after the Temptation scenes, while for some of the ladies the position would have been the reverse. This is no more than guesswork, of course; and even for a modern audience with no special interest in hunting, and no knowledge of its technical vocabulary, the hunting scenes convey an irresistible sense of delight in the contest between man and beast, and in vigorous activity in the open air. The emphasis in the words of the poem is often upon joy, both that of the lord—

> The lorde for blys abloy
> Ful oft con launce and lyght,
> And drof that day wyth joy
> Thus to the derk nyght (1174-7)

—and that of the poet, so entirely in sympathy with the feelings of his characters:

> Thenne watz hit list upon lyf to lythen the houndez,
> When alle the mute hade hym met, menged togeder:
> Such a sorwe at that syght thay sette on his hede
> As alle the clamberande clyffes hade clatered on hepes. (1719-22)

The violence hinted at here is unabashedly enjoyed; and how blessedly simple is the poet's delight in the very weather of these clear winter mornings:

> Miry watz the mornyng, his mounture he askes.
> Alle the hatheles that on horse schulde helden hym after
> Were boun busked on hor blonkkez bifore the halle yatez.
> Ferly fayre watz the folde, for the forst clenged;
> In rede rudede upon rak rises the sunne,
> And ful clere costez the clowdes of the welkyn. (1691-6)

The plain parataxis of the first of these lines seems to recapture for a moment the simplicities of the *chanson de geste* of the early Middle Ages:

> Clers est li jurz et li soleilz luisant.
> Li amiralz est issut del calan.[1]

The poet takes an almost childlike delight in the loud noises that accompany violent action, the shouting of men, the braying of the deer, the barking of dogs, the sounding of horns:

---

[1] *La Chanson de Roland*, ed. F. Whitehead (Oxford, 1942), lines 2646-7.

> The hindez were halden in with hay! and war!
> The does dryven with gret dyn to the depe sladez;
> Ther myght mon se, as thay slypte, slentyng of arwes—
> At uche wende under wande wapped a flone—
> That bigly bot on the broun with ful brode hedez.
> What! thay brayen, and bleden, bi bonkkez thay deyen,
> And ay rachches in a res radly hem folwes,
> Hunterez wyth hyghe horne hasted hem after
> Wyth such a crakkande kry as klyffes haden brusten. (1158–66)

Here and everywhere in the hunting scenes the vigorous onomatopo-
eia and the urgent drive of the rhythms plunge us into the very thick
of the chase.

One obvious function of the hunting scenes, then, is to contrast
with the bedroom scenes which they surround, not simply in appealing to different groups in the poem's audience, but in appealing to
different interests of individual members of that audience. Such
variety is an important part of any narrator's art when he has a long
story to tell. To pass from the hunting scenes to the Temptation
scenes is to move from an open air setting, crowded with men and
animals, full of loud noise and violent movement, to an enclosed
chamber, with its door locked upon a solitary couple, where sounds
are muted and movements stealthy. It is also to move, as it appears,
from danger and death to perfect safety. For the manifest delight of
the hunting scenes is inextricably involved with death. The closeness
of the connection between delight and death is obvious enough from
the last quotation, where 'What! thay brayen, and bleden, bi bonkkez
thay deyen' moves smoothly from one to the other. Each day the
lord and his men hunt and kill animals of a different kind: on the
first day a great heap of deer—

> Such a sowme he ther slowe bi that the sunne heldet,
> Of dos and of other dere, to deme were wonder (1321–2)

—on the second a huge swine, on the third a mere fox. There is
mortal danger for the hunters too, especially on the second day when
the boar tosses and presumably kills several hounds and then turns
at bay so fiercely that none but the lord dare approach him:

> He hade hurt so mony byforne
> That al thught thenne ful lothe
> Be more wyth his tusches torne,
> That breme watz and braynwod bothe. (1577–80)

In the end, however, it is only beasts that are killed, and their dead-
ness is brought home to us in the poet's descriptions of how they
were cut up. I have mentioned the importance of these episodes as a
kind of social ritual in the opening chapter, but they are also important as a means of emphasizing the death of the animals not just
as an idea but as an inescapable physical fact. Previously they were
living creatures, full of violent energy; now they are unmoving lumps
of meat, completely transformed from subjects to objects.

On the face of it, then, there could be few more striking contrasts
than that between the hunting scenes and the Temptation scenes.
And yet, underlying this contrast, there is an equally striking similarity. The two sets of scenes are carefully arranged to make us aware
that they are happening at the same time: 'Against the very nature of
narrative, we are plunged into two events happening simultaneously.
The *Gawain*-poet is one of the first poets in English to handle the
difficult problem of simultaneity in narration.'[1] This unusual skill in
organizing chronological perspective can plausibly be related to the
skill in handling spatial perspective which we have found elsewhere
in his work. With remarkably little of the machinery of transition
which is so often found in medieval narrative, the poet moves us on
each day from the forest to the castle—

> This day wyth this ilk dede thay [the huntsmen] dryven on this wyse,
> Whyle oure luflych lede [Gawain] lys in his bedde (1468–9)

—and back from the castle to the forest:

> The lede with the ladyez layked alle day,
> Bot the lorde over the londez launced ful ofte. (1560–1)

The 'framing' technique, by which the two sets of scenes are not
merely set side by side, but each bedroom scene is inserted into a
hunting scene, makes us experience their simultaneity with unusual
vividness. This in itself suggests some point to be made: why should
the effect of simultaneity be given if there is not some connection
between the two sets of scenes? It is well known that hunting is
commonly used in literature as a metaphor for sexual pursuit, a
metaphor supported by the possible pun on 'venery'.[2] The metaphor

[1] M. W. Bloomfield, '*Sir Gawain and the Green Knight:* An Appraisal', *PMLA*,
LXXVI (1961), 7–19; p. 18.
[2] The history of the image of love as a hunt, from Plato onwards, is sketched by Don
Cameron Allen, *Image and Meaning*, rev. edn. (Baltimore, 1968), pp. 45–9; Burrow

was familiar enough in medieval literature for it to become not verbal and explicit but narrative and implicit. In Chaucer's *Book of the Duchess*, for example, the Dreamer's encounter with the man in black is framed within a hunting scene. At the moment when the man in black releases the piece of information which the Dreamer has been pursuing, namely that his lady is dead, we are switched back to the hunt and are told that:

> They gan to strake forth; al was doon,
> For that tyme, the hert-huntyng. (1312–13)

We are left to deduce for ourselves that the Dreamer's questioning of the man in black in matters of the heart was also a 'hert-huntyng'. This surely is what takes place in *Sir Gawain and the Green Knight*: the insertion of bedroom scenes into hunting scenes forms a narrative metaphor from which we are to see that the Lady's pursuit of Gawain is also a hunt. Such an effect would not be unparalleled in Middle English romance. In *Amis and Amiloun*, for example, the knight Amis, while living in the household of the Duke of Lombardy, feels unwell one day and therefore stays at home while the Duke goes out hunting. But the Duke's daughter Belisaunt has fallen in love with him, and while he is alone asks him to be her 'lemman', threatening that if he does not she will accuse him of raping her. Amis is thus placed in a dilemma like Gawain's, though much cruder—

> Loth him was that dede to don,
> And wele lother his liif forgon[1]

—and he eventually prefers discretion to valour, and agrees to become her lover. Here, as in *Sir Gawain and the Green Knight*, we are surely to see, or at least to feel, that the lady is hunting her man while her lord (husband or father) is hunting animals.

In the case of *Sir Gawain and the Green Knight*, some critics have wanted to go further than this, and to find a detailed parallelism between the three hunts and the three Temptation scenes. They see Gawain's behaviour on the three separate days as similar to that of the three hunted animals, the cautious deer, the resolute boar, and the

---

(p. 86) quotes an example from Lydgate's *Pilgrimage of the Life of Man*, although he himself finds that 'the prime effect of the juxtaposition of hunt and temptation is one, not of parallelism, but of *contrast*' (p. 87).

[1] *Amis and Amiloun*, ed. MacEdward Leach, EETS OS 203 (London, 1937), lines 647–8.

wily fox.[1] This I find somewhat dubious; and, in any case, I believe
that the general parallel between the two sets of scenes is far more
important than any detailed parallels. A hunt is going on in the
castle as it is in the forest, and in both cases it is a hunt to the death.
On the third day the convergence in meaning of the two hunts is
indicated particularly strongly. When the Lady enters the room,
carefully prepared by her costume to make her most aggressive assault
on Gawain's senses, she flings open the window onto the clear morning that we have just seen the lord and the narrator enjoying:

> Ho comez withinne the chambre dore, and closes hit hir after,
> Wayvez up a wyndow, and on the wyye callez,
> And radly thus rehayted hym with hir riche wordes,
>   with chere:
> 'A! mon, how may thou slepe,
> This morning is so clere?' (1742–7)

And at the end of the Temptation scene, the simultaneity of Gawain's
failure with the killing of the fox is marked especially strongly by the
poet's choice of the perfect tense:

> Now hym lenge in that lee, ther luf hym bityde!
> Yet is the lorde on the launde, ledande his gomnes.
> He *hatz forfaren* this fox that he folwed longe. (1893–5)

Instead of the kill occurring, as on the two previous days, after the
Temptation, it *has occurred*, presumably at the moment of Gawain's
acceptance of the girdle. If one were making a film of the poem, one
might have the sound of 'The rich rurd that ther watz raysed for
Renaude saule' (1916) heard through the open window of Gawain's
bedroom at the moment when:

> he granted, and hym gafe with a goud wylle,
> And bisoght hym, for hir sake, discever hit never,
> Bot to lelly layne fro hir lorde; the leude hym acordez. (1861–3)

But perhaps that would make the point too obvious; for it is important that the hunting scenes are seen by us through the narrator's
eyes, but not through Gawain's. Gawain knows nothing of the joyful
and yet ominous activities in the forest, and he can therefore continue

[1] So H. L. Savage, 'The Significance of the Hunting Scenes in *Sir Gawain and the
Green Knight*', *JEGP*, XXVII (1928), 1–15. John Speirs interprets the parallelism
somewhat differently: 'The shy deer, the ferocious (yet courageous) boar, the cunning
fox are the qualities of the natural man which Courtesy has to vanquish or, at least,
civilize' (*Medieval English Poetry*, p. 236).

to think that his stay in the castle forms a pleasant if embarrassing interlude before he faces his real test at the Green Chapel. It is indeed an essential part of the Temptation that it should not be presented to Gawain as a special and formal test of his moral worth, but as part of the course of normal courtly life, though lived, no doubt, at an intenser pitch than usual. And while he is thinking this, and always looking ahead to the Green Chapel, the hunting scenes are repeatedly telling us that normal courtly life is not as safe as it seems, but that it too contains possibilities of violence and death. If the pentangle breaks, it may do so 'Wyth such a crakkande kry as klyffes haden brusten'. As we see from *Purity* and *Patience*, such apocalyptic possibilities are not to be discounted 'in the kingdom of men', since that kingdom is in fact at the mercy of greater and more terrible forces.

The significant parallelism between the Temptation and the hunt must prompt us, finally, to revert to that between the Temptation and the Beheading Game. Just as each separate Temptation scene is inserted into a hunting scene, so the Temptation as a whole is inserted into the Beheading Game; and once more we may find in this device not merely technical virtuosity, and not merely a means of keeping the audience on the edge of their seats, but a narrative metaphor. This time, indeed, the metaphor is explicit, because the link between the two plots is not merely hinted to us behind Gawain's back, but is openly disclosed to him at the Green Chapel. If the Beheading Game is a symbolic reflection of the Temptation, then it is reasonable to suppose that its qualities may disclose something about the Temptation. The Beheading Game is a contest even more ferocious than the hunt; if the 'breaking up' of the animals threatens Gawain obliquely, the Beheading Game holds over him the most open threat of death, and the Green Knight specifically tells him that what he in fact receives from his axe is directly related to his two successes and his one partial failure in the three days' Temptation. There is surely a similar relationship between the Temptation and the Beheading Game to that between the Temptation and the hunt. In both cases, a superficial contrast hides a fundamental similarity. On the face of it, there could be few more striking contrasts than that between the sufferings Gawain endures on his quest for the Green Chapel and the comfort he finds in the castle. He travels through the winter landscape 'in peryl and payne and plytes ful harde' (733), suffering physical discomforts that are sharply brought home to us by the poet's descriptions of the landscape itself—the 'naked rokkez', the 'hard iisse-ikkles', the 'bare twyges' (730, 732, 746). And he re-enters the same wintry waste when he resumes his journey early on New Year's Day, and finds its bleakness and barrenness redoubled when he eventually arrives at the Chapel: 'nobot an olde cave' (2182), as he caustically thinks to himself. The evocative skill of these descriptions of weather and landscape has been often and justly praised, and the ferocity of the Beheading Game itself needs no further comment. In contrast with them is the castle, in the latest fashion of the time, full of bright lights, warm fires, comfortable clothing, delicious food, and friendly and admiring courtiers. When Gawain is led in from the frozen outside world, and is brought to his luxurious bedroom, with its matching tapestries and carpet, its silk-covered bed, and the comforting 'chemné ther charcole brenned' (875), with a cushioned chair before it, he seems to have entered a different mode of existence, and to have put on a new identity with his new clothes. Yet he is still the same Gawain after all, with the same reputation to keep up; and, as he and we will eventually dis-cover, his host at the castle is identical with the Green Knight, his hostess is the Green Knight's wife, and her chaperone is Morgan la Fay, who sent the Green Knight to Camelot in the first place. The meaning of the relationship of the two plot elements, if something complex and concrete can be expressed in simple terms, is surely that there lies hidden in courtly society a danger as extreme and unpredictable as that so obviously represented by the Green Knight and his challenge.

As the poem proceeds, then, it gradually becomes clear, until eventually in retrospect it is completely clear, that Gawain's experi-ence at the castle, though comic, also contained a serious danger. The game of love is a game as deadly as hunting or as the Beheading Game. This is not to say, however, that in retrospect the comic aspects of the bedroom scenes are cancelled out, or that we should feel that we were wrong to find comedy in Gawain's situation. We must proceed to discuss just this: what judgment are we to pass on Gawain's performance in his test?

The verdict on Gawain's performance

For Gawain himself there is no doubt whatever about his perfor-mance in what he learns from the Green Knight to be his crucial test.

When he understands that his host was the Green Knight in another form, that the green girdle was his, and that he knew all about what had happened in the Temptation scenes, he is first silent, while he takes in this utterly unexpected news, and then is full of shame and anger. The anger is partly displaced from himself and directed onto the girdle, which he flings to the ground, but he is also angry with himself, and sees himself as a moral failure:

> Now am I fawty and falce, and ferde haf ben ever
> Of trecherye and untrawthe: bothe bityde sorwe
> and care!
> I biknowe yow, knyght, here stylle,
> Al fawty is my fare (2382–6)

His behaviour has been 'al fawty', he thinks. At a later stage in his final interview with the Green Knight, he once more allows his anger to be displaced from himself, this time to be directed on to the 'wyles of wymmen' (2415). He has been deceived by the Lady and her chaperone; but then even such great figures as Adam, Solomon, Samson and David were similarly deceived; and so,

> Thagh I be now bigyled,
> Me think me burde be excused. (2427–8)

Still later, he reverts to blaming himself for the weakness of his flesh, and he determines to keep the girdle as a reminder of this weakness, 'in syngne of my surfet' (2433). He will always wear it, to protect himself against pride. He keeps this resolve, and on his return journey to Camelot wears it as a baldric, 'In tokenyng he watz tane in tech of a faute' (2488). He tells his story to the courtiers at Camelot when he arrives, concealing nothing; and in the telling his sense of shame is renewed:

> He tened quen he schulde telle,
> He groned for gref and grame;
> The blod in his face con melle,
> When he hit schulde schewe, for schame. (2501–4)

The wound in his neck, which was the punishment for his failing, may be healed, but the fact of his failing remains, as something he can never get rid of, and so he will continue to wear the green baldric until his death:

> And I mot nedez hit were wyle I may last;
> For mon may hyden his harme, bot unhap ne may hit,
> For ther hit onez is tachched, twynne wil hit never. (2510–12)

Gawain's verdict on himself, then, despite his early wild searches for someone or something else to blame for his failing, is quite clear. He is permanently stained with sin.

And yet there are a number of factors in the poem which prevent us from meeting this unequivocal verdict with simple acceptance. One of these is that within the poem itself other, much less harsh verdicts are also passed on Gawain's performance. One of these is the Green Knight's own. In explaining to Gawain the trap in which he has been caught, he is quick to add, before Gawain can make any comment at all, that he sees his fault as comparatively trivial, and still thinks most highly of his moral standing:

> sothly me thynkkez
> On the fautlest freke that ever on fote yede;
> As perle bi the quite pese is of prys more,
> So is Gawayn, in god fayth, bi other gay knyghtez.
> Bot here yow lakked a lyttel, sir, and lewté yow wonted;
> Bot that watz for no wylyde werke, ne wowyng nauther,
> Bot for ye lufed your lyf; the lasse I yow blame. (2362–8)

And then, after he has heard Gawain's acknowledgement of his failing, he presents his experience to him in terms of sin, confession, penance, and absolution. Gawain's penance is the cut in his neck: absolution is what the Green Knight now offers him:

> I halde the polysed of that plyght, and pured as clene
> As thou hadez never forfeted sythen thou watz fyrst borne. (2393–4)

Thus he expressly contradicts what Gawain says later about the permanence of the stain of sin; and the metaphor of polishing and purification, reinforcing that of the pearl in his previous speech, will have all the more force for us, if we connect it with similar passages in *Pearl*. The Green Knight does his best to enable Gawain to come to terms peacefully and painlessly with his experience. He invites him back to his castle for New Year, and promises to 'acorde' him with his wife, 'That watz your enmy kene' (2405–6). But Gawain rejects these attempts at reconciliation, and goes back to Camelot determined to see himself, and proclaim himself, a sinner for ever. When he arrives at Camelot, there too a different verdict from his own is passed on his performance:

> The kyng comfortez the knyght, and alle the court als
> Laghen loude therat, and luflyly acorden

> That lordes and ladis that longed to the Table,
> Uche burne of the brotherhede, a bauderyk schulde have,
> A bende abelef hym aboute of a bryght grene,
> And that, for sake of that segge, in swete to were.
> For that watz acorded the renoun of the Rounde Table,
> And he honoured that hit hade evermore after. (2513–20)

For Gawain the green baldric is a badge of shame; for Camelot, and, the poet indicates, for posterity, it was a badge of honour.

What should be our response to these contradictory judgments within the poem itself? One possible response would be to accept Gawain's view of his experience as the right one. It is, after all, *his* experience, and this in itself might seem enough to dispose of the view of it taken by Arthur and his courtiers, who have stayed safely at home at Camelot. At the poem's opening, Camelot was shown as a place of innocence, ruled over by a boyish king, and seen by us at the very birth of a new year. By the beginning of the next year, this innocence has in Gawain's case been corrected by experience outside the protecting walls of the court; but the other courtiers remain arrested in their childlike condition. Hence their laughter when Gawain tells his story and Arthur comforts him; it is the laughter, one might say, of incomprehension, and it may remind us of the futile and nervous laughter of Arthur and the uninitiated Gawain after the Green Knight's first appearance:

> The kyng and Gawen thare
> At that grene thay laghe and grenne,
> Yet breved watz hit ful bare
> A mervayl among tho menne. (463–6)

In taking the green girdle as a badge of honour, the courtiers are perverting its true meaning, which is known only to Gawain himself. Thus the poem could be seen as ending on a note of bitter irony.

If this were accepted, we should still be left with the Green Knight's verdict on Gawain as an outstanding contradiction; but this too could be plausibly explained. When Gawain arrived at the Green Chapel, he immediately sensed that it was a diabolic place—

> Here myght aboute mydnyght
> The dele his matynnes telle! (2187–8)

—and the longer he stayed there waiting for the Green Knight to appear, the more convinced he became that this was so:

Wel bisemez the wyye wruxled in grene
Dele here his devocioun on the develez wyse.
Now I fele hit is the fende, in my fyve wyttez,
That hatz stoken me this steven to strye me here. (2191-4)

If we are to take Gawain as our guide to the significance of his adventure, why should he not be right in this conviction? It was well known that the Devil, like the Green Knight, dwelt in the north, and it was not unknown for the Devil, or a devil, to appear as a 'wyye wruxled in grene', as happens in *The Friar's Tale*. Perhaps the Green Knight is a devil, and the magic with which he is involved is black magic?[1] If this were so, then in offering Gawain absolution he would be tempting him to participate in blasphemy. Indeed, one might well argue that all the Green Knight's attempts to comfort Gawain and to persuade him not to take his failing too seriously were forms of diabolic temptation. Having failed to trap Gawain into committing more than a symbolic unchastity with the Lady, the Green Knight is in no position to seize his soul; but if he could persuade him that he had scarcely sinned at all, that his love of life was perfectly forgivable, and that he was as innocent as a new-born child, then he would really stand some chance of gaining him for evil. In this light, the Green Knight's apparently innocuous invitation to come back to his castle and be reconciled to the young Lady and her aged chaperone (whom we later learn to be the enchantress Morgan la Fay) would show diabolic cunning. If the fly, having escaped once from the spider's web, were to go back to it of its own free will, there would be no hope for it. But Gawain, whether consciously or by instinct, sees through this last temptation, and manages a courteous refusal. When he goes on to speak of the two ladies, however, his courtesy gives way to a raw sarcasm:

And comaundez me to that cortays, your comlych fere,
Bothe that on and that other, myn honoured ladyez,
That thus hor knyght wyth hor kest han koyntly bigyled. (2411-13)

He rightly sees how the Devil in the past has done his work through feminine wiles, as in the original case of Adam, and in thus giving

---

[1] Cf. D. S. Brewer, 'The *Gawain*-Poet: A General Appreciation of Four Poems', *Essays in Criticism*, XVII (1967), 130-42: 'Bertilak himself is a shape-shifting demon, with strong associations with the devil' (pp. 136-7). Cf. D. B. J. Randall, 'Was the Green Knight a Fiend?'

up at last the polite deference to ladies that *cortaysye* demands he is rightly abandoning the whole courtly system of values that has *cortaysye* at its centre. The pentangle has failed him, and he goes back to Camelot not as an ordinary knight, but as one marked out by a special token—one perhaps on the edge of the monastery. For the story has disclosed no middle way between the instability of Christian courtliness (revealed when it is put under the stress of an extreme temptation) and an ascetic denial of all earthly values. There need be no surprise at the suddenness and completeness of the collapse of the courtly synthesis. As has recently been written of another great work of the late fourteenth century:

Behind the story is the double standard of the times. It is difficult to recognise that the secular culture of Plantagenet England with all its brilliance, wit and elegance, and its social and administrative complexity, its achievements in peace and war, was only a sub-culture. It rested on no firm, comprehensive frame of its own, but relied for its intellectual cohesion upon the postulates of ecclesiastical thinking and the standards of monastic morality.[1]

I have been outlining one possible response to the contradictory judgments offered towards the end of *Sir Gawain and the Green Knight* from within the poem itself. But another possibility would be a diametrically opposite response. The view of the poem that I have been outlining depends on the assumption that Gawain is a reliable guide to the meaning of his own adventure. He must thus emerge as an acute and discriminating moralist, even in the most difficult case of all, his own. We have seen that at a number of points he is able to analyse his own situation with great clarity; but there is one part of the poem in which he appears as a highly fallible interpreter of the moral nature of his position. This is after he has accepted the green girdle from the Lady and agreed to conceal it from her husband. It is striking that at this point he shows no sign whatever of any feeling of guilt or shame; and commentators on the poem have often been puzzled by the fact that as soon as he has hidden the girdle he goes off and confesses to a priest and receives absolution from him:

> And he asoyled hym surely and sette hym so clene
> As domezday schulde haf ben dight on the morn. (1883-4)

[1] G. T. Shepherd, 'Troilus and Criseyde', in *Chaucer and Chaucerians*, ed. D. S. Brewer (London, 1966), p. 85.

This is indeed puzzling, because, under the Exchange of Winnings agreement, the girdle is due to the lord of the castle. If Gawain had included it in his confession, he would have been instructed by the priest to restore it to its rightful owner before absolution was granted; so we must conclude that Gawain did not include it in his confession. Why was this? Gollancz's view is that the poet simply failed to notice the omission; but this seems implausibly careless. Davis argues that 'The poet evidently did not regard the retention of the girdle as one of Gawain's "mysdedez, the more and the mynne" [1881], which required to be confessed.' But since the retention of the girdle is later treated so seriously, and is the reason why the Green Knight cuts him in the neck, this too seems unlikely. Burrow's view is that Gawain deliberately excludes the retention of the girdle from his confession, that the confession is therefore invalid, and that its imperfections are not made good until he acknowledges his fault to the Green Knight at the Green Chapel and receives 'absolution' (at least of a 'pretend' kind) from him.[1] This is an attractive explanation, particularly in its linking of the two confession scenes, but it is difficult not to feel that if we were to understand that Gawain was deliberately concealing what he knew to be a sin then the poet would have given us some insight into his consciousness at this point, in order to make the matter clear. A simpler and perhaps more plausible view is that it is precisely his consciousness, his self-awareness or *concience*, that is at fault. He does not include his intended retention of the girdle among his sins because he wrongly fails to recognize that it is a sin. This certainly seems to be the poet's meaning at the moment when Gawain is persuaded by the Lady to accept the girdle. The poet gives a most delicate analysis of the thoughts and feelings that passed through Gawain's mind at that moment, and the thought that he was about to commit a sin is not among them:

> Then kest the knyght, and hit come to his hert
> Hit were a juel for the jopardé that hym jugged were:
> When he acheved to the chapel his chek for to fech,
> Myght he haf slypped to be unslayn, the sleght were noble. (1855–8)

And later, of his attitude towards the Lady, after he has agreed to conceal the girdle from her husband:

---

[1] Gollancz, ed. *Sir Gawain and the Green Knight*, note on line 1880, p. 123; Davis, ed. *Sir Gawain and the Green Knight*, note on line 1882, p. 123; Burrow, pp. 105–10, 132–3; for a view similar to Burrow's, see also G. J. Engelhardt, 'The Predicament of Gawain'.

> He thonkked hir oft ful swythe,
> Ful thro with hert and thoght. (1866–7)

'With hert and thoght' is no doubt a formula, but it serves to assure us of the wholeheartedness of Gawain's response. The guilt that he might have felt and ought to have felt is drowned in thankfulness at the chance of saving himself from what seemed certain death. But this moral blindness of Gawain's is to be connected, I think, not only with his momentary surge of thankfulness, but with the habitual concern with his reputation which I mentioned earlier. For him, as for many chivalric heroes, the criteria of conduct are not fully internalized; what protects him from temptation is not entirely the private sense of guilt but partly the more primitive and public sense of shame. He has gone some way towards internalizing his moral impulses, as the scene with the guide makes clear. There Gawain is able to recognize, and to act on the knowledge, that even if the guide kept his promise to conceal Gawain's escape, so that no one else would know of his cowardice, he would still be 'a knyght kowarde, I myght not be excused' (2131). The passive form of expression in the second half of this line significantly bridges the gap between the public and the private, between 'People would not excuse me' and 'I could not forgive myself'. But in the scene with the guide the ethical situation is perfectly clear-cut—it is a straightforward choice between honourable courage and dishonourable cowardice—and in any case Gawain is faced by an accomplice whom he does not know whether he can trust. When the Lady offers the girdle, his difficulty, as I have stressed before, is precisely that the situation is not clear-cut. On the one side is his internal moral code; on the other side are both his sense of relief and the apparent certainty that his reputation will be safe, because (as it appears) it could not conceivably be in her interest to betray him to her husband. This would mean betraying her own unwifely conduct; and it is she who asks him, for *her* sake, not his, to conceal the girdle:

> And bisoght hym, for hir sake, discever hit never,
> Bot to lelly layne fro hir lorde. (1862–3)

Thus his honour seems to be engaged to the present wife rather than to the absent husband. In these circumstances, it is perhaps not surprising that, in the apparent absence of any possibility of shame, he shows no sign of feeling any guilt. What makes it clear that concern for his reputation is operative here is that it is not until Gawain

realizes that he has been found out that he starts to feel guilty. For
him, apparently, the important question is not whether he has been
unfaithful to his agreement with the lord of the castle, but whether he
is known by the lord himself to have been unfaithful to it. When he
discovers that the lord and his wife were acting in agreement, and
that his conduct has been under scrutiny all along, for once he loses
his self-control completely, and we see him full of impotent anger—
anger directed, as we have noted, not only against himself but against
the girdle and the Lady and her chaperone.

A good case could thus be made for arguing that Gawain does not
fully grasp the meaning of the test he undergoes: it is not that he sees
what the issues are and deliberately acts wrongly, but that, at one
crucial point, he fails to see what the issues are. And one could
pursue this interpretation further, and argue that he goes on failing
to be an adequate guide to the meaning of his adventure right up to
the end of the poem. One might well see something rather exaggerated
in the force of Gawain's reaction to the knowledge that he has been
found out, and one might well argue that he was being presented as a
partly comic figure here just as much as in the Temptation scenes.
There is perhaps a kind of self-regard, connected with his concern
for his reputation, in his very access of humility. Certainly he does
not take a balanced view of his situation. At one moment, before the
Green Knight explains things to him, his conscience is apparently
quite clear, and

> Never syn that he watz burne borne of his moder
> Watz he never in this worlde wyye half so blythe. (2320-1)

(The reference to his birth may connect his joy with the innocent
child's lack of any sense of guilt.) At the next moment, having
learned the truth, he is accusing himself of every sin he can think of.
As we have seen, his failing does indeed have many aspects; but
surely he is not really guilty of *covetyse*, of which he accuses himself
three times (2374, 2380, 2508)? It has been carefully emphasized that
Gawain did not accept or wear the girdle because he was attracted by
its material value:

> Bot wered not this ilk wyye for wele this gordel,
> For pryde of the pendauntez, thagh polyst thay were,
> And thagh the glyterande golde glent upon endez,
> Bot for to saven hymself, when suffer hym byhoved. (2037-40)

Now, however, in the extravagance of his remorse, he accuses himself of covetousness among his other sins,[1] and later, in accepting the girdle as a gift from the Green Knight, he seems to insist that *now* he will not wear it out of covetousness:

> That wyl I welde wyth guod wylle, not for the wynne golde,
> Ne the saynt, ne the sylk, ne the syde pendaundes,
> For wele ne for worchyp, ne for the wlonk werkkez,
> Bot in syngne of my surfet. (2430-3)

Gawain's situation is paradoxical. Previously, when he was truly guilty, he felt more joyful than he had done since he was a new-born child; now, when his offence is discharged, and the Green Knight assures him that he is

> pured as clene
> As thou hadez never forfeted sythen thou watz fyrst borne, (2393-4)

he has started to accuse himself of all kinds of sins. There is an obvious explanation for this. Gawain had his sights set on perfection, the endless knot of virtues symbolized by the pentangle; hence his intense and sensitive concern for his reputation. Now he finds that he is known not to be perfect, and, if his reputation for perfection cannot be complete, it is not enough for it to be almost complete. It is not enough for him to be, as the Green Knight assures him he is

> On the fautlest freke that ever on fote yede;
> As perle bi the quite pese is of prys more,
> So is Gawayn, in god fayth, bi other gay knyghtez, (2363-5)

for he has measured himself, not 'bi other gay knyghtez', but by a humanly unattainable standard of perfection. Now, if he cannot be a perfect knight, he is determined to be the most miserable of sinners. At least the great sinner is a heroic figure of the stature he has aimed at, and so he can now compare himself with such Old Testament heroes as Adam, Solomon, Samson and David. Seen in this light, there

---

[1] This interpretation was put forward by J. A. Burrow, 'The Two Confession Scenes in *Sir Gawain and the Green Knight*', *MP*, LVII (1959-60), 73-9, pp. 78-9, but is withdrawn in his book (pp. 135-6) in favour of the view that Gawain's action could rightly be classed as covetous 'objectively', though not 'subjectively'. Similarly, D. F. Hills, 'Gawain's Fault in *Sir Gawain and the Green Knight*', *RES*, n.s. XIV (1963), 124-31, argues that Gawain was truly covetous, in a strict theological sense, in loving the girdle more than God. The poet of keen theological interests we have found in the other three poems might have meant to make either of these points, but both seem a little fine-drawn.

is something comic about the speech in which he bitterly condemns the wiles of women, and takes up an attitude of Byronic cynicism towards them, quite at odds with his former *cortaysye*:

> hit were a wynne huge
> To luf hom wel, and leve hem not, a leude that couthe. (2420–1)

Such a reversal of attitudes is perfectly understandable in psychological terms as a reaction to the profound shock Gawain has undergone; but he looks a little absurd in these unaccustomed clothes.

He is absurd too in his petulant rejection of the Green Knight's attempts to comfort him and to achieve a reconciliation. He twice refuses the Green Knight's invitation to return to his castle and be reconciled with the two ladies, and his refusal may plausibly be seen to stem from his inability to achieve an *internal* reconciliation between his aspirations and his conduct. It may well be indeed that the explanation the Green Knight gives of the elder lady's identity makes it even more impossible for Gawain to feel that he can meet her again. For she is not merely the legendary enchantress who wished to terrify Guinevere—'Morgne the goddes' (2452)—she is also, as the Green Knight goes on to point out, someone intimately related to Gawain himself. She is Arthur's half-sister, and therefore Gawain's aunt. The Green Knight evidently thinks that this will make it easier for Gawain to come back to the scene of his failure—'Therfore I ethe the, hathel, to com to thyn aunt' (2467)—but in fact it makes it far more difficult, because to meet her *as* his aunt would mean facing the fact that he has not been trapped by a malice totally disconnected from himself. As Benson points out, Gawain in his opening speech at Camelot speaks only of Arthur's blood flowing in his veins:

This kinship, Gawain says, is his only claim to merit. After the return-blow is delivered, when Gawain is brought to true humility, he is forcibly reminded that Arthur is not his only kin, that the blood of Morgan la Fay also flows in his veins. She is the symbol of the evil that Gawain discovers in his flesh, a discovery that angers and shames him.[1]

If this were indeed the poet's point, it would make clear why he made the Green Knight offer Morgan's enmity for Guinevere as the spring of the whole plot. This explanation has caused much discomfort among modern critics, who have either simply dismissed it as unsatisfactory or else made it satisfactory only by distorting all the rest of

---

[1] Benson, p. 32.

the poem to fit it.[1] But if its point were Gawain's inability to come to terms with his own failing, then the Morgan la Fay explanation would at least fall into place as part of the poet's presentation of Gawain as a fallible interpreter of his own experience.

When Gawain rides back to Camelot wearing the green girdle as a baldric, he still has in mind his reputation. There is something noble about his determination to wear the token of his failing publicly, but there is something a little absurd too. He will not wear a hair shirt secretly under his armour against 'The faut and the fayntyse of the flesche crabbed' (2435); he will punish himself openly in his reputation, by wearing something that will call other people's attention as well as his own to his imperfection. And yet, without judging him unsympathetically, may we not feel that there are still traces of pride in the feeling that one's own imperfection deserves such ostentatious treatment? He wears the baldric 'In tokenyng he watz tane in tech of a faute' (2488): we note the 'he watz tane' as a sign that being found out, rather than committing the fault in the first place, is still uppermost in his mind. And Gawain seems to be behaving as though he were the only person in the world who had ever done wrong and been found out, or as if he were such a special person that in him human imperfection was especially remarkable. It is along these lines that we may interpret his reception at Camelot when he returns. When the court laugh at his story, their reaction is a healthy one, and should guide our own, for they see that he is giving excessive importance to a minor failing in an impossibly difficult task. He is not the only human being, or even the only knight of the Round Table, who has some taint of sin about him. The only sinless human beings are those who, like the Pearl Maiden, die before they emerge from infancy; hence the prayer quoted from the Psalter:

> Lorde, thy servaunt draw never to dome,
> For non lyvyande to the is justyfyet. (*Pearl*, 699–700)

When the court determine that henceforward they will all wear the green baldric, they are in effect reminding Gawain that he is not alone in his imperfection. At the same time they are preventing him from being the outstanding figure he wishes to be. Henceforward he

[1] For the former approach, see Speirs, *Medieval English Poetry*, p. 218; for the latter, Moorman, 'Myth and Mediaeval Literature', and Mother Angela Carson, 'Morgain la Fée as the Principle of Unity in *Gawain and the Green Knight*', *Modern Language Quarterly*, XXIII (1962), 3–16.

will be indistinguishable among them, not the notorious sinner he takes himself to be.

I have been presenting two alternative views of the later stages of the poem: one that sees Gawain's understanding of his adventure as being essentially the same as the poet's, while the Green Knight is misleading and Camelot mistaken; the other that sees the poet as sharing the lenient judgment on Gawain that he attributes to the Green Knight and to the court, and as presenting Gawain's own perception and understanding as seriously flawed. I may as well say at once that, faced with a simple choice between these two views of the poem, I would opt for the second. The central figures of *Patience* and *Pearl* are both men in whom failures of moral awareness are revealed through a meeting with the supernatural; they are both would-be heroes of a partly comic kind; it would not be surprising if Gawain were similarly conceived. But I do not believe that one is necessarily faced with a simple choice between two views of Gawain. This at least is what is suggested by the subtlety of the poet's handling of point of view. We have seen in the *Gawain*-poet's other work the skill with which he opens up the space of the poem, and enables us to move freely about inside it. More than one recent critic has called attention to this aspect of *Sir Gawain and the Green Knight*, and has noted how cinematic is its treatment of space. Sometimes the poet enables us to follow the moving cine-camera-like point of view of a neutral narrator, as when in the banquet at Camelot, having made the general statement that many dishes of delicate and rich food were served, he uses the characteristic film device of close-up to show us silver dishes closely crowded together on the table-cloth (121–5). At other times, the poet permits us to share the point of view of one of the characters, as when the Green Knight is about to strike his first axe-blow at Gawain, and we see it from Gawain's point of view, whistling down on us from above—and with him we flinch. It was exactly effects of this kind that terrified the viewers of early films, as steam-engines appeared to hurtle towards them out of the screen. Or, to take a third technique, a scene may be presented alternately from the points of view of two (or more) characters within it, as in gun-duel scenes in Western films, where the two opponents walk slowly towards each other, and we see alternately A through B's eyes and B through A's. The *Gawain*-poet employs a somewhat similar technique at the beginning of the first Temptation scene, when he alternates between Gawain's view of the Lady and the Lady's of

Gawain.[1] This resourceful use of spatial perspective readily merges into a similar treatment of moral perspective: just as we feel the poem to be a spatial solid because we can in imagination move about inside it, so, one might say, we also feel it to be a moral solid. In an earlier essay on *Sir Gawain and the Green Knight* I wrote that 'the centre of consciousness in the poem is unmistakably Gawain himself',[2] but, as more recent work on the poem has shown, this is an oversimplified view of the matter. It is true that Gawain's point of view often acts as a kind of magnet, so that it and the assumptions by which it is shaped are sometimes projected onto the narrator himself. This is perhaps the explanation of the discrepancies noted by Burrow during Gawain's stay at the castle, when 'We know that Gawain is deceived; but we do not respond to his hosts merely as deceivers'.[3] Thus we may say that the reason why Sir Bertilak does not recognize Gawain when he first sees him is that Gawain does not expect to be recognized, and the reason why we are told that the Lady loved Gawain as well as that she was deliberately tempting him is that he assumed that her apparent feelings were genuine. (So they may have been, of course; that question is never settled.) But the magnetic force of Gawain's point of view is not irresistible. We *are* told (what he is supposed not to know) that the Lady is deliberately tempting him, and we are even given some encouragement to speculate about her motives:

> Thus hym frayned that fre, and fondet hym ofte,
> For to haf wonnen hym to woghe, what-so scho thoght ellez. (1549–50)

Throughout the three days of the Temptation, we see the violence of the hunt, and respond to its possible metaphoric effects, but Gawain does not. As the Temptation proceeds, and particularly after Gawain has committed the fault of agreeing to conceal the girdle, his point of view becomes steadily more resistible. It is never replaced by any consistent alternative point of view, though I have mentioned the vertiginous effect of the shift of perspective in lines 2333–5, by which we suddenly see Gawain through the Green Knight's eyes. Indeed, as the end of the poem approaches, the narrator's point of view takes

---

[1] The three examples given are all singled out by Borroff, pp. 123, 126, 92, though she is not responsible for my comments on them. Cf. Renoir, 'Descriptive Technique in *Sir Gawain and the Green Knight*'.

[2] Spearing, *Criticism and Medieval Poetry*, p. 29. Cf. Brewer, 'The *Gawain*-Poet': 'All is told from the point of view of Gawain' (p. 137).

[3] Burrow, pp. 56–7.

over, and it moves to a point completely outside the action, and therefore tantalizingly neutral. Earlier the narrator had adopted a certain intimacy with Gawain, addressing him directly—'Now thenk wel, Sir Gawan...' (487)—and calling him 'oure luflych lede' (1469) or 'oure luflych knyght' (1657). Now Gawain and everything else in the poem seem to recede into the distance, to become small and incomprehensible. Gawain rode back to Camelot, he told his story (we see him blushing clearly enough, though), the courtiers laughed, they adopted the baldric as a badge of honour—and suddenly the poem has receded into the legendary history from which it originally emerged.

There is no reason to suppose that the *Gawain*-poet manipulated point of view in *Sir Gawain and the Green Knight* with the self-consciousness shown by Henry James in his novels. It is scarcely possible to imagine that, in giving us the first of our two brief glimpses of Gawain through the eyes of his host—'Loude laghed he therat, so lef hit hym thoght' (909)—he did so as consciously as James did in taking up for a moment the point of view of a minor character in *The Bostonians*: 'If we were at this moment to take, in a single glance, an inside view of Mrs Burrage (a liberty we have not yet ventured on), I suspect we should find....'[1] On the other hand, our second glimpse of Gawain through the eyes of his opponent, when he leaps up to defend himself against any further axe-blow, is so startling in its effect of reminding us that Gawain may be judged from outside as well as from inside that it is difficult not to believe that it was carefully planned. Whether consciously or instinctively, the poet seems to have intended in his hero a character such as James, with the wisdom of hindsight, saw that the hero of his early novel *Roderick Hudson* ought to have been:

The very claim of the fable is naturally that he *is* special, that his great gift makes and keeps him highly exceptional; but that is not for a moment supposed to preclude his appearing typical (of the general type) as well; for the fictive hero successfully appeals to us only as an eminent instance, as eminent as we like, of our own conscious kind.[2]

---

[1] *The Bostonians* (1886), chapter XXXII.

[2] *The Art of the Novel: Critical Prefaces by Henry James*, ed. R. P. Blackmur (New York, 1934), p. 12. As Burrow rightly remarks of Gawain (p. 10): 'He is, for all the poem tells us, "primus"; but he is "primus *inter pares*", and it is there that he differs from the "elect" heroes of the sophisticated French religious romances.'

As we have seen from *Purity, Patience* and *Pearl*, there was for the *Gawain*-poet something *essentially* comic in the condition of 'our own conscious kind'—a comedy that lay above all in the seeming impossibility for human beings of achieving a full consciousness of their status in the face of the divine. The Green Knight has certain similarities to the representations of God in *Patience* and *Purity*: he shares their omniscience with regard to the motives of his human antagonist, and his cool explanation that events too are under his control—

> Now know I wel thy cosses, and thy costes als,
> And the wowyng of my wyf: I wroght hit myselven (2360–1)

—is strongly reminiscent of the emphasis on God's creative power in the earlier poems. But the Green Knight is given no hint of a place in any theological scheme, and we cannot say that man in *Sir Gawain and the Green Knight* is confronted, directly, or indirectly, with the divine. But, equally, the world of *Sir Gawain and the Green Knight* is certainly not one from which the divine is excluded: it has many references, as we have seen, to God, the Blessed Virgin, and other saints. We may surmise that for the poet the world of this poem, more than that of any of his others, was the everyday modern world, though of course heightened and idealized. It was not that of Biblical times, in which God spoke directly to man, nor even that of *Pearl*, in which man could at least approach God. It must therefore be a world in which it was at least possible to see the hero as comic, and yet not necessary to do so. The conception of the poem seems to require that we should perceptively *watch* Gawain being entangled in the situation to which his acceptance of the Green Knight's challenge leads him, and that we should see more clearly than he does the nature of his strengths and weaknesses (which means, too, those of Camelot and, by an easy extension, those of any civilized society); and yet we must also ourselves be entangled in and rebuked by the mystery he has to face.

If this is so, it has consequences for the treatment both of Gawain and of his antagonist. So far as Gawain is concerned, he must, in Jamesian terms, combine the role of Roderick Hudson with that of Rowland Mallet, through whose eyes Roderick's 'adventure' is viewed:

The centre of interest throughout 'Roderick' is in Rowland Mallet's consciousness, and the drama is the very drama of that consciousness—

which I had of course to make sufficiently acute in order to enable it, like a set and lighted scene, to hold the play. By making it acute, meanwhile, one made its own movement—or rather, strictly, its movement in the particular connexion—interesting...It had, naturally, Rowland's consciousness, not to be *too* acute—which would have disconnected it and made it superhuman: the beautiful little problem was to keep it connected, connected intimately, with the general human exposure, and thereby bedimmed and befooled and bewildered, anxious, restless, fallible, and yet to endow it with such intelligence that the appearances reflected in it, and constituting together there the situation and the 'story', should become by that fact intelligible.[1]

This means that the *Gawain*-poet could not have used for *Sir Gawain and the Green Knight* the method James used in *The Ambassadors*, and presented the whole story through the eyes of a single character. He could not say, as James wrote of Lambert Strether, the seeing eye of *The Ambassadors*: 'with other persons, save as they were primarily *his* persons (not he primarily but one of theirs), I had simply nothing to do'.[2] On the contrary, we must be given some glimpses behind the scenes, some hints of the plot against Gawain, and must even occasionally be allowed to share the point of view of his opponents. We may see Gawain's story more through his own eyes than through those of anyone else, but the significance of his story is not limited to what he makes of it. What Gawain makes of his story is, from a point of view we are momentarily allowed to imagine as the Green Knight's and as Camelot's, only enough to send him veering from one extreme to another—from aiming at perfection to feeling himself the most miserable of sinners, from *cortaysye* to something like misogyny. If the story of *Sir Gawain and the Green Knight* is, as James saw that of *The Ambassadors* as being, a 'drama of discrimination',[3] it is a drama of our discrimination as well as Gawain's. In an earlier study of *Sir Gawain and the Green Knight* I wrote that Gawain returns to Camelot after his adventure 'both wiser and sadder',[4] but in fact the poem allows the possibility that he is sadder without becoming much wiser, while *we* may become wiser through, and at the expense of, his sadness.

It is equally important, though, that we should not be able to feel our wisdom certain and complete. We must ourselves be entangled in and rebuked by the mystery Gawain has to face; and so it must remain a mystery. I have pointed out the poet's notable failure to make the

---

[1] *The Art of the Novel*, p. 16.   [2] *Ibid.* pp. 320–1.   [3] *Ibid.* p. 316.
[4] Spearing, *Criticism and Medieval Poetry*, p. 38.

Green Knight consistently 'intelligible', either by giving him any openly interpreted symbolic device like Gawain's pentangle, or by letting us see the poem for more than a moment through his eyes. Everything about him is ambiguous, from his opening appearance as a creature half-man and half-giant, half-knightly and half-brutish, with a symbol of peace in one hand and a symbol of war in the other,[1] to the final disclosure that he is two apparently different people, both the terrifying challenger and the jovial host. And it is very much to the poet's purpose that, in answer to Gawain's request for an explanation, he gives one which makes Gawain uncomfortable without in fact 'explaining' the substance of the poem. If Gawain did accept his invitation to go back to the castle, we should no doubt get some further insight into the mystery of his true nature and into the intentions and powers of Morgan la Fay. But this the poet does not allow us. Instead, Gawain rides back to the familiar world of Camelot, the Green Knight rides off 'Whiderwarde-so-ever-he wolde' (2478), and the mystery remains unsolved. It remains to be pondered by us; and thus we have in *Sir Gawain and the Green Knight* a poem more 'open-ended' than the poet's three others, because it is not firmly placed in a perspective of absolute values. If it was 'modern' for the poet, it is likely to seem, whether fortuitously or not, modern for us too, in its striking relativism and the striking freedom of choice it grants us. In telling of this adventure of Gawain's, the poet has given us a richly suggestive concretion of material. That material does not fall of itself into a single pattern of organization and significance, but into a number of alternative patterns. The choice and the adjustment are ours.

[1] The ambivalences in the opening description of the Green Knight are well brought out by Burrow, pp. 12 ff.

Index